D0210909

*f*P

THE POWER OF CO-CREATION

Build It With Them to Boost Growth, Productivity, and Profits

Venkat Ramaswamy
Francis Gouillart

Free Press

New York   London   Toronto   Sydney

*f*P

Free Press
A Division of Simon & Schuster, Inc.
1230 Avenue of the Americas
New York, NY 10020

Copyright © 2010 by Venkat Ramaswamy and Francis Gouillart

All rights reserved, including the right to reproduce this book or portions
thereof in any form whatsoever. For information address Free Press Subsidiary Rights
Department, 1230 Avenue of the Americas, New York, NY 10020.

First Free Press hardcover edition October 2010

FREE PRESS and colophon are trademarks of Simon & Schuster, Inc.

For information about special discounts for bulk purchases, please contact
Simon & Schuster Special Sales at 1-866-506-1949 or business@simonandschuster.com.

The Simon & Schuster Speakers Bureau can bring authors to your live event.
For more information or to book an event contact the Simon & Schuster Speakers Bureau
at 1-866-248-3049 or visit our website at www.simonspeakers.com.

Designed by Carla Jayne Jones

Manufactured in the United States of America

10 9 8 7 6 5 4 3 2 1

Library of Congress Cataloging-in-Publication Data
Ramaswamy, Venkatram.
   The power of co-creation / build it with them to boost growth, productivity, and profits
Venkat Ramaswamy, Francis Gouillart.
      p. cm.
   Includes bibliographical references and index.
1. Creative ability in business. 2. Business networks.
3. Interorganizational relations. I. Gouillart, Francis J. II. Title.
   HD53.R35 2010
   658.4'0714—dc22   2010006297

ISBN 978-1-4391-8104-1
ISBN 978-1-4391-8106-5 (ebook)

Dedication

To Brahman & Swami Krishnananda,
Ishvara & Shivashankar,
Bhumi Devi & Soulmate Bindu,
Prakriti & Joyful Adithya and Lalitha,
And Co-Creators of the Future everywhere.

—Venkat Ramaswamy

To Laura for singing in the morning,
Emily for keeping me young,
Gregory for teaching me to see the world from a different perspective,
And all those in emerging nations who are excited about life.

—Francis Gouillart

In Memory of C. K. Prahalad,
who inspired us with his
visionary thoughts, insights,
teachings, mentorship, and friendship.
May God bless his soul.

—Venkat Ramaswamy and Francis Gouillart

Contents

PART ONE
VALUE CO-CREATION

Chapter 1

Becoming a Co-Creative Enterprise

All around the globe, the expectations of informed and connected people have dramatically changed in recent years. Whether as customers, employees, or citizens, people demand more engagement with providers of goods and services, with their employers, and with their governments. People today are highly connected and networked, sharing their experiences of using products and services. They want to help design the value of the products and services they use; they want an ongoing conversation with the organizations they do business with and with each other; and they want their voices heard. Yet, in spite of their best efforts, many organizations are locked into a firm-centric paradigm of value and its creation. They fail to engage people in generating better products and services that the organization can deliver. Technology gives innovators and marketers more and more options in designing and delivering products and services, yet they struggle to connect with what people value, and this further frustrates people. As a result, satisfaction ratings are declining or flat across many industries, and loyalty is increasingly a thing of the past.

During 2000 to 2004, Venkat Ramaswamy (together with C. K. Prahalad) wrote a series of articles on the implications for business and society of the more connected and empowered customer. They detailed the shifting of competencies toward a network of customer communities and global talent outside the firm on one hand, and the emergence of global resource networks of firms on the other. The authors suggested that customer experience is central to enterprise value creation, innovation, strategy, and executive leadership.[1] These broad changes in business and society, they argued, called for *co-creation*—the practice of developing systems, products, or services through collaboration with customers, managers, employees, and other company stakeholders. Their book, *The Future of Competition* (Harvard Business School Press, 2004), offered a series of compelling examples showing that value is being increasingly created jointly by the firm and the customer, rather than created entirely inside the firm. The authors held that customers seek the freedom of choice to interact with firms through a range of experiences. Customers want to define choices in a manner that reflects their view of value, and they want to interact and transact in their preferred language and style. *The Future of Competition* provided a new frame of reference for jointly creating value through experiences.[2] Just three years after its publication, a number of businesses had capitalized on opportunities anticipated by the book—whether start-ups such as Crushpad, which made winemaking a more democratic process using Web 2.0 technologies, or established businesses such as Brother, which breathed new life into a century-old product, the sewing machine, by networking the product and nurturing active user communities.

In many ways *The Future of Competition* portrayed the digital and consumer universe we know today. It also commenced an ongoing journey for Venkat Ramaswamy. In 2005 Francis Gouillart joined the journey, and the authors started developing a transformational framework for co-creation. Through their interactions with thousands of managers globally who had begun experimenting with co-creation, they discovered that enterprises were building platforms that engaged not only the firm and its customers, but also the entire network of suppliers, partners, and employees in a continuous development of new experiences with individuals. In some cases, they found that organizations had gone further in extending their resource base through practices such as crowdsourcing, mass collaboration, and open innovation. In other cases, they were tapping into user communities and social networking among customers. Some organizations had also begun allowing their customers to personalize products. Others were engaging suppliers in new forms of vendor relationships. Still others had developed new ways of interacting with their employees and were able to mobilize their workforce to unheard-of levels of performance through co-creation. In all these cases, companies were succeeding by paying attention to how they *engaged* people. Managers had to make the fundamental shift to go beyond their conventional goods-services mind-set to an *experience mind-set*—defining value based on human experiences rather than features and processes, whether downstream or upstream, in the value chain. They further observed that success lies in using people's engagement experiences to generate insights to improve the nature of *interactions* as a result, including inside the enterprise. Interactions among people inside and outside the firm became the connective tissue where new insights, learning, and innovation were generated.

As shown in **Figure 1-1,** the activity chain of the enterprise no longer solely creates value, nor is its value proposition unilaterally defined by the organization. The activity chain remains key in creating goods and services, but customers, suppliers, partners, and employees are no longer limiting their experience to just "receiving" what is being offered by the enterprise's activity chain. They increasingly want to insert themselves into that activity chain, and also open up to the possibility of enhancing value in their own activities. In other words, people want to be personally engaged in co-creating value through human experiences. In doing so, the traditional distinction between production and consumption gets blurred.

Figure 1-1: Becoming a Co-Creative Enterprise

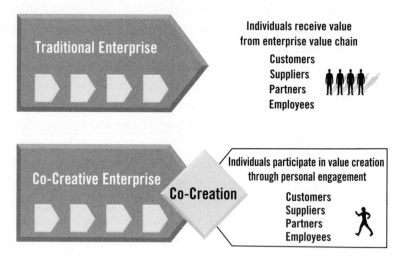

Although the co-creation principle applies equally for suppliers, partners, and employees, let us start by illustrating how value co-creation works with customers. In the conventional enterprise, customers are largely passive in the process of value creation. They are researched, observed, segmented, targeted, marketed at, and sold to by people in the organization, but they are not engaged in any meaningful interaction with the organization, on their terms. To use common business terminology, the organization has established "touch points" for them, but these touch points are scarce and brief, and they are all staged from the perspective of the organization. The organization decides what those touch points are and how the relationship with the individual is defined. Individuals do not get to decide what they are to share with the enterprise, but instead answer the questions asked of them at the focus group. They do not participate in the design of the product or service or program, but are only presented with an offering designed for them by the organization. They do not participate in the marketing of the offering, but only get to see the campaign aimed at them. They do not sell the offering to each other; the organization sells it to them. They are left with a yes-or-no decision, a modern capitalistic equivalent of Shakespeare's *Hamlet*: "to buy or not to buy." Throughout, the organization views value as a function of its activities, ignoring the role of individuals and their activities in the shaping of value. This firm-centric paradigm of the conventional enterprise has served us well for many years, but it is rapidly becoming obsolete.

As we will see in this book, the future belongs to the *co-creative enterprise*. Co-creation involves both a profound democratization and decentralization of value creation, moving it from concentration inside the firm to interactions with its customers, customer communities, suppliers, partners, and employees, and interactions among individuals. Once an organization accepts this premise, it starts on a journey that will require it to develop new capabilities. First, the organization needs to use the experience of individuals as the starting point, rather than its own products and services. In addition, the development of compelling experiences with individuals requires that they be allowed to engage in interactions of their own choosing. In co-creative enterprises, individuals participate in the design of value through their own experiences, which leads to a recasting of the conventional role of strategy, innovation, marketing, supply chain management, human resources management, and information technology.

The co-creative enterprise is also a formidable productivity engine that can pay for itself many times over, in the same way that the quality movement and Six Sigma process-based practices have increased productivity by increasing worker engagement. In addition to cutting costs and improving efficiency, co-creation reduces business risk. Most important, the co-creative enterprise is a growth engine. It enhances strategic capital, increases returns, and expands market opportunities. Co-creation draws innovative ideas from customers, employees, and stakeholders at large. It increases the capacity of firms to generate insights and take advantage of opportunities they might not have identified, while reducing risk and capital needs by using global networks and communities. To illustrate a co-creative enterprise in action and the power of value co-creation, consider Nike.

Nike as a Co-Creative Enterprise

After Apple introduced the iPod in 2001, employees on the Nike campus started to notice many runners sporting ubiquitous white earbuds. As Nike's senior managers traveled globally, they came back seeing the connection between running and music in a different light. In the words of Nike's president and CEO Mark Parker, "Most runners were running with music already. We thought the real opportunity would come if we could combine music and data."[3]

In 2006, Nike launched Nike+ (pronounced NikePlus), an initiative in partnership with Apple to engage more deeply with runners and the running community at large. Nike+ consists of a smart sensor on the shoe that can communicate with a built-in wireless receiver on the iPod Touch or iPhone. As you listen to music and run, the sensor electronically logs the time and distance of the run, keeping track of any records being set. When a new record is set, a voice-over recorded by Lance Armstrong offers congratulations and provides encouragement. And once you are done running, you can go online to the Nike+ website (www.nikeplus.com), upload data from your run, chart it, analyze it, and share it with other runners. Runners can set individual goals, track their progress, and challenge other runners.[4]

Nike+ goes beyond an agglomeration of devices and websites, however. To appreciate the co-creativity of Nike+, let us see how a runner actually engages with this platform and with other runners. Meet our protagonist runner, "Youtou," as she is affectionately called. She has had a passion for running from a young age and takes running seriously. She works with a global firm and enjoys watching soccer and sports in general. Youtou is not just a statistic in a company database or someone to be "targeted," but a living, breathing human being who cares about the quality of her running experience.

Youtou is training for a half-marathon in London in five months. She has set a goal of finishing in less than an hour and a half, a highly ambitious time given where she is today. It is an opportunity to prove her competitiveness to herself and others. Let us identify the various interactions Youtou can engage in through Nike+. Her experience is ultimately the result of all those interactions. First, using the Run Tracking feature, she can now automatically plot distance, time, pace, and calories burned. She can display a friendly, colorful histogram of any set of data over time, assessing whether she is making progress. No need to log her runs into spreadsheets on her laptop manually every day as she used to, serious runner that she is. She can also issue running challenges to others through the Challenge Others feature. Here, she may let her competitive streak run free and dare the kids at her office to beat the time she recorded yesterday on their favorite "run around the Park Plaza" course. She may issue her challenge as an individual or as part of a team. The challenge may be, for example, about the total number of miles that her team can run over a set period of time—say, 30 days— thereby fostering motivation within each team. "Hey buddy, how about logging a couple of miles for the team this evening?" Youtou can also put herself out there and publish a Running Resolution, whereby she intends to run at least 1,000 miles over the next five months. She can already hear the electronic cheering coming from friends and relatives as she accumulates a few more miles every day, not to mention the emotional lift she receives from congratulatory messages from Lance Armstrong as she passes certain milestones.

Youtou can now Map and Share Her Runs. Every time she establishes a new course, she can view it on a Google map, through a partnership between Nike and Google. She can also make that map available to others, annotating it with detailed data such as the nature of the road terrain and whether the course is well lit or not. When Youtou is sent to London on business, she can now download local data and find the popular running places around the hotel where she is staying. Of course, Youtou can Listen to Music on her iPod Touch. In the words of the Nike+ website, she can "hear how she runs." Many athletes will tell you that there is a unique symbiosis between sports and music rhythms, which Nike+ capitalizes on. Youtou can also Publish Her Running Playlists. And who knows? Her iTunes iMix playlist tuned to the running rhythm of people like her may become a hit. She might become a contributor to popular iMixes and stoke the teenage aspiration she once had to become a music producer.

Through Nike+, Youtou can also join local Nike Running Clubs. There, she will be able to attend running clinics and participate in runner reward programs. She can also sign up for Nike-Sponsored Events such as a five-kilometer run on Valentine's Day in the streets of New York. Youtou can engage in virtual Training with a Running Coach or Interact with Running Stars. There, she can get into a personal discussion on how quickly she should start running again after her pregnancy, or why her running pace seems to be hitting a wall after steadily improving for the last year. More broadly, she can join a variety of Blog and Discussion Board interactions with the larger running community, covering topics as diverse as running shoes, clothing, personal stories, and, as the Nike+ website indicates, "everything running."

Notice how active Youtou can be throughout in defining her running experience. She can create her own running courses, potentially building on what others have devised before her. She can decide whether to engage with training specialists or professional runners, based on the specific issues she faces. She can share her wisdom and running tips, based on what works for her. She can decide to seek encouragement and support in training for the half-marathon in London in five months. In all those cases, *she* initiates the contact, rather than passively wait for someone to reach out to her. She can share feelings or data about herself. She can be creative and exhibit her personality. She can be imaginative and whimsical and have fun in a way that suits her mood at any one time.

Thus, for Youtou as a runner, value is now a function of her running experience. This is created partly by herself—how she decides to run—and partly by Nike+, which provides the *engagement platform* that reaches out to her on her own terms and invites her to connect not only with Nike but also with a vast community of runners (more than 2 million registered as of 2009).[5] As a result, Youtou's running experience can be co-created between herself and Nike+. Note that if Youtou prefers the passive orientation of the traditional model occasionally, she can do that as well. (The co-creative enterprise also has conventional one-sided value chain capabilities.) In other words, Youtou can engage and disengage when she wants to.

For Nike's part, the Nike+ system allows the company to engage runners and their social networks in rich conversations that generate deep knowledge and insights into the running experience, not to mention all that real, live data to which it now has access. Says CEO Parker, "In more ways than one, the genius of the Nike+ system is the software that allows generation of deep insights and facilitating social connections among the community of runners."[6] For instance, in 2009, Nike learned that the average duration of a run worldwide is about 35 minutes, and that the most popular Nike+ "PowerSong" that gave runners extra motivation was "Pump It" by the Black Eyed Peas. Nike also found that it took five runs with music uploads, on average, for a runner to get hooked on Nike+. The community conversations also provided key qualitative insights; runners not only liked the information they got, but the positive feedback from the body after five runs also propelled their motivation. Thus, Nike now has a live laboratory from which it continuously learns and generates insights from the data about customers' running mileage and music tastes. Nike watches runners using the system as they map their routes, graph distances for each run, record their speed, and chart their overall progress.[7] Nike+ is a foundation of interaction that allows the continuous enhancement of its offerings. For instance, as runners started to "mash up" their runs with Google Maps, Nike made it possible for runners to annotate the routes of their runs and to view and discuss popular routes in their neighborhoods with the Nike+ community more easily.

Nike+ is a great example of a co-creative engagement platform that allows Nike to:

- learn directly from the behavior of its customers;
- generate new ideas rapidly;

- experiment with new offerings quickly;
- get direct input from customers on their running preferences;
- build deeper relationships and trust with the community; and
- generate "stickier" brand collateral.

These benefits to the enterprise constitute what we call *strategic capital*. Nike+ is a two-way learning engine, facilitating dialogue with and among the running community. Nike can identify and act upon new growth opportunities with this enhanced global resource network continuously. Besides attracting new adherents to its brand through the largest community of runners ever assembled, Nike boosts product sales and enhances returns through the increased motivation and involvement of runners that Nike+ generates. The payoff has been impressive:

- By the end of 2007, the company had captured 57 percent of the $3.6 billion U.S. running shoe market, compared with 47 percent in 2006. Nike had sold more than 1.3 million Nike+ iPod Sport Kits (at $29 apiece) and more than 500,000 Nike+ SportBands (at $59 apiece). More than 600,000 runners from more than 170 countries used the Nike+ website in just a year, with over 40 million running miles uploaded.
- The growth has been relentless. Near the end of 2008, runners logged the 100th million mile on Nike+. By August 2009, despite a sluggish economy, over 150 million miles had been uploaded by more than 1.3 million runners burning more than 14 billion calories. Nike's share of the U.S. running shoe market had increased to 61 percent by mid-2009.

Seeing the growth potential, Charlie Denson, president of the Nike brand, set a stretch goal in 2007 of having 15 percent of the world's estimated 100 million runners using the Nike+ system.[8]

But Nike is not only accelerating its growth through the strategic capital it generates. It is also *reducing its risk and costs*. With Nike+, the company shifted its spending away from traditional media like TV networks. Conventional advertising expenditures, for example, were down 55 percent at the end of 2007, and the portion of Nike's advertising budget devoted to traditional media declined from about 60 percent of the total in 1997 to 33 percent in 2007. Says Trevor Edwards, Nike's marketing director, "We're not in the business of keeping the media companies alive. We're in the business of connecting with consumers. Nike+ is a very different way to connect with consumers. People are coming into it on average three times a week. So we're not having to go to them."[9] Instead, Nike is making investments in building out the Nike+ platform further and enhancing its social media capabilities to enable runners to connect with each other and with Nike in new ways. By 2007, Nike's nonmedia spending was more than its traditional media spending: $457.9 million to $220.5 million. For Nike, the benefits of Nike+ include:

- Reducing the cost of marketing through the positive word of mouth created
- Sharing the risk of product/service development with partners such as Apple by getting them to co-invest and participate
- Mitigating the risk of capital investment through enlightened experimentation, because it can now test major investments through its engagement platform

Building a successful engagement platform of this kind is a sophisticated process that requires a good deal of teamwork and is likely to involve some false starts. Nike+ wasn't the company's first such effort. In 1987 Nike had launched the Nike Monitor, a clunky device about the size of a thick paperback book, with a waist strap and sonar detectors, a far cry from the miniature sensor + software + online database that is Nike+. Michael Tchao, head of Nike's Techlab, notes, "You can imagine that this device, a little big, maybe not the most fashionable, wasn't the runaway success we had hoped."[10] Nike+ was a huge step forward that involved collaboration between areas of the company that had never directly interacted before, as

13

well as with Apple. And melding jogging, music, social networking, and technological collaboration with Apple was no easy feat. Doing so required managers from apparel, technology, research, footwear design, and music to come together as a new kind of team. As Michael Donaghu, Nike's director of footwear innovation, notes, "The best teams get a little borderless. We got really borderless."[11]

So far, we have described the Nike side of mutual value creation. But there are also considerable benefits generated on the customer side of co-creation. Nike managers have escaped the conventional product-centric view of value and are, instead, focusing on the real *human experience* of running. They now understand how runners want to connect with their own running experiences and recognize how experiences are not only personal but also social—shaped by interactions with other runners, trainers, and coaches. Nike designed the Nike+ website to facilitate these interactions and engage in conversations with the running community at large to learn rapidly from their interactions. As a result, the enterprise can bring all of its strategic capital to bear on continuously enhancing the human experiences of runners through the Nike+ platform.

The runner's researching of gear, buying shoes, and occasionally invoking customer service—the only parts of the runner's processes that truly line up with the conventional enterprise processes—are only a small part of the running experience. Most of what a runner does has no matching counterpart in the product-service activity chain—until Nike+ came along. Nike+ goes beyond conventional goods and services thinking as the basis of value creation. In the words of Nike's Stefan Olander, Nike's global director of consumer connections, "In the past, the product was the end point of the consumer experience. Now it's the starting point."[12] Nike+ expands value as a function of new types of experiences of value to individuals. Specifically, Nike+:

- Allows runners to track their runs with unparalleled precision
- Enhances their productivity
- Enables them to integrate music and running
- Propels their motivation

- Makes it easier for them to make and state running resolutions
- Connects them with running buddies and events happening locally and globally
- Encourages them to take part in a new social network of runners, trainers, and coaches specifically focused on the running experience

These are all new types of valuable experiences that did not exist before Nike+ enabled them. The record of runs belongs uniquely to each individual runners as does the social network they build, the resolutions they make, the motivation they create, the buddies they elect to run with, and the music they pick. As a result, Nike+ significantly enhances customer engagement.

The Nike+ platform also reduces *risk and cost for individuals* engaged with the Nike+ system. Specifically, the Nike+ platform:

- De-risks the initial cost of equipment for runners, by giving them access to people who have already experienced that equipment
- Reduces the runner's risk of training, by giving them access to professional trainers and experienced runners
- Reduces the runner's search cost of finding local buddies and events through the web

In summary, Nike+ has been able to harness the four key powers of co-creation, as shown in **Figure 1-2:**

- Nike+ increases returns and strategic capital for the enterprise.
- It lowers risks and costs for the enterprise.
- It allows individuals to gain new experiences of value.
- It lowers risks and costs for individuals.

As we will demonstrate later in this book, this same *Four Powers Model* applies whether the individual involved in co-creation is a customer, supplier, partner, or employee.

Figure 1-2: The Four Powers of Co-Creation

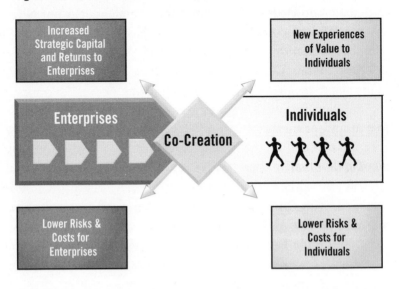

The co-creative enterprise reenergizes its people and discovers new sources of sustainable growth. It can also generate efficiencies by recognizing and eliminating many hidden costs of the current ways of doing business, such as traditional (and expensive) advertising campaigns. For Nike, every one of the people and organizations contributing to its extended network is a potential (and often actual) buyer or advocate for Nike shoes, clothing, accessories, and equipment. From another perspective, they have (or can) become even more engaged: a part of the Nike co-creation system, through which they can generate new sources of mutual value. Individuals as co-creators enjoy differentiated experiences and better economics, while the enterprise is able to generate new strategic capital for itself and dramatically improve its economic model.

From the company's standpoint, not only has Nike redefined how it interacts with customers, it has also enabled a full system of interactions. Nike no longer attempts to control the value system, but has instead opened up to multiple types of co-creators, leveraging the skills and talents of millions of people willing to contribute their knowledge. As a result, the "value system" of Nike is now open and co-creative. As Olander, Nike's global director of consumer connections, has remarked, "The more we can open up Nike+, the better. The only reason to close it out is because you actually don't believe that you have a strong enough product for others to want to take it and do good things with it."[13] The more applications out there, the more Nike can sell.

Inside-Out Co-Creation Opportunities at NIKEiD and Nike Soccer

There are two ways to discover new co-creation opportunities (see **Figure 1-3**). Nike, like all companies, has existing interactions with its customers. For example, Nike advertises shoes directly to customers through different media and sells its shoes to customers through independent retail channels and Niketown stores. Customers are by definition also involved in these interactions, since they watch Nike ads or buy shoes in the stores. (Existing interactions are represented in the central portion of **Figure 1-3**.) But the art of co-creation lies in the dual realization that:

- The vast majority of customer processes do not involve any matching process on the enterprise side, therefore opening up the possibility of *outside-in co-creation,* as represented in the upper part of **Figure 1-3**. Nike+ is an example of outside-in co-creation since it starts with the human experiences of individuals running and then develops a platform that connects their running experiences to the company in new ways.
- Most enterprise processes are not transparent to customers, which precludes those customers from interacting with those processes and thereby generating new experiences for themselves. This constitutes an opportunity for *inside-out co-creation,* as represented in the bottom part of **Figure 1-3**. We now turn to this part of the Nike strategy. What would Nike's customers and stakeholders want to do if every en-

terprise process were visible to them? Where would they get involved? How could they participate in those processes and derive new types of experiences?

Figure 1-3: Outside-In and Inside-Out Co-Creation

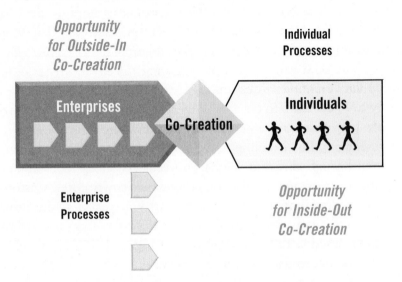

To illustrate the inside-out approach to co-creating value, consider Nike's design process. Traditionally, Nike's in-house shoe designers would design shoe models and offer them for distribution with limited involvement from customers. The customer input would be limited to focus groups and traditional market research. Through its NIKEiD engagement platform, Nike has now opened up the design of the shoe to the customer. Youtou, our protagonist runner, can go online and personalize her running shoes (or apparel). For example, she can enter different sizes for each foot (many people have slight variations in the sizes of their feet) and choose colors for some nine components of the shoe: base, tip, heel, swoosh, tongue-top, lining, lace, sidewall, and outsole. She can even inscribe her name on the tongue of the shoe. Further, at the NIKEiD Studio at select Niketown stores, she, along with other customers and enthusiasts, can be engaged in "live" creative inter-actions of defining new styles of shoes through intimate one-to-one design sessions. Here, she can have access to shapes, colors, and materials that are not offered on the NIKEiD website.

Thus, through both its online NIKEiD platform and its NIKEiD studio platform, Nike engages customers deeply in how its shoes are designed and used. What we have just described is not just mere personalization of products. NIKEiD is far more than inscribing one's name on a product and determining the color. It is also not just about creating a personalized experience for the customer. Rather, Nike *learns deeply, and continuously, about what personalization options are valuable to its customers and why, and then connects better with their experiences of personalization.* Moreover, the opening up of shoe design to co-creativity applies not only to Youtou as an individual, but also to communities and any team as a collective. The Team Locker section of NIKEiD allows individuals to enter and share their designs, invites team members to rate one another's designs, and facilitates the rallying of the group around a unique shoe design for the team. This group application is of par-ticular value for team sports such as (American) football or soccer.

NIKEiD was part of an innovative platform that Nike created for soccer lovers before and during the 2006 World Cup. To improve its position in the competitive soccer shoe market, Nike set up a social networking platform called Joga.com, in partnership with Google, in fourteen languages across 140 countries. (The name Joga was drawn from the phrase *Joga Bonito*, which means "play beautiful" in Portuguese.) Joga.com leveraged ideas from a number of recent digital and social media innovations. In the same vein as YouTube, Joga.com invited individuals to film their soccer skills and upload videos, and then invited the user community to comment on, rate, and share them. The community was the judge of a winner every month. Joga.com also invited individuals to create their own pro-files and to network with one another, and the site encouraged users to identify inspired soccer blogs. Nike also brought professional soccer players on the site to connect with their fans.

The best engagement platforms are multifaceted. Just as NikeID involves both online and offline interactions, the Joga initiative also tapped into live interactions, in this case among the fans themselves. Nike sponsored street soccer competitions called Joga 3, inspired by the traditional game of futsal, which is played indoors or outdoors on small courts with an emphasis on skill over power. In Nike's version, teams of three competed in three-minute games. Nike organized Joga 3 tournaments in thirty-nine countries around the world, with national winners qualifying for the world finals in Brazil. The word spread beyond the social networking on Joga. com through many non-Nike websites, as soccer amateurs sought to co-opt others.

A third part of the Joga platform involved a connection with NIKEiD. Nike invited shoe designers to compete in designing a new soccer shoe. The firm structured the competition as if it were a reality show and then invited its community of customers and enthusiasts to vote on the best designs. The winning designs were then produced and offered to the Joga community. In addition to these community-mediated designs and Nike's new designs for the 2006 season, fans personalized their own soccer shoes on NIKEiD with various styles and colors, including leather embossing of the flags of the countries they wanted to support on the rear heel of their shoes. Nike provided software tools for local soccer teams and professional leagues to co-design their personalized soccer shoes.

Through these multiple linked initiatives, Nike connected with and learned from millions of soccer fans around the globe, cultivating customer relationships on a scale as never before. A key lesson of the Joga initiative is that unless enterprises build requisite engagement platform capabilities, they cannot sustain co-creation efforts. Also, once these capabilities are built, the nature of engagement will morph for both the enterprise and its customers, as enterprises learn from interactions on the platform.

Becoming a co-creative enterprise means using both "inside-out" and "outside-in" approaches to co-creation, in continuous fashion, among all functions of the enterprise. Eventually, it is about a complete *transformation* of the capabilities and culture of the enterprise, in conceiving, designing, and executing value. To appreciate the significance of this transformation, consider the metaphor of color mixing. Think of the conventional enterprise as represented by the color blue and the individual (a customer or any other stakeholder) by the color yellow. The outside-in co-creation approach (as in the case of Nike+) is about starting with the "yellow" side (human experiences) and mixing in "blue enterprise processes" to create new experiences of value to individuals. The inside-out co-creation approach (as in the case of NIKEiD), in contrast, starts with the "blue-side" (enterprise processes) and blending them with "yellow-side thinking" by opening up enterprise activities to customers and other stakeholders. Both approaches result in co-created value and are necessary for the total transformation to a co-creative enterprise. (If you are wondering about the significance of the resulting color "green," think both profitability and sustainability in that "green" is the color of the U.S. dollar and connotes planetary responsibility.) The main organizational challenge is in institutionalizing the power of co-creation enterprise-wide, in everything the enterprise does. To show this, we look at the example of Starbucks and its makeover embodied in a new tagline in 2008: "You and Starbucks. It's bigger than coffee."

Enterprise Transformation at Starbucks

From its initial public offering in 1992 to its peak in 2006, the stock value of Starbucks increased by nearly 5,800 percent. By 2007, Starbucks was a $10 billion company serving 50 million customers a week with some 10,500 stores in the United States and more than 4,500 stores internationally. In the process of the company's rapid expansion, however, management had not only decreased its attention to the Starbucks Experience, but it also had to contend with rising customer and market risks from an erosion of its loyal customer base, due to competitors who had caught on to espresso drinks—from Dunkin' Donuts to McDonald's at the low end, to other fast-rising premium coffee shop chains like Peet's Coffee and Caribou Coffee, and the hordes of local coffeehouses that had begun to upgrade the customer experience. In a memo he had circulated the previous year within the Starbucks organization, CEO Howard Schultz raised concerns that Starbucks stores "no longer have the soul of the past" and outlined the risks to its culture that had been built around experiences of value to customers.[14]

In a bid to revitalize the Starbucks customer experience, Schultz, who had returned as CEO of Starbucks in January 2008, launched the MyStarbucksIdea.com website two months later, with these words:

> Welcome to MyStarbucksIdea.com. This is your invitation to help us transform the future of Starbucks with your ideas—and build upon our history of co-creating the Starbucks Experience together . . . So, pull up a comfortable chair and participate in My Starbucks Idea. We're here, we're engaged, and we're taking it seriously.

On MyStarbucksIdea.com, everyone is invited to help co-shape the future of Starbucks with their ideas—in ways Starbucks might not have thought of—to check out other people's ideas, and vote on the ones they like best. Starbucks has been proactive in laying out areas of experience on the website, including ordering, payment, and pick-up of goods; atmosphere and locations; social responsibility and building community; product-related ideas concerning drinks, merchandising, and the Starbucks Card for frequent customers; and any other ideas to enhance the Starbucks experience. Within a month, many constructive ideas were posted. One that quickly gained traction was to embed a customer's regular order on the Starbucks Card—for example, "a tall, nonfat, no-foam, extra-hot caramel macchiato with light caramel and a dash of vanilla"—which would speed up the personalized transaction for an individual customer. From Starbucks' perspective, it could serve more customers faster, generating a "win-win" for both sides. Other customers called for the ability to send in orders by phone or web, for gift drinks, for ice cubes made out of coffee so when they melt they won't dilute cold drinks, and for a stopper to plug the hole in lids to prevent sloshing (which Starbucks implemented through reusable "splash sticks," a solution that originated from customers in Japan).

Chris Bruzzo, Starbucks' CTO, says the purpose of MyStarbucksIdea was to "open up a dialogue with customers and build up this muscle inside our company." By 2008, there were nearly fifty Idea Partners active on the site—specially trained employees who act as hosts of the discussion, take specific ideas to their internal teams, and advocate for customers' suggestions, so "customers would have a seat at the table when product decisions are being made," as Bruzzo puts it, and "close the loop in an authentic way." The goal is to adopt customer ideas into Starbucks' business processes, including product development, store design, and customer experience.[15] In the first year alone, more than 65,000 ideas and 658,000 votes were cast. In late 2009, the company announced that fifty distinct ideas drawn from the site had been approved, including healthy food options as a major initiative for the company. This is no small feat for an organization the size of Starbucks. For instance, after Schultz returned as CEO, Starbucks announced that breakfast sandwiches would be discontinued in order to return the stores to a more coffeehouse-style experience. Through MyStarbucksIdea, however, customers asked that Starbucks retain sandwiches but said they wanted more nutritious and healthier options (more whole grains, more fiber and protein, smaller portions, and so on). Starbucks Idea Partner Katie Thomson, a registered dietician and senior nutritionist at Starbucks, engaged in dialogue with the community, with Starbucks internally, and with the company's supply chain, finally implementing a new range of nutritious, tasty sandwiches in late 2008, with small ingredient changes that would reduce aromas so as not to interfere with the smell of coffee. Not only did the community vote (up and down) and decide, but members also discussed the ideas with Starbucks Idea Partners and helped make them even better. Says Bruzzo, "There are advantages to having that kind of transparency because it creates more engagement, and we actually get to iterate on our solutions while we're building them."[16] Ultimately, the MyStarbucksIdea community can not only see which ideas were the most popular but also engage with the company in dialogue as it reviews ideas, watch as the company takes action, and provide real feedback based on actual experiences.

Following the success of MyStarbucksIdea, the company had expanded it presence in social media. Starbucks overtook Coca-Cola as the most popular brand on Facebook in 2009 with more than 5 million fans, where it uploads videos and alerts people to events. More than 700,000 people follow Starbucks on Twitter, where the company broadcasts information, answers questions, and engages with many people one-on-one. On its YouTube channel, nearly 5,000 subscribers receive advertisements and informational videos on the company and coffee. A series of videos about its new product, Via instant coffee, garnered 130,000 views. Starbucks allows people to embed its videos anywhere on the web, in contrast to many companies concerned that their videos might end in places they don't want to be associated with.

This kind of continuous, iterative engagement between Starbucks and its customers—as well as its customer-facing employees (whom Starbucks refers to as "partners" and who have also chipped into the conversation), its supply chain, and stakeholders at large—enables the brand to be co-created and managed in ways that challenge traditional brand management orthodoxies. Companies that engage customers in co-creating brands through their human experiences can create a "seeing culture," as Schultz puts it, and help employees inside the company "get" customer-think. It is important to drive co-creative thinking into the management of human capital and the (re)design of business processes, and then back to points of interactions with customers.

In June 2009, Starbucks raised the bar on its food even further. Sandra Stark, VP, Food Category, said, "Starbucks customers have been telling us that they want better tasting and healthier food options when they visit our stores. We answered their call with a delicious new menu of food made with real ingredients and more wholesome options." The company removed the artificial trans fats, artificial flavors, artificial dyes, and high-fructose corn syrup in all its food items. Some of the healthy food items rose to the top of the company's food sales chart within just a few weeks.[17]

Partly in response to calls on MyStarbucksIdea.com for an increased commitment to increased environmental and social responsibility, the company also created a new website in 2008 called Starbucks Shared Planet (www.starbucks.com/sharedplanet). On this platform, the company makes a commitment to do good for its community and the planet, ranging from the way it buys coffee to minimizing its environmental footprint, to involvement in local communities. As with MyStarbucksIdea.com, the company engages directly with its customers and other stakeholders on the interactive Shared Planet website. The company encourages individuals to interact with its Global Responsibility annual report in key focus areas, inviting them to create their own custom reports of portions that matter to them and to share and discuss aspects with friends via social media.

Starbucks Shared Planet has three key areas of focus: ethical sourcing, environmental stewardship, and community involvement. The main goals, supporting goals, and KPIs (Key Performance Indicators) in each focus area are stated publicly and progress is reported with full transparency. Take environmental stewardship. Starbucks customers have the opportunity to pledge to bring in a reusable mug or tumbler for their beverages, reducing their drink price by 10 cents (in North America) and reducing their environmental footprint. For its part, Starbucks has taken steps in using renewable energy, conserving energy and water usage in its stores, and undertaking "green construction" of its stores. Most important, these pledges provide transparency and access, inviting customers to engage in a dialogue around company activities. Authentic engagement breeds trust over time. We believe there is no other way in an openly networked society to build the trust that many institutions have lost.

Starbucks Shared Planet is in keeping with the company's revitalized mission statement: "to inspire and nurture the human spirit—one person, one cup, and one neighborhood at a time." As part of

Shared Planet, Starbucks promises "reinvigorating the in-store experience for its customers by focusing on the aspects of stores that makes each one unique." These stores feature the "elevation of coffee and removal of unnecessary distractions," use local materials and craftsmanship, emphasize reused and recycled elements, and promise "storytelling and customer engagement through all five senses." Arthur Rubinfeld, president of Starbucks Global Development, said, "We recognize the importance of continuously evolving with our customers' interests, lifestyles, and values in order to stay relevant over the long term. Ultimately, we hope customers will feel an enhanced sense of community, a deeper connection to our coffee heritage, and a greater level of commitment to environmental consciousness."[18]

Starbucks' community involvement is not just online but offline as well. In early 2009, Starbucks launched a "Pledge5" initiative to get people to donate five hours each to community service, toward a total of 1 million hours. Yet another company website (pledge5 .starbucks.com) makes it easy to find volunteer opportunities by partnering with HandsOn Network, providing a list of hundreds of thousands of local volunteer opportunities in the United States. Pledge5 extends to a Facebook application, so you can remind yourself and show others that you have pledged. By fall 2009, the total service hours pledged easily exceeded 1 million. In addition, the company partnered with V2V, an online platform that connects volunteers to service organizations. The connection with V2V was originally made by a Starbucks employee in Connecticut, and was soon extended to a Starbucks V2V platform, which seeks to be a "catalyst for conversation and connection that inspires people to contribute to a cause greater than themselves."[19] Starbucks has set a public global goal of facilitating more than 1 million hours of community service every year. It continues to find ways to connect with nongovernmental organizations (NGOs) and other partners to build joint engagement platforms that harness the collective reach of community involvement in the neighborhoods of Starbucks stores worldwide.

Starbucks is also extending customer involvement all the way into its supply chain. In the past, the company found itself in challenging situations with its coffee bean suppliers over fair trade issues and the branding of coffees based on their origins. The company is now attempting to tackle the issue more directly, through what it calls "ethical sourcing" and collaborating with partners such as Conservation International to buy responsibly grown, ethically traded coffee. The goals are to help create a better future for farmers and to mitigate climate change through farmer incentives, ranging from preventing deforestation to providing capacity-building resources, including loan programs through social investment organizations. In 2009, about 85 percent of Starbucks coffee was grown on small-scale family farms with less than 12 hectares of land. Through its Small Farmer Support Initiative, a joint engagement platform with the Fairtrade Foundation (part of a global network of "fair trade" labeling organizations), Starbucks is now more actively engaged in dialogue with farmers in east Africa and Latin America. And the results show. For instance, since the opening of the company's Farmer Support Center in Costa Rica, Starbucks has seen improvements from participating growers in quality evaluation scores, a 20 percent increase in yields per hectare, an 80 percent reduction in use of pesticides, and a 5 percent increase in suppliers' performance scores for sustainable practices.[20] Customers can even insert themselves into this sustainable supply chain, through the Shared Planet website. An interactive coffee map lets customers see the positive impact Starbucks is having in communities where their coffee is grown. Moreover, the company also gives its customers the opportunity to connect with entrepreneurial artisans from local communities in its supply-side regions—artisans who are creating a better life for themselves and their families. For instance, in the summer of 2009, Starbucks stores began featuring merchandise created by Rwandan artisans such as fabric tumblers and hand-sewn totes, through its relationship with Fair Winds Trading.

The company also sought to "relocalize" its stores, changing their feel from that of a cookie-cutter corporate giant to the local neighborhood coffee shop. It began offering different types of beans in different regions, rather than insisting on batches large enough to distribute across all its stores. It allowed store managers and employees to change the look of individual branches to appeal to local sensibilities. After a series of brainstorming sessions where Schultz told employees to "break the rules and do things for yourself," some of them came up with plans to launch a new pair of shops in Washington, D.C., called 15th Ave. Coffee & Tea. These shops looked aggressively anticorporate, featuring décor scrounged from local shops and coffee servings ground to order.[21]

Thus, through multiple engagement platforms, Starbucks emphasizes that "You" as an individual are an integrative part of its "social ecosystem"—from the farmers and communities on its supply side, to the in-store experience and local neighborhood communities on its demand side, to its employees inside, to the larger fabric of human experiences.

It is important to recognize, however, that a co-creative enterprise is not antithetical to process efficiency, as Starbucks discovered during the economic downturn of 2008–2009. According to Scott Heydon, the company's "vice president of Lean Thinking" (formerly the VP of Global Strategy), reducing waste frees up time for baristas/partners to interact with customers and improve the Starbucks experience. As he notes, "Thirty percent of the partners' time is motion: the walking, reaching, bending." And so in a big efficiency drive, Starbucks used classic lean thinking principles to shave precious seconds in filling each order, cutting the labor required at each store. Because every store is configured differently and has its own customer-traffic patterns, local employees are encouraged to come up with their own solutions rather than apply a single solution sent from headquarters.[22]

In the first quarter of 2010, Starbucks returned to profitability, despite the Great Recession having hammered spending on luxuries (such as gourmet coffee) nationwide. Schultz credited both "the successful innovation and enhancement of the customer experience" and "a transformed, more efficient cost structure."[23]

The Starbucks example also illustrates how *existing* interactions with customers, employees, and all other stakeholders can be made co-creative—by redesigning relationships with people and the environments of interactions as engagement platforms, incorporating an experience mind-set. Further, while enterprises still need to carefully design internal processes and deliver consistently high-quality experiences, rooting out all internal variations in the delivery system, at the same time they must paradoxically "free" how they approach the design and specifications of outcomes (experiences). It is neither consistency in the delivery system nor flexibility in what is delivered, but consistency *and* flexibility." In the co-creative enterprise, every employee who interacts with customers—from the call center operator to the service representative, from the sales associate to the logistics manager, from the engineer to the product developer, from the supply chain partner to the community manager—all have the same responsibility of making interactions more co-creative, human experiences more meaningful, and generating more mutual value.

Build It *With* Them

So far, we have seen examples of engagement platforms in the design of new offerings (Nike+), involving customers in the design (NIKEiD) or marketing process (Nike soccer), ideating with customers (MyStarbucksIdea), or being transparent regarding socially responsible corporate activities (Starbucks Shared Planet). Although these initiatives in and of themselves would be a big step forward in many organizations, co-creation is more than that. It is a full philosophy of business. As illustrated by Nike and Starbucks, companies can use engagement platforms to involve customers, employees, and all stakeholders systematically in a continuous process of value discovery. Ultimately, co-creation is about learning how to create meaningful and rewarding experiences. Co-creation is both the means and the end, in a continuous cycle.

Why does the co-creative enterprise give any manager the

power to create stunning results? The simple but powerful concept of co-creation underscores what leading neurologists tell us: that meaningful interactions among individuals enable people to both learn faster and remember more of what they learn. It tells us what the most exciting brands know—that neither customers nor employees want "take it or leave it" business decisions anymore; they want to be involved in what is created for them and share their experiences. It tells us what the new science about networks and communities has found—that engaged minds in collaboration generate creative solutions even the smartest minds alone may not find.

Co-creation goes well beyond the conventional goods and services view of the past hundred years, where "demand" was conceived to be just "supply looking in the mirror." The co-creative enterprise is *not* about "build it and they will come." Rather, it is about *"build it with them, and they're already there."* Co-creation can be applied to most any type of innovation—from operational and product-service innovation to business strategy and management innovation. In the future, enterprises that do not embrace co-creation principles are likely to see an erosion of value.

Enterprises, whether private, social, or public, all have to engage people, individually and collectively. Fundamentally, enterprises must stop thinking of individuals as passive recipients that they can just deliver to, but must instead *engage individuals as active co-creators in defining and delivering value.* This surely is a substantial challenge. We have found that while many individuals (customers, employees, and all other stakeholders) around the globe are ready to engage with organizations in co-creating value, many enterprises aren't quite ready. That said, dozens of leaders from a wide range of enterprises have approached us with the challenge to awaken and engage others within their organizations to co-creation. The global financial and economic crisis of 2008 and 2009 has created a further sense of urgency in "resetting" value creation—to echo the words of Jeffrey Immelt, CEO of General Electric.[24] As Samuel J. Palmisano, chairman and CEO of IBM Corporation, said during this crisis, "A period of discontinuity is, for those with courage and vision, a period of opportunity . . . And though it may not be easy to see now, I believe we will see new leaders emerge who win not by surviving the storm, but by changing the game."[25]

Figure 1-4: Book Examples

Sector	Organizations	
• Agricultural Life Sciences • Automotive • Capital Intensive Equipment • Commodities • Consumer Durables • Electronics • Energy • Entertainment • Fashion • Fast Moving Consumer Goods (FMCG) • Financial services • Healthcare • Industrial Goods and Services • IT Services • Manufacturing and Contract Services • Media • Pharmaceuticals • Professional Services • Public and Citizen Sector • Retail • Social Sector • Software • Telecom • Travel	• ABB • Amazon • Apple • Ashoka • BEME (Chile) • Brother • Caja Navarra (Spain) • Camiseteria (Brazil) • Cisco • Club Tourism (Japan) • Crédit Agricole (France) • Crushpad • Dassault Systèmes • Dell • ERM • GE Healthcare • GlaxoSmithKline • Google • HCL Technologies (India) • Hindustan Unilever (India) • IBM • Infosys (India) • Innocentive • Intuit	• ITC (India) • Jabil Circuit • Kaiser Chemicals (disguised) • La Poste (France) • LEGO • Mozilla • Nestle • Nike • Nokia • OASIS (S. Korea) • Orange (France) • Rio Grande do Sul (Brazil) • SAP • SEBI • Shell • Sony • Starbucks • TiVo • Toyota Scion • Wacoal (Japan)

In interacting with many leaders worldwide who have begun their own journeys to transform their enterprises, we have discovered a host of brilliant examples of co-creation (see **Figure 1-4**). In the rest of this book, we will present and discuss many of them. Collectively, these examples illustrate the universal applicability of co-creation across a variety of industries and business domains, across the private and public sectors, in both developing and developed countries. We have found that as managers begin exploring value expansion with their peers, employees, and customers, their thinking and actions begin to change. Through their stories in this book of how both traditional and internet-era firms have elevated themselves to a higher orbit of value creation, you will learn how any enterprise, and any group in an enterprise, can harness the immense power of co-creation. Becoming a co-creative enterprise energizes the whole organization.

The Power of Co-Creation is structured into two parts. The rest of part one (chapters 2 to 6) describes value co-creation in more detail. Chapter 2 discusses the core principle of co-creation, as well as the various types of engagement platforms that enterprises can build through interaction linkages. Chapter 3 shows how organizations can expand the space of human experiences and co-create innovation. The aim of chapter 4 illustrates how organizations can expand the scope and scale of interactions by engaging people across business networks. In chapter 5 we show how expanding stakeholder relationships—both for profit and nonprofit organizations—can turbo-charge social innovation and economic development, expand markets at the bottom of the economic pyramid, and extend the social legitimacy of enterprises as a whole. Chapter 6 concludes part one with a discussion of how the design of engagement platforms and the building of co-creation capabilities evolve over time, because this is itself a co-creative process.

When you're done reading Part One: Value Co-Creation, ask yourself as a manager and leader:

- How does the enterprise currently connect with customers and external stakeholders? Can it be more co-creatively engaged in these interactions? Where and how can interactions be made more co-creative?
- What assets and resources—the product or service itself, mobile devices, social media, call centers, retail channels, websites, and communities—can we leverage as engagement platforms? How can we generate better and more experience-based insights with customers and stakeholders through these platforms?

- Where are the operational, product-service, and business innovation opportunities for expanding value? Are there activities and processes inside the enterprise that can be opened up to co-creation? With whom? How can the innovation process be made more co-creative? How do we engage our innovation partners in building engagement platforms together?
- Who are the different types of customers and stakeholders in our business network? How do we currently engage with them? What are the current experiences of people, across the value chain system, as they engage with our platforms and our products, services, and processes? Can we build more meaningful experiences with them?
- What social, environmental, and economic development activities is my organization engaged in? What types of stakeholder interactions can we change for the better? Can we involve our stakeholders in different and new ways to expand mutual value?
- How do we keep platforms alive in embracing value co-creation consistently and across all functions in the organization?

Part two discusses how co-creation can guide the building of new management capabilities. In this new vision of the enterprise, the job of managers is to co-create employees' experiences of management processes and connect them with the experiences of customers, partners, and all other stakeholders. First, organizations should mobilize their customer-facing functions around this transformation to a co-creative enterprise (chapter 7). Leaders must also set up organizational processes so that many different constituencies can co-create with the firm, from employees and managers inside the firm to external customers and stakeholders (chapter 8). Ultimately, co-creative enterprises must go beyond management processes to co-creative engagement (chapter 9) and open up their strategy management processes to new stakeholders (chapter 10). We conclude this book by discussing how enterprises can co-create philanthropic and civic change, and how the institutions of public governance can be transformed through co-creation (chapter 11).

When you're done reading Part Two: Management Co-Creation, ask yourself as a manager and leader:

- Where and how can managers and employees inside the organization be engaged co-creatively? Where and how can we add new stakeholders to management processes? Where and how do we begin the process of change and governance in the organization to become a co-creative enterprise? What organizational capabilities do we need to build?
- Where and how do we enable new and better organizational linkages among our engagement platforms? How do we build the technology and social architecture that enhances these linkages?
- How do we design new human resource processes that enable more meaningful employee experiences? How do we enhance and nurture a culture of co-creation inside the enterprise?
- Where and how do we make the processes of strategy and decision making, and performance management more co-creative? How do we open up these processes, and to whom, inside the enterprise and its business network?
- Where and how can we contribute to and benefit from partnerships among public, social, and private enterprises? How can we enhance our social legitimacy and build trust?

Ultimately, becoming a co-creative enterprise is not just about "thinking outside the box," but about "transforming the box." This transformation results in a "win more–win more" approach to doing business that benefits the enterprise's employees, customers, suppliers, partners, investors, and all other stakeholders. We hope this book inspires you to become a co-creator and your organization to become a co-creative enterprise. We invite you to visit powerofcocreation.com and share your thoughts on the co-creation paradigm as expounded in this "living" book.[26]

Chapter 2

The Co-Creation Principle

In chapter 1, we showed how companies such as Nike and Starbucks have implemented co-creation, unleashing its four powers in the process. The core principle underlying the transformation of enterprises toward co-creation is this: *engaging people to create valuable experiences together while enhancing network economics.*

This co-creation principle has four components, as shown in **Figure 2-1**:

- *Experience mind-set*
- *Context of interactions*
- *Engagement platforms*
- *Network relationships*

Put together, these four components liberate the four powers of co-creation described in chapter 1.

Figure 2-1: The Core Principle of Co-Creation

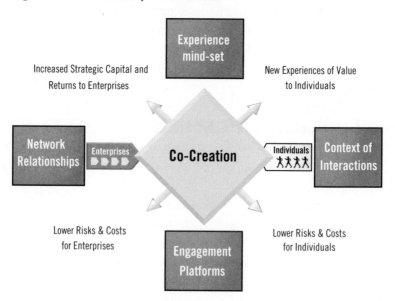

Co-creative enterprises respond to insights originating from the actual engagement experiences of people—customers, employees, suppliers, and other stakeholders—continuously designing and re-designing what is of value, together with them. These enterprises innovate new types of experiences shaped by the context of people's interactions, creating unique value. To make the process effective and affordable, they design engagement platforms that "industrial-ize" the scale and scope of interactions, driving their costs down and reducing risk through co-creative engagement. Doing so re-quires building an expanded, reconfigurable network of resources that goes beyond the traditional boundaries of the organization to expand stakeholder relationships (including private-public-social enterprise partnerships), generating radically new economics for all participants in the ecosystem.

This expansion of value creation in "win more–win more" fashion leads to more and more transformational results, as its scope of application expands over time. In the early stages of co-creation, an organization might experiment by connecting with adjacent elements of the individual's experience, modestly expanding the scope of experience it attempts to influence. Over time, the organization gains the confidence to venture into new experiences for the individuals involved. The same is true of interactions. At the beginning, most organizations experiment with the opening up of a few interactions, then gradually get bolder and end up devising entirely new types of contextualized interactions. Similarly, most enterprises start with a modest expansion of their co-creative network, usually with a small group of players to engage in the initial stage. Over time, though, they gain the confidence to involve a larger and larger set of players, thereby lowering the cost of each new interaction that becomes part of the co-creative ecosystem and energizing new strategic capital that ignites new growth through new network interactions.

There is an iterative, experimental nature to the building of these capabilities. Most organizations start by setting up one platform in one particular corner of the enterprise, then realize that this platform can be linked to other platforms, allowing the co-creation of a broader, more unique experience for the individuals involved. Sometimes companies enter the world of co-creation through the experience door, for example when the marketing department initiates a customer experience program, HR aims to build a different employee experience, or supply chain people realize the vendor experience is an integral part of their competitiveness. Other organizations get started by having process owners attempt to transform single processes into co-creative interactions, for example, in sales, customer service, or product development. Co-creation is sometimes introduced by designers of engagement platforms, such as people who facilitate meeting processes, new technology groups that design interactive devices, or IT departments that promote interactive technologies with business owners. Finally, the move to co-creation can come from the drive for improved competitiveness or a new business model from senior financial people or general managers.

Regardless of where the transformation starts, engagement platforms are the cornerstone of co-creation that support the other three components of co-creative engagement, which we will discuss at length in subsequent chapters. The rest of this chapter focuses on illustrating how co-creative enterprises are building and linking many types of engagement platforms—live meetings, websites, physical stores, physical and digital products, mobile devices, call centers, and private or public community spaces. In some cases, the engagement platforms are integral to the offerings themselves (e.g., Nike+), and in other cases they support and augment product-service offerings (e.g., MyStarbucksIdea). In all cases, engagement platforms are fertile ground for enabling new types of valuable experiences for the individuals involved.

The examples featured in this chapter are:

- **Club Tourism** of Japan, which shows the power of face-to-face live interactions. It also highlights the influence of individual employees over and above technology as a vital element of the best engagement platforms.
- **Dell,** which had to contend with the anger of the blogosphere before realizing the positive side of online engagement with customers. Dell now seeks to harness the ideas of millions of customers through interactions on its websites.
- **Apple Retail Stores,** which have become engagement platforms rather than simply places that sell products. By paying attention to the customer experience in myriad ways—in the store layout and product display, in encouraging customers to browse and use products, and in "high-touch" employee interactions with customers—Apple has redefined how retail stores can work.
- **LEGO,** which illustrates how new types of interactions can be layered around a company's physical and digital offerings, engaging customers and enthusiasts in new ways.
- **The Apple iPhone,** which illustrates the promise of mobile devices for enabling co-creative engagement. In particular, the iPhone's App Store creates an engagement platform

among the company, independent software developers, and its end customers.

- The call centers of **Nestlé** and **Nokia India,** one captive and the other outsourced, show how these companies have transformed them into a powerful capability of co-creating insights through dialogue with customers, and even for customer experimentation.

- **GlaxoSmithKline's Alli** product, which demonstrates the usefulness of private community interactions for co-creating a brand's positioning and product usage. The company used a prelaunch online community to shape usage guidelines for Alli and maintains an ongoing online community for users to support one another.

- The public online communities championed by **Hindustan Unilever (HUL), SAP, & Intuit** show how companies can make use of interactions in public communities to revitalize products and reshape brands (HUL Sunsilk), how community members can support one another to the benefit of all participants (SAP), and how community contributions can improve a product (Intuit).

Live Meetings at Club Tourism

The simplest form of engagement platform is the meeting where people congregate with a specific purpose and a structured process through which they will co-create, thereby playing a central role in defining the product or service experience. A good example of this approach is Club Tourism. A division of Japan's second-largest tourist agency, Kinki Nippon Tourist, Club Tourism has more than 7 million community members and exemplifies the power of building such thematic communities.[1] Club Tourism not only sells tours, it also co-creates experiences with its customers, employees, and travel partners, which include airlines and hotel chains. The enterprise has generated more than two hundred different theme-based clubs for people with a common interest—say, tea drinking.

At Club Tourism, specially designated employees called "Friendly Staff" constantly interact with the clubs to brainstorm ideas about new trips, modifications to existing trips, and desirable new experiences. Through this process, the company generates early ideas of new potential trips and related activities. Now, imagine being invited by Club Tourism to a large Tokyo or Osaka office building with ten or fifteen people who share your passion for tea. With the help of a Friendly Staff facilitator, the Tea Drinking Club designs a trip, identifying activities of potential interest such as visiting tea plantations or learning about the medicinal virtues of tea. Club Tourism taps expert resources like tea connoisseurs and specialists relevant to the club's theme. The Club engages customers who have been on previous related trips, encouraging them to contribute photos and other content. One of the authors attended just such a club meeting, at which a member and a staff person shared photos in a slide show, while other members began conversing and offering ideas about how to enhance future trips, for instance by sampling different types of tea and activities involving the rituals of tea drinking. The Club Tourism facilitator has a dual role. On the one hand, the facilitator listens to suggestions from the people in the room and tries to incorporate those into travel arrangements. On the other hand, she (facilitators are women, in most cases) relays to the group specific deals its travel partners may have offered for particular times or places. The key is that people can ask questions and engage in dialogue about what it all means for their travel experience. Because Club Tourism attracts many elderly people who can travel off-season, the firm can take advantage of cheaper accommodations, which reduces the cost of the trip and allows Club Tourism to retain more margins, away from the bargaining power of tour operators during peak vacation periods. People who have been on one of these pioneering trips are the best agents to sell to the next customers. Many of the initial club members are also recruited as facilitators or travel guides on subsequent trips.

Once the trip concept has been fully developed and the first trip has taken place, Club Tourism moves to mass marketing. Its methods are largely low-tech; the mass marketing involves the distribution of catalogs delivered door-to-door on bicycles by part-time employees, often hired from among customers. These employees, called Echo Staff, play an important customer relations role for Club Tourism, as they often represent the high point of the day for elderly people living alone. In addition to acting as evangelists for Club Tourism, Echo Staff also cycle back to the organization new insights on what people are interested in, thereby generating new ideas for potential clubs. Through this *systematic elevation of customers to the role of company insiders,* the firm is able to concentrate singlemindedly on customer experience. Moreover, this process removes most of the risk typically associated with new hires, since these former customers represent a known entity to the firm.

Before tours, club members gather at Club Tourism's classroom, which is called Chie House (*chie* means knowledge), for free study sessions of the history of the tour destination. After tours, customers share their travel experiences with each other and the Friendly Staff, who take notes and learn from customer experiences. The instructors at these sessions are also recruited from Club Tourism's customer base, and many are former schoolteachers.

Club Tourism is an example of the co-creative power of live, face-to-face interactions with consumers. While some conventional travel agencies do some of these activities as well, Club Tourism's uniqueness is that it also focuses attention on the before- and after-travel experiences. The company describes the travel experience as a cycle that starts with an imaginative design, carries through the actual trip, involves a formal debrief of the trip, and eventually generates memories. Employees view their business as supporting the entire cycle, not simply organizing the trip in the middle.

Club Tourism has been successful because it has redefined its role as that of a "nodal" company—connecting customers with travel partners and community resources—which allows it to escape the commodity dynamics of the travel business. As a result, Club Tourism grew to be one of the parent company's main businesses in both sales revenue and profits.[2]

Engaging Customers at Dell

We may not think of physical meetings as natural places for co-creation, but we more intuitively see the web as the vanguard of customer interaction and co-creation. With everything from blogs to videos, wikis, podcasts, and the plethora of social interaction technologies on websites, conversation online has boomed. The paradox is that few companies use this technological explosion to engage their customers in productive and creative ways. Instead, they leave it to consumers to engage in conversations among themselves, where they share their often-negative experiences of dealing with companies. Transforming corporate websites into engagement platforms constitutes a huge opportunity in just about any industry. As Michael Dell, CEO of Dell Inc., put it in 2008, "If we don't do this at Dell.com, it's going to be on CNET or somewhere else. I'd rather have that conversation in my living room than in somebody else's."[3] But it took a customer-induced storm, and the enlightenment of Michael Dell himself, for the company to embrace this conversation.

Many stories of successful web-based co-creation start with a corporate crisis. In June 2005, Jeff Jarvis, a Dell customer (and a professor of journalism) posted a blog entry called "Dell Hell." He had recently purchased a new laptop, paying a high price for a four-year, in-home customer service warranty. He experienced many problems with it, from overheating and network connectivity problems to microprocessor usage issues and machine hang-ups. The service representative who came to Jarvis's house couldn't fix the problems—he did not seem to ever have the necessary parts—ultimately forcing Jarvis to send the laptop back. It turned out that the replacement machine did not work properly either. Only after emailing Dell's chief marketing officer did Jarvis get someone to resolve the issue and receive a full refund. Jarvis ended up buying an Apple computer, and in August 2005 he blogged an open letter to Michael Dell articulating how his intent was to help rather than harm the company. Jarvis suggested that Dell management read blogs, ask customers for guidance, and participate in the conversation that customers were having *without* Dell.

Dell already had active programs in place for customer satisfaction, service quality, and market research. In fact, the company was considered by many to be highly customer-oriented. After all, Dell had largely invented the "direct model," in which the company interacts directly with its customers. It relied on excellent phone and online customer support to connect with them. The problem was that all of Dell's customer-oriented activities were largely *the company's view of the customer experience, not the customer's*. In other words, Dell's customer orientation was largely *product-centric and service process–centric, and, therefore, firm-centric*. Dell treated its customers as passive recipients of its offerings and processes, disproportionately influencing the nature of customer value and staging— rather than co-creating—the customer experience. The focus at Dell was on connecting the company's offerings to the customer, not on allowing customers to interact with Dell's products and processes on their own terms. Dell's model was being challenged, not by new competitors, but by Jarvis and legions of connected, informed, and active customers who wanted their view of value to be recognized.

The Dell Hell blog post gave a voice to thousands of frustrated customers who had been experiencing poor customer service from Dell and unleashed a raging customer storm that had been simmering in the market.[4] The blog discussion was a leading indicator of Dell's problems. Once a stalwart on *Fortune* magazine's list of "America's Most Admired Companies," Dell saw its customer satisfaction metrics plummet. The American Customer Satisfaction Index (ASCI) commented in August 2005 that at Dell, "Customer service in particular has become a problem . . . Customer complaints are up significantly with long wait times and difficulties with Dell's call center abound . . . Whether Dell's declining satisfaction will have a negative impact on the company's stock performance remains to be seen; however, ACSI history has shown that changes in customer satisfaction often signal similar changes in future financial performance." And indeed, Dell's stock price began a sharp decline soon after Jarvis's initial blog post. In the fall of 2005, Dell had to issue a profit warning.

In April 2006, Dell finally joined the conversation. The company began tracking blog posts, and it launched a "blog resolution team" to offer customer service and technical support, dispatching technicians to complaining bloggers and earnestly trying to solve their problems. In July 2006, Dell launched its Direct2Dell blog, with Dell's Lionel Menchaca giving the company a human face and a no-nonsense voice. The company took a while to find its stride. Bloggers, including Jarvis, blasted Dell's first blog posts as classic corporate communications gobbledygook. Deeply etched ways of "enterprise think" limited Dell's ability to exhibit authenticity and shift to co-creation mode. To its credit, the firm became more humble. It acknowledged that Jarvis and other bloggers "were kind enough to tell us what we're doing wrong" and that it would "keep working to get it right." The company asked for patience: "Give us some time and we'll prove it."[5]

Dell has indeed come a long way. For starters, Michael Dell made a point of personally meeting with Jarvis. Michael Dell later remarked that "these conversations are going to occur whether you like it or not, okay? Well, do you want to be part of that or not? My argument is you absolutely do. You can learn from that. You can improve your reaction time. And you can be a better company by listening and being involved in that conversation."[6] Michael Dell sees co-creating insights with customers as the linchpin of his strategy for Dell 2.0, saying, "We need to think differently about the market and engage our customers in almost everything we do. It's a key to regaining momentum as a technology industry leader."[7]

And so, in February 2007, Dell launched its IdeaStorm website. Users post their ideas on the site, the community votes, the most popular ideas rise to the top, and the company responds to those ideas. Just five days after launch, there were 1,384 ideas, voted on 122,388 times with 2,189 comments. In a year, 8,859 ideas had been submitted, voted on 613,638 times with 66,882 comments. The company had implemented more than twenty of those ideas in the first year, but most important, it had learned a whole lot about how customers think. For instance, there was overwhelming desire on the part of customers to get rid of the "trial-ware" on their PCs and all those things that clog up system resources. The technology industry may believe that giving more to customers equates to greater value, but customers told Dell it has negative value. Other popular ideas included newer product configurations with Microsoft's older operating system (XP rather than Vista), a "no OS" option, pre-installed Linux (Ubuntu), reduced plastic wrap, and more standardized accessories.

Dell has retrained staff to take on more problems and responsibility, e.g., higher-end techs can scrap their phone scripts, and techs in some countries have been trained in empathy. Dell stopped counting the "handle time" per call that rushed conversations by motivating reps to transfer customers promptly, pushing them to become someone else's problem. "In order to become very efficient, I think we became ineffective," said Dick Hunter, the former head of manufacturing turned head of customer service.[8] At Dell's worst, more than 7,000 of the 400,000 customers calling each week suffered transfers more than seven times. The transfer rate fell from 45 to 18 percent. The minutes per resolution of problems now run in the 40s. Dell trained a squad of 42 employees to spend their workdays engaging with customer communities on Facebook, Twitter, and other social media. The percentage of negative blog posts about Dell has dropped from 49 to 22 percent. A key learning from the company's social media crew: potential customers spend 99 percent of their time on the web doing research and just 1 percent actually buying.[9] As a result, Dell is now dialing down the hard sell, helping customers make more informed choices, and focusing on generating insights usable for new products and markets. For example, in 2008, Dell engineers took the collective learning from IdeaStorm and generated a new laptop with a keyboard that lights up in the dark, faster connection component technologies, longer battery life, and extra security. The new laptop embodied Dell's new ability to co-opt customers early on and engage in continuous, iterative interactions with those who actually used the new laptops. As a result, the company's reaction time improved and the development cycle time started shrinking.

With Michael Dell returning as CEO of Dell in 2008, the company further expanded its engagement with customers. Said Michael Dell, "I'm sure there's a lot of things that I can't even imagine, but our customers can imagine. A company this size is not going to be about a couple of people coming up with ideas. It's going to be about millions of people and harnessing the power of those ideas."[10]

Although Dell's sales fell in the Great Recession of 2008–2009, one of the few bright spots has come from embracing the social media website Twitter. Dell had attracted 1.5 million followers on Twitter by late 2009, and its Twitter feed led directly to sales of $6.5 million in PCs, accessories, and software. The company received kudos for the authenticity of its engagement with Twitter users, and recognition for its efforts to engage with customers across a range of social media. One journalist wrote, ". . . there is more to the company's social-media thinking than a Twitter campaign, and the reason is that it learned about social-media engagement the hard way."[11]

Changing the Retail Experience at Apple Stores

The bricks-and-mortar retail store is the workhorse of traditional, pre-web selling. Yet retail stores can be more than places that sell products; they can become engagement platforms. One of the best ways to see how this can be done is to contrast Apple retail stores with Sony's stores. Compared to Apple, Sony has a much larger suite of products it is now offering through Sony Style stores, where the customer is invited to play (on the PlayStation game console), photograph (Sony cameras), watch (Sony TVs), create (Vaio computers), listen (Walkman MP3 players), and read (electronic book downloads through the Sony Reader, comparable to Amazon's Kindle). In addition, Sony offers its own music and videos through its media store (including some of its own productions from Sony BMG Music, featuring artists such as Beyoncé, and films from its own Sony Pictures studio). It also offers the Sony Ericsson line of mobile phones (e.g., the Walkman phone).

With such a broad lineup of offerings, one might expect Sony stores to win the battle for customer loyalty against Apple hands-down. Unless, of course, you've been to an Apple Retail Store. The Sony stores are far less successful than Apple's, and the core reason for this is Sony's ferocious focus on products. The Sony Style store epitomizes the challenge of having an *experience mind-set*. Sony has opened sixty such stores, but they have been unfavorably reviewed because of their "me, too" nature and failure to engage customers. The Sony flagship store in New York City—close to Apple's Fifth Avenue store—was described as offering "the hush of a mausoleum."[12] A *New York Times* reviewer offered the following advice to Sony regarding its stores: "Just connect." Sony characterizes the stores as "fashion retail boutiques" that happen to carry electronics rather than clothing, yet the stores have been criticized for simply displaying goods rather than enabling an emotional connection with games, photos, TV shows, and music.[13]

Responding to the criticisms and lack of consumer interest, Sony launched the Backstage service offering in 2007, which attempts to duplicate Apple's Genius Bar and one-on-one training. Backstage offers a five-stage process that involves setting up software on the customer's machine, protecting data through backup, educating customers through personal trainers, enhancing the speed of the customer's computer through new memory or software, and repairing hardware and software as needed. Only time will tell if Sony makes headway with these changes.

Now consider the wildly popular Apple Retail Stores. What is it that Apple got so right? Apple has brought to life new experiences not only for its customers but also for its employees. In 2008, the 280-plus retail Apple Stores around the world registered sales per square foot of about $4,700 (versus under $1,000 for Best Buy, for example).[14] Total sales at Apple Retail Stores reached $6.3 billion in fiscal year 2008, barely seven years after the first one opened. More than half the computers sold at Apple Stores in 2007 went to people new to the Macintosh platform—whether novice personal computer users or converts from a PC platform.[15] This rate has boosted the Mac's share of the personal computer market to around 7 percent in 2009, from a base of 2 to 3 percent in the years before the retail stores launched in 2001.[16] The operating margin on Apple Stores was an impressive 21 percent of sales in 2008, with Apple Stores contributing more than 20 percent of revenues and 25 percent of profits for Apple.

The central stroke of brilliance in Apple's success is that CEO Steve Jobs recognized that the personal computer had evolved from a productivity tool to a hub for experiencing video, photography, music, and information of all kinds. Computer sales had become less about the physical product, the machine, than about what the user could do with it. Jobs conceived of the Apple Retail Store in large part because he felt Macs were poorly sold by the general-purpose consumer electronic stores, which typically allocated space and attention to the Mac in proportion to its low market share, meaning that store employees did not know how to engage customers in discovering the Mac's true abilities.

In 2001, Jobs hired Ronald Johnson away from Target to run Apple Stores. The two of them decided to rent a warehouse, build a prototype store, and experiment. As the first warehouse took shape near the Apple campus, Jobs recalls that the two men winced when they looked at their mock-up store. The hardware was laid out in conventional product category format—in other words, according to how the company thinks, conditioned by how it is organized internally—and not by *customer experience think*," i.e., how a customer might actually want to experience and buy things.[17]

Jobs and Johnson scrapped the product-oriented store layout

and replaced it with a design aimed at getting customers to play with products as they would use them if they already owned them. Rather than designing the store as an extension of Apple's internal processes, they started from the *processes through which customers interact with electronic products and create their experience of those products*. As a result, Apple Stores display comparatively few products spaciously arranged on large wooden tables, which removes the traditional display cacophony of most retail stores. Customers can try on the earphones of an iPod Touch, pick out a song, and listen to music actually loaded onto it. Apple employees are nearby if you need them, from the concierge who orients entering customers to the roving salespeople who perform checkouts.

Ironically for a high-tech company, the Apple Retail Store is a low-tech, high-touch engagement platform. While the products are technology oriented, the Apple Store relies on a well-considered utilization of physical space, coupled with personal advice provided by employees to support the customers' discovery of new experiences. Great attention was paid to how customers browse the store and experience the offerings, and how they learn to use the products.

A crucial appeal of the in-store interactions is the ability for consumers to bring the *personal context* of their own experiences to the store. For example, they may bring in a digital camera and test how easy it is to create their family's photo album. Few other manufacturers of electronic products offer consumers the opportunity to learn how to use their products *before* the actual purchase. Apple has set up its stores to allow this presale discovery. Both customer and company gain from this new interaction, since customers reduce their risk of picking a product they don't like and Apple increases its chances of making a sale. Apple Stores also offer a Personal Shopping service that allows customers to book an appointment with a knowledgeable specialist who will discuss any product the customer is interested in and provide a demo of that product in the unique context of what the customer wants to learn, without any sales pressure or obligation to buy.

Another appealing part of the Apple learning experience is the option to sign up for a "personal trainer" to continue acquiring new skills in using a product, often long after it's been purchased. As of 2007, more than 1 million Apple customers had spent $99 a year to have the right to make a one-on-one appointment with a personal trainer—by phone or online—for whatever the customer wanted to learn. This is a very effective means for people to combat "feature-itis," the common tendency by technology companies to overemphasize features of products rather than the experience they provide. At Apple Stores, actual or would-be customers no longer have to wonder whether RAM refers to a goat, megahertz to an oversized car rental company, or Gig to a dance. Instead, they can get answers to simple yet confounding questions such as "How can I transfer music into and photos out of my iPod, Mac, and iPhone?"

At the Apple Store, one can learn how to create and share music playlists, turn photos into a calendar, record an audio podcast, or shoot a movie of a child's birthday party. The prepaid flat fee reassures customers that there are no hidden sales agendas on the part of Apple employees, allowing them to lower their guard and concentrate on learning. Yet while Apple does not use the training sessions for a hard sell, the sessions often result in additional sales on their own, induced by the lessons rather than the conventional sales push. Once a customer has gotten good at photography, she is more likely to want to upgrade her photo-editing software, boost the amount of memory she has, or even buy a new computer.

One of the most effective features of the Apple Store is the now-famous Genius Bar. Instead of offering a faceless call center that prevents customers from physically demonstrating their struggles, the Genius Bar allows them to make an appointment, show up at the store with the actual device in hand, and talk at no cost with a designated Apple Genius who will have a dialogue with them and diagnose the repair or service issue. The Genius Bar itself is a carefully designed space. It is typically located in the back of the store, with a big sign above it and a clear display of the appointment schedule. Customers sit shoulder-to-shoulder on high stools, leaning over a long wood bar, speaking with employees who wear the obligatory T-shirt of the creative set. The Genius Bar's success lies in encouraging a two-way dialogue, thereby removing the intimidation and condescension of the traditional repair interaction. (The term "Genius" may seem arrogant, but Apple Geniuses are trained to convey parity in the exchange with customers; also, they're arguably part of an elite since the firm hires only one of twenty applicants.)

Thus, Apple Stores have expanded the scope of the traditional customer experience in a retail shop. While most retailers focus on the moment of purchase transaction—getting the customer to buy as quickly and as much as possible, through the exasperating "cross-sell"—the Apple Store invites interactions that offer a new and unique customer experience long before the purchase (browsing and touching) and long after it (one-on-one trainer, Genius Bar). Following the Apple Stores example, the challenge for many retailers over the next few years will be to foster co-creative customer experiences inside their stores, rather than use them as a "push channel."

LEGO's Physical and Digital Experiences

LEGO has been a pioneer in co-created product design. Although LEGO's approach to co-creation has increasingly become high-tech over the years, at its core it relies on a highly standardized, unmistakably physical product: the LEGO block of our childhoods. By building technology-enhanced communities at the edge of a physical product, LEGO has shown the world that co-created experiences can take place around a physical product.[18]

The LEGO Factory was the first of several co-creative initiatives launched by the company. Using LEGO Digital Designer software, customers can design and build any model they can imagine. They simply download the software, free of charge, and can then start designing from scratch or choose one of a number of starter models.

They can then upload their designs to the LEGO Factory Gallery, where designs can be stored and shared with other users. Designers can choose to have their own products manufactured for a fee. Customer-designed products feature the customer designer's picture on the box, along with an auto-generated building guide. LEGO chooses some of the most popular customer designs for mass production. All custom products are based on LEGO's standard bricks and other decorative pieces. The company also works closely with individual retail stores and develops unique offerings with them.

Within the LEGO Factory, the company has created an online community that engages more than 400 million people through message boards and a website called My LEGO Network. The dialogue created through these forums allows enthusiasts to exchange ideas. The company's core audience is children, but a large group of adult "superusers" also participates in the generation of product ideas, or downright invention of new products.[19] A case in point is the LEGO Architecture series of kits for noted buildings. Cecilia Weckstrom, who heads LEGO Group's Consumer Insight & Experience Innovation team, calls LEGO Architecture "a great example of a fan-created enterprise on the LEGO platform [that] has come to completely revolutionize the souvenir industry and also to become a great product appealing to a different audience than we would normally do." Through the Architecture series, LEGO has become the supply chain for an architect turned superfan, producing the bricks for his products, which he and the LEGO community distribute around the world.[20]

LEGO's latest online offering is a virtual world called LEGO Universe. It involves a massive multiplayer online game where players can create online versions of themselves—the ubiquitous "avatars." LEGO Universe blends animated environments with characters and buildings made of digital plastic pieces. Each player's avatar is a customizable digital version of the "minifigs," the tiny characters included with most standard LEGO kits. Players can create, enact battles and destroy, or just plain fiddle with bricks. As LEGO chief experience officer Mark William Hansen notes, "We want to make the connection between digital play and physical play. The physical experience is our core; the digital experience will never replace the physical experience, but it's a nice add-on."[21] And as in LEGO Factory, consumers can order the physical versions online and have the actual bricks delivered to their door. All the while, LEGO's classic products continue to be among the most popular toys ever.

Thus, LEGO's strategy spans traditional building kits and customized, personalized products designed by customers through LEGO's online tools. LEGO also shows how community-based co-creation approaches in established firms can mix in the new with the old.

LEGO's Mindstorms robotics line constitutes the third co-creation initiative of LEGO. It allows consumers to create robots using the familiar LEGO bricks. Mindstorms 1.0 was released in 1998, featuring a microcomputer and snap-on infrared sensors. Using their PCs as a sandbox, users could write computer code and snap together blocks of code to build their robot—just like they would do with the studded LEGO bricks. To LEGO's surprise, Mindstorms rekindled the child in thousands of adults, who made up more than half of Mindstorms users. Independent websites sprang up, allowing enthusiasts to share instructions on how to build robots ranging from sorting machines to intruder alarms to land rovers. Over time, Mindstorms fans began to experiment with advanced programming design software made available by other firms such as National Semiconductor (NSC). To sustain the interest of these enthusiasts using its software, NSC then reciprocated by showcasing their work at robotics leagues. An entire ecosystem was born.

Opening up its design, LEGO invited enthusiasts to take part in the programming of the user interface of Mindstorms. In the fall of 2006, LEGO introduced Mindstorms 2.0 NXT, which features programmable "intelligent bricks" and new capabilities for motion and touch, as well as a range of new sensors such as gyroscopes and accelerometers. NXT includes a programming interface called LabVIEW, which was co-developed with a select group of LEGO enthusiasts, some of whom have advanced degrees in robotics. For the launch, LEGO selected several robotics buffs from a large pool of applicants (many of whom already had their own blogs dedicated to Mindstorms), gave them access to inside information, and encouraged them to write about their impressions of NXT. LEGO also set up a message board allowing users to discuss their experiences with the new product generation, and encouraged them to share pictures of their creative inventions. At that point, LEGO was no longer solely engaging a community of fans in designing, developing, and marketing Mindstorms NXT. It was now encouraging the community to evolve beyond the firm's control, doing much more than act as an extension of the firm's development resources: they represented a whole new competence base, in creative conjunction with employees of the firm.

Apple iPhone as a Mobile Engagement Platform

Mobile devices are another means to engage partners, customers, and stakeholders. When Apple launched the iPhone in 2007, it took its focus on customer experience to another level: first, in what the users can do with the device; then, by opening the iPhone to software developers everywhere, resulting in tens of thousands of applications that users can choose from.

As a device-based platform that enables users to create personalized experiences, the iPhone ups the ante for customer experience. For starters, it's a smart phone with internet capability and a camera. Many other smart phones share these features, but the iPhone became the market leader by offering superior capabilities in each application, and, most important, by linking them together more effectively in one device. Still images and videos can be manipulated and shared in intuitive fashion, for example. Phone commands are quite easy to use. Calling and web surfing can be done simultaneously. The device is motion- and position-sensitive, which opens up a world of possibilities for location-based activities. The iPhone links to other Apple devices effortlessly. It enables users to browse the iTunes music store online, sample a song, and instantly download it to their phones. The iPhone is itself a computer. Apple sold 11.6 million iPhones in 2008, the first full year of sales, exceeding its publicly announced goal of 10 million phones.[22]

The truly amazing story of the iPhone, however, is the opening up of Apple's software to new applications developed by individuals or organizations around the world. By making its internal Software Development Kit (SDK) available online at no cost to software developers, Apple has stimulated a wildly popular new dimension of consumer experience. The online App Store is a viral phenomenon that "has reinvented what you can do with a mobile handheld device," Jobs has said.[23] The myriad applications offered for the iPhone tap into users' desire to participate in shaping the devices they use. Apps enable new types of personalized experiences for each iPhone user.

The App Store achieved an impressive 100 million downloads just two months after its introduction, and maintained its blistering pace with more than 3 billion downloads in about two years, exceeding even the speed with which iTunes took off. It has caught the attention of thousands of developers who offer their wares on the iPhone and iPod Touch, making it a cauldron of exciting new applications appearing every day and driving a huge buzz around the device. By autumn 2009, over 125,000 software developers had joined Apple's iPhone Developer Program and had made more than 85,000 apps available on the App Store. Apple made it easy for developers to distribute their offerings. Ads for the iPhone feature the App Store as one of its most valuable features, touting the snazzy applications developed by third parties. This free marketing for developers of popular applications is a boost to the traditional developer experience. Further, the prices of the applications are set by the developers themselves (after basic screening by Apple) and range from "free" to "fee," with most priced at under $5. Apple splits the revenue with developers on a 30 to 70 percent basis. The new iPad, launched in January 2010, offers publishers the opportunity to sell e-books as "apps" on the same 30 to 70 percent basis, a larger margin than heretofore experienced by publishers with retailers or Amazon.

The development of the App Store marked a dramatic shift in Apple's approach to applications development, as it is the first time the company has opened up its internal product development processes to co-creation. Apple has long been known for its secrecy about its operating systems and its suspiciousness of any external attempt to open up any element of its hardware or software.[24] With the advent of the App Store, however, Apple became a co-creative firm engaging individuals and communities, at both the customer and developer ends of its value chain, and went beyond consumers and traditional software developers to media, brand managers, entrepreneurs, and superfans, and partnering with firms such as Nike (on Nike+). The power of the App Store was extended in 2010 with the launch of Apple's iPad, which was based on the iPhone operating system and ran the 100,000+ apps of the iPhone right from the start. In the first two months, Apple not only sold more than two million iPads, but more than 8,500 iPad apps were downloaded over 35 million times. As Steve Jobs put it, "the iPad is changing the way we experience the web, email, photos, maps, video, you name it. It's a whole new way to interact with the internet, apps, content, and media."

Transforming Call Centers at Nestlé and Nokia

One of the most consistently frustrating customer experiences comes from call centers, which many companies use as their first point of contact with existing customers after they have bought a product or service. Interestingly, call centers are equal opportunity offenders in that they often provide a negative experience for both the customer and the call center agent. It does not have to be that way. The enterprise call center, in particular, represents a powerful but underused opportunity to co-create insights with customers.

One of the authors witnessed an innovative use of a call center in Kyoto in 2005, where Nestlé was experimenting with one of its four captive call centers in Japan—"captive" referring to the fact that these call centers are staffed with company employees rather than contractors.[25] The head of Customer Relationship, Junpei Fujisaki, was spearheading a new initiative dubbed "CRM as Dialogue" that was vividly emphasized around the call center. Agents seemed more relaxed than in a conventional outsourced call center. As we walked, Fujisaki explained that his focus was on ensuring that employees were happy, because they otherwise would not be able to engage customers in a dialogue. Most important, he said, was the quality of the conversations and the "active listening and probing mind-set" of employees. These employees had undergone a qualitatively different kind of training. The call center overlooked the beautiful Kobe Bay, and employees had the best view. These customer-facing employees were referred to as "line managers" rather than staff, to reflect their disproportionate influence on the customer experience.

Every so often, one of the call center employees would get up, go to the center of the room, and write down some insights she had gleaned (all the employees were women), identifying herself as the source of the comment. Occasionally, someone from the product development group or the interactive marketing group on the other side of the floor (without a direct view of Kobe Bay) would stop by and look at the comments. If anything caught their attention, they'd arrange for that particular issue to be explored further. In this way, call center employees were actively engaged in the new product development process and in fine-tuning the marketing of new products, along with customers. Each month, an award was given for "best co-created insight," as judged by departmental managers. Now, contrast the sense of self-worth generated for the Nestlé Japan's call center employees with the experience of typical call center employees measured on "average handle time." The same jump in experience quality applies to the customers who called the center and were encouraged to share their experiences—in 2005, more than 1.5 million people contacted the Nestlé call center.

In emerging markets, customer call centers can be a rich place for customer experimentation and generating insights. Consider the Customer Care Center at Nokia India, which handles customer service and repair of Nokia's mobile handsets. Every year, Nokia launches a large number of new mobile phone models, producing a service challenge of major proportions. India is one of Nokia's fastest-growing markets, and in 2006 the company had a commanding 70 percent market share there. Sanjeev Sharma, then CEO of Nokia India, told the authors that market leadership wasn't good enough for Nokia: he wanted the firm to become "invincible." This meant focusing on customer retention as much as customer acquisition.

Given the fast pace of new product introductions into the market, Nokia had to contend with several issues involving malfunctioning handsets. In a high-growth market like India, where more than 70 million mobile phones were being sold annually at the time, it was hard to keep up with the relentless flow of customer service calls coming through the call center and retail care centers. Shivakumar (Shiv), head of Service Operations at Nokia India, was working relentlessly to reduce Turn-Around Time (TAT) and provide an excellent service experience at every touchpoint. Shiv's group had previously launched several TAT-related initiatives to reduce response time and improve service, by improving process quality, and Nokia had run several successful Quality Management, Six Sigma, and continuous-process improvement programs. In 2006, Sharma got together with Shiv to explore how co-creative thinking could enhance their approach to customer care.[26]

After a series of workshops discussing co-creation opportunities, call center employees started listening to customer calls with a "different ear," as Shiv put it. By focusing on customer experience in addition to call productivity, customer care managers began to see new co-creation opportunities. They started imagining new experiments. For example, what would happen if the call center sought out customers rather than waiting for customers to call them? By contacting previous callers for a dialogue, they discovered that many customers would pay to have their phone picked up at home or at work. If the phone could not be repaired, they would be happy with a substitute handset, as long as the individual's contacts and content were transferred over to the new phone and it was fully charged. This retrospectively simple insight triggered the implementation of more creative ideas, such as the development of a "floating mobile van" that stops at selected Nokia dealers, makes simple repairs on site, takes phones to a central repair center, and returns them on the next round a few days later. Many dealers got very excited about the van and started competing with each other to have it park outside their stores, even offering to share in the cost of mobile van operations. In this fashion, Nokia dealers became involved, as a community, in the co-creation of the new repair process between customers and Nokia.

The Nokia co-creation team also began imagining what would happen if the repair process at the centers was made transparent to customers. Several customers had expressed the desire to know what was happening to their expensive phones as they were being repaired. As Nokia listened to the dialogue with customers in the call centers, it became evident that much of the "soft" contextual information about service problems was not being captured in the database, e.g., the fact that the handset had been dropped into water, or that the same problem had occurred several times before. The Nokia co-creation team realized the best way to guarantee that the problem description was accurate was to open the call center database to customers, i.e., let customers add the information themselves. This move eliminated multiple calls to ensure the information was accurate, thereby reducing Nokia's costs while creating a better experience for the customer.

Nokia also began recognizing the potential role the call center could play in channeling customer insights to the teams that were developing new mobile phone software tailored to the Indian market. Software development is a delicate art in that developers, no matter how talented or thorough they are, cannot anticipate all the circumstances in which the phone will be used. This results in user difficulties, bugs, and shortcomings in how the software works. The problem is further compounded by the high frequency with which mobile phones are launched every year. Realizing the company could not fix this situation alone, the co-creation team decided to partner with talented users and hackers in identifying and correcting the problems. For example, a New Delhi disc jockey called the Nokia service number to suggest a change in mailing list software. In the conversation that ensued, the team discovered he had redesigned the software for big mailing lists. They invited him to the Gurgaon headquarters of Nokia India, where he showed the team how he had tinkered with the software. All they had to do was import his fix into the software, and a new application was born. With that, the team realized the call center was more than a repository for problems: it was in fact an engagement platform for co-creating insights with millions of Nokia users, some of them even acting as augmented developers.

Using Private Community Spaces for GlaxoSmithKline Alli

Online communities are powerful engagement platforms for co-creation. One of the best ways to build a community is to invite a group of customers to share their experience of a product or service with the firm in a private, insiders-only setting. This allows companies to understand in more nuanced ways their customers' needs and desires, while giving customers unique access to some of the company's resources. The pharmaceutical company GlaxoSmithKline (GSK) used this approach with great success in launching a new over-the-counter weight-loss pill called Alli in 2007.

Technically, Alli is a reduced-strength version of orlistat (also sold by Roche as Xenical), a prescription drug to treat obesity. It promotes weight loss by decreasing the absorption of fat in the intestines. As the only FDA-approved over-the-counter weight-loss product, Alli had a distinct market advantage. But GSK also faced several challenges. The drug is meant to be used in conjunction with a low-calorie, low-fat diet and regular exercise, which means that behavioral change is integral to using Alli. Because Alli impedes the body's ability to metabolize fat, if a user eats more than the recommended 15 grams of fat in a given meal, they run the risk of potentially unpleasant and embarrassing "treatment effects," in the form of diarrhea or leakage. In short, if a customer isn't compliant with a low-fat diet, the customer experience can be strongly negative. Also, most of the weight loss from Alli takes place in the first six months of use, and a big challenge for users is that they may well regain the weight when they stop taking the medication. Thus, while Alli can be a supplement to a weight-loss regimen, it cannot substitute for it.

GSK knew that to be successful in Alli's launch, it had to build a customer base for whom the drug worked, optimizing the likelihood that good candidates—those willing and able to change their eating and exercise behavior—would buy the product, and that poor candidates—people looking for a "miracle drug" instead of long-term lifestyle changes—would not. Because word-of-mouth and peer-to-peer recommendations have such influence in this product category, Alli consumers might be able to help each other identify whether or not the drug was right for them.

Enter Communispace, a company whose specialty is in helping companies set up, manage, and leverage private online communities quite rapidly. In April 2007, Communispace and GSK Consumer Healthcare invited 400 overweight women and men to be part of the Alli "First Team"—an online community of early users, facilitated by Communispace, who would help design the Alli program, share personal experiences, and discuss how to support community members. The core insight in developing this program was that the desire to lose weight is a psychological crucible for many people. It would be a great benefit for them to be able to share their experiences about Alli with one another, and to take part in a community of others going through the same struggle. There was also great value for the company. Communispace put it this way: GSK "needed a way to understand the rational and emotional tugs of war overweight adults face every day in order to help the company develop, and inspire, a new behavioral model, while carefully managing consumer expectations."[27]

The site that GSK and Communispace set up allowed the first users to provide candid feedback about their experiences with Alli in an effort to help others succeed on the program. One of the First Team members wrote, "In beginning the Alli program, I learned that there are 'treatment effects,' so if you cheat (by eating foods that are high in fat), you will pay the price. Luckily, I've stayed within the plan so I have not had any treatment effects. However, I pushed the envelope once."[28] Another First Teamer said, "I committed to losing the weight with Alli and have lost twenty pounds in ten weeks. The treatment effects have been manageable and have kept me honest about my diet."[29] The site was an open and honest forum that made it clear that Alli is not a magic pill. The online conversation illuminated for GSK the nature of the problems that users had in sticking to the regimen that would allow the pill to have its optimal effect.

Based on insights from the First Team community, GSK then designed a website for Alli users to help them appreciate the importance of behavioral modification and to assist in keeping them on track. The website contains a clear explanation of how Alli works in the body (including a warning about treatment effects), stories of real Alli users, tips for healthy eating and exercise, and a community section called Allicircles in which registered members can commiserate and celebrate. GSK also created a separate website for health care professionals, including doctors, dieticians, and pharmacists, with clinical information about Alli and how to counsel patients using it. Also on the consumer website is "Myalliplan" for each person purchasing Alli, developed by nutrition and weight management experts in conjunction with users. This platform features an individually tailored online action plan, including meals and recipes for a healthy diet, online tools to record food and lifestyle information, and connection to a social network of other users. The site also sends personalized emails offering encouragement and suggestions for weight loss, delivering lessons about managing hunger, dealing with setbacks (with links to community members as a support group), and making the food and lifestyle changes to help people succeed—all with the intent of helping Alli users develop the skills to lose weight and keep it off. Myalliplan became a centerpiece of the Alli program. The effectiveness of the site is expressed well by this post from one user: "I have never seen a pharmaceutical company go to such lengths to provide such education, support, and valuable tools to the consumers who will buy their product. This has totally changed my notions about the 'greedy pharmaceutical industry.' Thank you all."[30]

After the Alli website was launched nationwide in the United States in June 2007, more than 2 million starter packs of the product were sold in the first four months, more than 200,000 people enrolled in the online behavioral support program, over 5 million unique visitors logged on to the Alli websites, and consumers posted more than 125,000 messages on the official Alli message boards. GSK reported $156 million in Alli sales in the first six weeks after launch, and sales in the first six months totaled $290 million. Though revenues from Alli dropped sharply in 2008, GSK reported that U.S. sales increased 12 percent in the first half of 2009, and sales boomed in Europe, where the product was introduced in early 2009 and recorded revenues of $92 million in one quarter.

In October 2007, GSK launched a new Alli advertising campaign. To design the campaign, Alli's advertising agency, Arnold Worldwide, recruited close to 100 users from the First Team and asked for YouTube-style videos of their stories, even flying seven of them to New York for filming. Arnold creative director Kate Murphy said, "Consumers today want to hear that a product works from other real people. It's one thing for a manufacturer to say its product is effective, but getting that information from an actual user with actual experiences to share is much more powerful."[31]

Diane Hessan, CEO of Communispace, told the authors that a key to Alli's success was that GSK was able to connect with the "world of weight loss" from the user's perspective and thus generate the language and imagery that communicated both the usefulness and limitations of the product. This prompted people who were highly motivated to lose weight to try Alli. Not all members of the Alli First Team stayed with the product, but because of their long-term, personal engagement with GSK, they nonetheless became informed brand advocates out in the marketplace, recommending Alli to those friends who they thought could follow and benefit from the program, and discouraging it for those they thought would be likely to fail. In the words of one First Team member, "I know that at this point in my life, Alli is not for me. But I also know that it works for people more ready for long-term change than I am, and I won't hesitate to recommend it to them."[32]

Leveraging Public Community Spaces at HUL, SAP, and Intuit

Public community spaces in the world of social media are the most visible form of engagement platforms. The essence of social media is to build a network of like-minded individuals. These networks often form around a common passion, such as a brand.

One of the best-known uses of community co-creation around a brand is user-generated advertising. Frito-Lay Doritos' Super Bowl Ad campaign in 2007 was one of the pioneering examples of such an approach. The Doritos product management group simply opened up the design of its commercial as a contest to anyone willing to submit an amateur video about the product, and the winning clip—about a distracted Doritos eater flirting with a woman walking alongside his car—was professionally inserted into the Super Bowl campaign. The Doritos commercial was the top-rated Super Bowl ad of 2009 (displacing the longtime leader, Budweiser), according to *USA Today*'s Ad Meter system, while also saving the company several million dollars that a conventional agency-developed ad would have cost.[33] In the 2010 Super Bowl, the Doritos spot "House Rules," featuring a young boy telling his mother's date to keep his hands off both his mom and his Doritos, was rated the most engaging ad.[34] Co-created ads have now become an integral part of the marketing landscape.

But community co-creation can go much deeper than user-generated ads; it can place people at the center of the market and brand-building processes. Hindustan Unilever Ltd. (HUL), India's largest consumer goods company, scored a big success in using this approach to breathe new life into Sunsilk, one of its leading brands. India boasts one of the world's largest youth populations, and HUL needed to attract more girls between the ages of seventeen and twenty-two to its products. Sunsilk, a leading brand of shampoo in India for many years, was increasingly viewed as outdated, as "Mom's brand." To change that perception and rejuvenate the brand, the company decided to launch the Sunsilk Gang of Girls (GoG) online community in June 2006.[35]

HUL understood that girls enjoy the process of communication itself, not just its end result, and therefore the goal of establishing the community was to make Sunsilk GoG a place for them to express themselves. HUL first conducted some traditional market research, interviewing its target market and learning that young Indian girls wanted "dollops of fun," "a dose of advice," "lots of sharing," "personalization of beauty care," and "professional growth." The company then repurposed a previous website, sunsilknaturals.com, which had more than 100,000 registered users and a popular message board feature. HUL observed that site visitors tended to go beyond discussions of hair care and talk about celebrities, their favorite films, and other life issues. Using its global marketing expertise and working with a conventional advertising agency, HUL launched a media campaign to draw consumers to the new site, including a classic media blitzkrieg campaign in print, on television, and online, supplemented with offline events involving product displays and activities at malls and cinemas. It also organized the site to enable interactions between Sunsilk GoG members, HUL, HUL's partners, and its extended network of hair care professionals and beautification experts.

GoG was designed to maximize the participants' engagement with one another—around any topic of their choosing, not just hair care—through group blogs for each "gang" and a "talent show," in which site members voted on contributors' uploads. HUL even partnered with Monster.com to post résumés of registered members. Mentions of HUL products were few on the site; instead, the site focused on general hair-related topics. One of the most popular features was the "hair makeovers" option, which provided icons that consumers could select from to test new looks for themselves, including changes to hairstyle, hair color, lipstick, lip liner, eyeshadow, eyeliner, blush, and even contact lenses. The site also allowed users to converse with hairstylists at HUL salons about their specific hair and makeover needs. This aspect was inspired by Apple's Genius Bar, and HUL called it the Hair Care Bar. Users were also offered a chance to win a "tress-busting experience," i.e., an invitation to a social event and an appointment with a renowned hairstylist, if they purchased a bottle of Sunsilk.

Gangs of girls flocked to the site. Eighteen months after the launch in June 2006, Sunsilk GoG had 614,000 registered users, forming 37,154 gangs (limited to 50 members per group). Sunsilk's sales growth rose from 2 percent annually to 17 percent, and its market decline reversed, as Sunsilk's share in the Indian market rose from 18 percent in 2002 to 40 percent in 2006. Brand metrics, such as recognition and identity, also saw meaningful gains, as the brand scored its highest-ever score on "modernity" (up by 27 percent). Sunsilk became more popular among teens and younger adults. In 2009, Unilever opened up its innovation process to external talent, inviting seven well-known hairstylists to co-create new offerings for different hair concerns, and then connecting these offerings with the global Sunsilk user community. The hair concerns included straight, curly, and damaged hair; shaping, volumizing, and coloring hair; and scalp care and hair loss—each addressed by hair professionals with relevant expertise. HUL rolled out the co-created products as the Sunsilk Co-Creations line.

Whether shampoo or software, online communities can take on

a life of their own, expanding mutual value, when properly constructed and supported. For example, the German software maker SAP has fostered a series of online communities with more than 1.3 million members in total, bringing together a wide range of parties, of which the company's internal experts are only a small fraction. The communities create a powerful center of gravity around SAP products, and they have taken over part of the role of the company's customer support function. The largest of SAP's online communities is the SAP Developer Network (SDN). Established in 2003, this community for developers, analysts, consultants, integrators, and administrators centers on the use of SAP's offerings. More than 900,000 individual members across 195 countries share their experiences and insights on a range of forums, blogs, and a wiki, and have access to an e-learning catalog, technical articles, white papers, how-to guides, and software downloads. And the community is growing fast: in 2008, 5,500 members posted in forums, compared to just 2,000 in 2007. A second online community that SAP supports is the Business Process Expert (BPX) network, which is the IT world's largest business process community, with over 300,000 members covering 15 industries. This community connects SAP customers, SAP internal experts, business analysts, application consultants, IT managers, and enterprise architects, through a series of resources similar to those on SDN.

The great potential of this kind of community is illustrated by SAP's substantial savings in customer support. Prior to the establishment of SDN, queries from customers were forwarded to SAP's support organization, which was quite costly to maintain. Now, 10 to 15 percent of queries are resolved via SDN forums, translating into savings of more than $10 million in 2007. Participation in this problem solving is boosted by a point system and public acclaim. Community members reward each other with points based on the quality of their answers to problems. They also offer points for blogs, code samples, wiki editing, white papers, and technical articles based on effort and quality. There is a public ranking of contributors, helping individuals make a name for themselves in front of the community and within their own organizations (e.g., Indian software integrators advertising themselves as top contributors on SDN).

In 2009 SAP announced the launch of additional communities, including one dedicated to understanding International Financial Reporting Standards (IFRS) and another supporting a partnership with PlaNet Finance to give new businesses access to microfinance and technology. The communities are linked into a single network: members can use the same identity across all the communities, and topical searches lead to a wealth of content and links. Members from more than 200 countries make 6,000 posts per day, and there are a million topic threads in the communities. As Mark Yolton, senior vice president SAP community network, noted, "The SAP community network provides a trusted and validated environment to exchange ideas, discuss needs, and identify solutions for co-innovation that leads to more revenue, growth, and value for customers."[36]

Senior executives can play a critical role in stimulating and leveraging customer communities and user contributions. Consider Intuit, a maker of popular business software. Scott Cook, who co-founded Intuit, recognized the impact of co-creation with customers when the Intuit customer service team began experimenting with online support forums moderated by employee enthusiasts. He thought there was great potential in these "user contribution experiments," as he called them, and in 2005 at the company's annual off-site gathering, he put the following question to the company's top three hundred executives: "How might we leverage user contribution at Intuit, both to enhance existing businesses and create new ones?"[37]

Right away two executives came up with an idea for enhancing the company's tax preparation software for tax professionals. Intuit has long included tax help tutorials and tips in its products. But could the company build a new community around in-depth advice on obscure tax issues, getting professional tax preparers to interact with one another and collectively answer each other's questions? A team cobbled together a wiki-forum site for this purpose and launched it just five weeks after the offsite meeting. Cook was skeptical that even a minority of tax professionals would spend time on the site in the midst of the busy tax season, but to his surprise, the wiki quickly attracted a following. Today, TaxAlmanac, as the site is known, has been used by more than 400,000 unique visitors (about equal to the number of tax preparers in the United States), contains more than 170,000 pages, and draws on the collective expertise of thousands of tax professionals.

The site has proved to be of direct value to Intuit in several ways. The company has been able to learn continuously about the kinds of tax prep questions that its professional customers have, and they often go on to buy tax prep software. Intuit has embedded a Q&A community into TurboTax, which is for nonprofessional tax filers; there is now a user forum on every page of TurboTax, with questions and answers relevant to the topic of the particular page. Originally, Intuit moved cautiously, including the user forum only with the least popular product variants of TurboTax Online in 2007. Within just five weeks, however, a third of the questions posed already had answers. The team moderating the forum was surprised to see the quality of the answers, particularly as users built on other answers in an organic process of continuous improvement. Called TurboTax Live Community, the idea is spreading to other Intuit products, inspiring others within the company to experiment. This example show how co-creation can be proactively stimulated by good leadership and tried in an experimental fashion at first, to be rolled out more widely over time.

In summary, the examples in this chapter suggest how enterprises can take advantage of many different kinds of engagement platforms. Engagement platforms can be located downstream in the value chain, creating new user experiences with products (LEGO, Apple iPhone), retail sales and support interactions (Apple Stores), user community and customer support interactions (SAP, Intuit), or customer service and customer relationship interactions (Nokia, Dell, Nestlé), or engagement platforms can be used to reshape a firm's marketing and branding (GSK Alli, HUL Sunsilk, Nestlé). They can involve connecting employees with customers throughout the entire life cycle of products and services (Club Tourism). Engagement platforms can also be located upstream in the value chain (Dell product development, Nokia software testing, and Apple applications development). In all these instances, the engagement platforms enable new environments of interactions, resulting in better human experiences.[38]

As you read the stories in the rest of this book about the many ways to achieve success with co-creation, keep in mind its core principle. In the next chapter, we delve into how enterprises are opening up their processes of innovation to customers and external talent, and how to migrate these processes to *innovation co-creation*.

Chapter 3

Innovation Co-Creation

For many organizations, innovation is the number one challenge. Many are attempting to open up innovation by leveraging talent from outside the organization—from the product/service development function in discrete manufacturing, durable goods, and consumer goods industries, to the R&D function in science-oriented industries such as pharmaceuticals and high-tech. Popular approaches to opening up innovation include crowdsourcing and mass collaboration. These aim to tap into talent outside the enterprise to widen the competence base of innovation, and bring new perspectives into the innovation process.

While these methods broadly proceed from a co-creative intent, they often miss a key ingredient: the need to build a compelling experience of innovation with participants. For instance, crowdsourcing and mass collaboration do indeed involve the building of platforms to engage with external constituencies. Where they fall short, however, is in incorporating participants' experiences of interactions on the platform, and their experiences of enterprise offerings and processes. We have repeatedly found this step to be a hurdle for companies, leading to partial or failed attempts at opening up innovation. The solution lies in continuously generating insights from the engagement experiences of all participants, and then building the innovation process with them in a mutually valuable manner. Such innovation co-creation also addresses the challenge of opening up existing innovation processes in large, established organizations, which have to pay as much attention to their own people's experiences as to the experience of outsiders.

Co-creative innovation entails the application of the co-creation principle to innovation in all enterprises—regardless of whether they are start-ups or established organizations; whether operations, products and services, or new business models are at issue; and whether the offerings are mass-produced, custom-built, or personalized. In all these cases, enterprises can make their innovation processes more co-creative by providing a better experience for innovators. In the co-creative innovation process, participants can range from knowledgeable people outside the organization (such as developers, scientists, and entrepreneurs) to passionate contributors (such as consumers and enthusiasts) to employees inside the enterprise who otherwise would not be tapped for ideas.

The examples featured in this chapter are:

- **Camiseteria,** a Brazilian clothing company that uses crowdsourcing as a business model, so that participants can experience the joy of creating their own T-shirts (and wearing them)
- **Wacoal,** an established Japanese apparel maker, which designs unique garments by mobilizing very busy, dual-career young women in its product development process
- **Orange,** the operating brand of France Telecom, which highlights how the enthusiasm of employees and multiple external communities leads to supercharged innovation
- **Mozilla** and **InnoCentive,** which illustrate the rigor that is required for platform providers to be successful in innovation co-creation
- **Apple** and its Software Development Kit (SDK) initiative, which focused on the experience of developers working on

the development of applications for its iPhone, iPod Touch, and iPad

- **Infosys and IBM,** which represent examples of firms specializing in providing expertise and IT support in building powerful engagement platforms for innovation co-creation

Customers as Chief Designers at Camiseteria

Camiseteria.com is a virtual Brazilian T-shirt shop where customers both design T-shirt images and approve designs submitted by others. Camiseteria calls itself the "fashion *you* make."[1] As members of this online community, customers can post designs, which are voted on by other members, and the most popular are produced. Winners are given a prize in cash and products, but the greatest value received is arguably the fun of seeing one's work publicized on the website and sold in the market.

By making customers into active agents in the choice of T-shirt designs, Camiseteria has transformed the traditional relationship between apparel companies and customers. Camiseteria delegates a large part of the product creation process to user communities on the website. According to founder Fabio Seixas, "The motivation was derived from the opportunity to develop the Brazilian design market, which had largely been stagnant around 2004–2005, offering few interesting projects in the country. Camiseteria is not only a good business opportunity, but also the expression of our wish to have Brazilian T-shirt designs recognized."[2] Passion for Brazilian design is his fuel, and Camiseteria the incarnation of his passion.

The company had quick success, with 150,000 registered users throughout Brazil visiting the website—about 20,000 times per day. They have co-created more than 25,000 T-shirt designs in less than five years, resulting in estimated sales of about $1 million in 2009. This may look small by global sales standards, but it is no small feat for a new Brazilian start-up.

From the start, Seixas knew Camiseteria's distinguishing aspect had to be a unique and emotionally engaging experience to attract people. He was aware of two other similar websites for co-created apparel, one in France called laFraise.fr and another in the United States called Threadless.com. Seixas understood how critical it was to have an attractive and easy-to-use web tool to make the design creation and submission a compelling experience. The steps for creating a new T-shirt design are simple: design the image, download the basic template, save and upload the files, and publicize the design. Designs are highlighted in Camiseteria's virtual shop window. The designs gaining the most points from site visitors go into the Hall of Fame. The relative celebrity status resulting from publication is what attracts the best designers to Camiseteria, but there are also tangible rewards such as prizes and points to be traded for T-shirts. Camiseteria also supports blogs on its site, on which members can post about their work. There is a strong community effect: designers get to know each other by their nicknames and discuss designs. The website makes a wide range of information transparent to the community: designs and votes generated by each participant, best designs, worst designs, history, site visits, and personal photos. Of course, not everything is co-created at Camiseteria. The customer experience also relies on more traditional features such as fabric comfort, choice of payment options, and guaranteed delivery across the country.

Beyond the dramatically different customer experience resulting from the outsourcing of its design function to customers, Camiseteria fundamentally changes the economic model of the apparel industry. Camiseteria's model reduces both the cost and the risk involved in designing and launching a new T-shirt. On the cost side, it eliminates the professional designers traditionally involved in the process. On the risk side, it dramatically decreases the chances of investing in a design that won't take off with customers.

Because the community is an integral part of the business design, the company cannot succeed without their continued participation. To continue growing his community, Seixas plans to create a network of physical shops and extend the opening up of the design process to offline customers in those stores, which will require the development of new tools. He's already connected the customers' T-shirt wearing and design experience. He now wants to link the online and offline experiences. Listening to Seixas, one gets the feeling he won't rest until product design is massively entrusted to customers.

Opening Up Product Development at Wacoal

In the case of Camiseteria, the company had a crowdsourced business model. But how can an established company with in-house design professionals *also* successfully harness talent from outside the enterprise? Wacoal Corp. is Japan's leading intimate apparel fashion company.[3] Its operations include the planning, design, and manufacturing of lingerie, innerwear, and outerwear products. Revenues in fiscal year 2009 were 173.2 billion yen ($1.87 billion), with about two thirds coming from sales in Japan and a third from overseas. Wacoal has become a leading brand in Asian countries such as Thailand, Taiwan, and South Korea, and it has manufacturing subsidiaries in Japan, China, southeast Asia, and Dominica.

The company has a long tradition of focusing on customer experience in crafting its products. In its Human Science Institute, thousands of women's figures, from teenagers to senior citizens, are measured each year. With its accumulated knowledge of body types, design possibilities, and product options and costs, the company has consistently pioneered new product concepts, such as the iBra, a stitchless, seamless, and tagless bra. But in the late 1990s, Wacoal faced a leveling of sales growth. In response, the company experimented with a semitailored product line, for which customers' bodies were measured and lingerie was customized to fit. In developing this line, the Wacoal design team gained many "soft insights" from their interactions with customers, a precursor for the broader co-creation to come.

In May 2001, Yasuyuki Cho was tasked with developing Wacoal's business and innovating new product lines, with a focus on online and other emerging technologies. Cho had spotted a latent market opportunity he dubbed "home fashion" for the style-conscious consumer. While many apparel manufacturers concentrated on fashion in the workplace and others on comfortable apparel for the home, there seemed to be a "white space" opportunity at the intersection of fashion and comfort. This led to the development of a "house wear" concept, known as *Ouchi wear* in Japanese.

Cho sought to use online technology to design the new line. As he told the authors, he wanted to find a way to engage young working women in Japan in a dialogue about the new Ouchi wear concept. To do so, he approached Cafeglobe.com, a popular web community and social interaction platform for Japanese working women (akin to iVillage.com in the United States). Cafeglobe has more than 60,000 members, mainly working women in their twenties and thirties. The idea was to create a Cafeglobe subforum dedicated to intimate fashion. To generate traffic to the site, Cho hired a popular young fashion model to act as facilitator of the conversation with Cafeglobe members. As hundreds of women came to the site, the Wacoal design team introduced to the community what Cho called "joint collaboration with potential customers," inviting all to participate in the shaping of the new Ouchi wear line. More than 1,200 women ultimately joined in as co-creators.

The Wacoal design team had already developed concept sketches for the line and presented those ideas, complete with detailed drawings and explanations about the thinking behind the clothes. The initial goal was simply to collect feedback, but at the urging of several participants, the Ouchi team began encouraging the community to comment in more depth on the designs. At this point, Cho realized his team was not quite tapping into the potential of the rich conversations happening in the community. He saw that some women in the Cafeglobe community were discussing their own design ideas—some of which modified the original sketches and others that offered unique starting points. His first insight was triggered by the receipt of faxes from community members showing hand-drawn sketches for new garments and matching accessories. This meant having to convince his team this was an opportunity rather than a problem. In a pilot experiment, Cho created a set of online tools and invited community members to make changes, submit original designs, and vote on the design, color, and material for the garments offered. Cho describes the results as amazing to him and his team: somehow the community was suddenly breathing new life and energy into an already exciting new line.

Perhaps the greatest surprise came from the fact that the women involved in the design were busy young professionals. Three-quarters were between the ages of 25 and 35, and 80 percent of them worked. Most also had children. And yet they found the time to look at patterns, suggesting different shapes for a collar here, moving buttons and redesigning buttonholes there, or going through the trouble of changing shoulder fits or pockets. When Cho actually met some of these women later on, he realized he had offered them a new experience: the ability to channel their creative tendencies and become designers. Through the tools the team had designed, Wacoal had revealed the artist inside each of them, making it extraordinary fun and giving them a new sense of self-worth. For that, busy young professional women were finding the time.

For the internal team, this meant going back to the drawing board and revising the collection, based on the new community ideas. The Ouchi wear team started developing prototypes of the new collection, and Cho sweet-talked Takashimaya, a leading department store in major cities in Japan, into showcasing the line in a live trial in one of its stores. He was directed to sales managers at the Shinjuku branch in downtown Tokyo, with whom he organized a visit by members of the Cafeglobe community to come and try out the new collection. The Wacoal design team, company planners, marketing personnel, store sales managers, and community members came together face-to-face at the event. Cho could see the Takashimaya sales managers and salespeople were excited, which made him feel confident they would eventually want to adopt the new line because of their early involvement. The Cafeglobe community members were delighted to have a chance to meet each other in person and interact with the Wacoal design team. Cho saw that they shared a sense of pride and ownership in working together. Once this live connection was established, Wacoal managers and the customer community continued their interactions online, allowing the team to finalize the collection and move it into production and launch mode.

The resulting collection turned out to be a big hit for Wacoal, with sales exceeding $1 million the first year. The end-to-end process proved a lot faster than usual: while Wacoal's conventional product development process typically required eleven months from planning to sale, the Ouchi wear development took only three months. There have been more than a dozen new launches since then, all considered highly successful. These launches have followed the model devised by Cho, involving a series of co-creative stages for each product launch—from concept planning, design proposal, voting and suggestions, and sample production, to in-store trial, production, and sales.

Cho has since moved on to other responsibilities within Wacoal, but is taking his pioneering views of co-creation wherever he goes. When the company faced a quality disaster in its bra line, he immediately saw the potential to engage customers again, this time to learn about the experience of actually wearing the garments. The problem started with a deluge of calls to the company's call centers, because some bras were falling apart as the glue used to hold a new model together had a tendency to lose its adhesive capability over time. He told the authors, "Wacoal's most loyal customers were the ones contacting the call centers, and they had much information to reveal."

This gave him the idea of turning the call centers into another engagement platform for consumers, rather than remain as mere service centers. Cho realized with the bra incident the competitive advantage he had in the structure of Wacoal's call centers, as small, Japan-based, high-quality staff groups trained to solve problems and able to discuss customer experience. Today, Wacoal's call centers have turned into an insight machine, connecting the customer usage experience with the product development group where he had pioneered co-creation earlier. In Cho's vision, the garment-wearing experience is just the other side of the design experience, and he views his mission as connecting the two. When asked where his passion for co-creation will take him next, he smiles enigmatically and says, "Co-creation is everywhere."

Innovation Without Walls at Orange

Employees are a big part of companies' competence base, of course, but even their role can be amplified. Indeed, in most established organizations, this is an immediate opportunity. Orange, the operating brand of France Telecom, is a case in point. Orange's "intrapreneurial" engagement platform, idClic, totally changed the way the company innovates by supercharging the employee suggestion box. Any employee can come up with ideas—for instance, on process improvement, facility optimization, or product revamping—promote his idea through a blog, and gain visibility by acquiring points for comments on other employees' ideas. Orange received more than 21,000 ideas in just one month in 2007, a total that practically doubled in the same month of 2008. Over 2,300 of these ideas have been implemented, generating more than 400 million euros of earnings and savings for the company. By promoting internal entrepreneurship, Orange has unleashed innovation that did not find expression in its traditional hierarchical organization.[4]

Emboldened, Orange then opened up its innovation process to the outside world through its Livebox Lab, a web-based platform that provides information ranging from technical specifications to contacts and connections about Orange's home gateway (called Livebox). The Lab encourages individuals to submit B2B partnership ideas and small companies to propose products. Access to information is key for potential external partners who want to work on complementary products. The risk of sharing "home recipes" with competitors is a key question, says Alban Martin, social network specialist at Orange, but in the end, the benefit of opening up access is higher. Orange has received many ideas through Livebox Lab and has already launched several products initiated through this channel, such as Live-Radio, a Wi-Fi device enabling the streaming of hundreds of web-radio channels.

Dream Orange is the equivalent of Livebox Lab for the mass market. This web-based engagement platform enables what Martin calls "ascending innovation": rapidly co-testing concepts, mock-ups, or just early-stage ideas with a population of early adopters, including students from various engineering and design schools. Orange researchers otherwise would not have such a chance to test ideas and concepts so early in the process of innovation. The early adopters, in turn, get direct access to Orange R&D and can communicate directly with them.

There are two key benefits of these newly opened doors of innovation at Orange. The first is an increase in the audience for its products or services, since the company can now attract a new audience interested in early-phase information, which is richer in technical details than mass-market communication at the end of the value chain. The second benefit is that these lead users and early adopters contribute to the R&D and marketing processes. Estimating that Orange's community consists of about 1 percent content creators, 10 percent reviewers, and 89 percent free riders, Martin believes that without the early adopters in the system, there would be no free riders and thus no mass-market audience in the end.

Orange Partner Camps are the company's community for "deepening the relationship with entrepreneurial developers," Martin says. The camps have two areas in which to develop and test new products and services: a developer play zone and a "mosh pit." At a camp held in 2008, one hundred sessions and workshops, some involving community-voted contests, resulted in thirteen APIs (Application Programming Interfaces) being launched. Orange also connects start-up firms with venture capitalists, going so far as to devote employees to accompany the firms when they meet with

VCs. As one of the entrepreneurs noted, "I found Orange Camp's atmosphere very casual and cool in order to build personal relationships while discussing business opportunities."[5] The Orange Partner Program is another initiative aimed at connecting with the community of developers. Developers are encouraged to mash up Orange products and use Orange APIs, which Orange sometimes develops on-demand especially for them. The company created a platform with technical resources for anybody who wanted to tweak Orange web services. The number of subscribers to the website grew from about 200 in 2003 to more than 60,000 in 2008. As one enthusiast notes, "It is most encouraging to see a major operator like Orange genuinely embracing innovation in mobile technologies, applications, and services from outside."[6] Live events are a key element of this program, replicating the camp model, where participants propose a theme to discuss with Orange.

The atmosphere is very relaxed at the partner events, which are held in resort locations around the world such as Cadiz in Spain, Faro in Portugal, and Cape Canaveral in the United States. New ideas of product evolution are tested live during the Orange Partner Camps, with Orange and the developers working hand-in-hand in focus areas. The company also uses these camps to organize what it calls "speed dating" between external developers or start-ups and Orange product managers. Several commercial ideas have come from these camps, including Mob-it, from the start-up firm NPTV, which lets people upload content from mobile phones. This service was a feature missing from Orange's photo-sharing platform, Pikeo. Mob-it then became "Pikeo to go." In return, NPTV received financial and business support for its development.

Tapping into Talent from All Over at Mozilla and InnoCentive

Orange provides an example of how companies can benefit from co-creative innovation driven by multiple open communities of employees, developers, and entrepreneurs, as well as customers. It also illustrates that putting in place engagement platforms of that type is no easy task. Figuring out which interactions lend themselves to co-creation and which ones need to be controlled is a major challenge. As noted by Jimmy Wales, one of Wikipedia's cofounders, "Any company that thinks it's going to build a site by outsourcing all the work to its users . . . completely misunderstands what it should be doing. Your job is to provide a structure for your users to collaborate, and that takes a lot of work."[7]

Many firms and researchers attempting to co-create innovation have been disappointed because they've failed in one of two areas. Some have not designed the right platform. Others have failed to understand that they must enable a compelling engagement experience for both the external and internal stakeholders. Merely providing an open platform does not guarantee that people's experiences in using that platform will be good.

Mozilla and the Firefox browser provide a good illustration of the precision required in establishing the right co-creative innovation platform. Mitchell Baker, the chairperson and former CEO of the Mozilla Foundation, recognized early on the need to strike the balance between maintaining control and letting motivated people run with their passions. Mozilla has more than 120 employees—without whom, Baker says, "we'd be a good open-source project, but nothing like a force on the internet." Mozilla's decision-making process is highly distributed, crowdsourcing a volunteer community for product development, software coding, distribution, and promotion. But as Baker notes, they must have extreme discipline for some things at the center of the process. She says, "If you're touching code that goes into Firefox, the process is very disciplined. But there are lots of areas for participation—whether it's building an extension or localizing the product or building new products—that don't need that degree of discipline."[8]

If Mozilla is the heart of the system, its community is the arms and legs. For example, Firefox couldn't be distributed to its more than 300 million users without its community. Mozilla provides the platform—a "scaffolding" for people to work from—so that anyone in the community can innovate. Some of the people who make decisions about code are not employees. Some people with a high degree of expertise and specialization cannot be hired, Baker says. As long as Firefox provides co-creation experiences that are meaningful to these rare individuals, it will be successful.

The other challenge of co-creative innovation lies in fostering productive collaboration for both external and internal designers. Attracting external talent is hard, but getting internal development people to accept the intrusion of the new open system can be even more challenging.

InnoCentive is further along than most in dealing with this challenge. InnoCentive is a web-based company focused on matching external research solutions with internal company problems. It has largely mastered the ability to attract external problem solvers but is in the midst of figuring out how to overcome the internal challenge of its clients. Founded in 2001 with funding from pharmaceutical maker Eli Lilly & Co., the company is a clearinghouse for problems filed by companies including Eli Lilly, Procter & Gamble, Avery Dennison, Solvay, and many others. These "seeker" companies draw "solvers" with cash prizes ranging from $5,000 to $1 million. More than 200,000 engineers, scientists, and garage inventors from over 200 countries are registered as solvers. A study of challenges posted on InnoCentive by Swedish firm SCA showed that its solutions had an average return on investment of 74 percent with a payback period of less than three months.[9] By late 2009, 930 challenges had been posted on the site, with $22.5 million in awards offered. The solution rate had increased to 45 percent, up from 30 percent in 2006. Solvers registered 15,875 solutions, with 539 awards made totaling $4.65 million. Many of the seeker companies are proven innovators that have large in-house R&D staffs of their own, yet they have found InnoCentive to add value beyond their own research capabilities. The odds of a solver's success have been found to increase in fields in which he or she has no formal expertise.[10]

As InnoCentive CEO Dwayne Spradlin states, "Diversity is the secret sauce. We go outside a company's R&D department to entrepreneurs and chronic problem solvers from around the world. They can connect the dots that you and I can't."[11] InnoCentive understands it must manage the diversity of experiences on the site, and has learned to pay close attention to the engagement interactions and experiences of both seekers and solvers. For example, InnoCentive redesigned its online "project rooms" in 2009 to facilitate a better dialogue between solvers and seekers. It is also credited with having figured out how to protect the intellectual property of all parties involved, a complex challenge for an insights-brokering platform.

InnoCentive also must overcome the resistance posed by internal development people in client organizations, who do not always view the incursion of external professionals onto their turf with a favorable eye. Recall that Orange succeeded in getting its employees to accept external collaboration after it engaged them in innovation co-creation *inside* the firm. InnoCentive, as a platform provider, has undertaken two initiatives recently that are squarely aimed at this issue. First, it has developed an internal version of its software that allows problem seekers to find problem solvers inside the firm. The new software has its own market—which involves helping InnoCentive's client companies "know what they already know"—but the idea is also to familiarize researchers with the tool and make them comfortable with the experience of using this tool to work with outside resources later on. InnoCentive also launched a second initiative that deploys a small consulting services team to guide and accompany the behavioral transformation that the new software platform requires. The tipping point for InnoCentive's development is no longer the software platform itself, but the creation of a comfortable experience for professionals in client companies who let go of their development monopoly.

Apple Inside

Apple has changed the world by linking iTunes (content and applications) with the iPhone/iPod Touch—software and hardware, in a seamless combination with its human-ware at Apple Stores. The result is an extraordinary human experience. But where does this experience come from? One of our favorite quotes from Steve Jobs, *Fortune*'s CEO of the Decade (2000–2010) is "the software *is* the user experience."[12] We saw in the previous chapter how Apple opened up applications development for the iPhone/iPod Touch through its SDK platform. What is less widely understood is that Apple's success stems from its paying attention to the experiences of large and small developers—whether established entrepreneurs or a kid testing out his software development skills—anywhere in the world.

How so? Apple makes it easy for anybody with software development talent to create new mobile end-user experiences through its SDK platform. Users, software developers, entrepreneurs, and partnering firms can play together in a giant sandbox organized by Apple. Yet the core layers of the technology behind SDK and its integration through the Mac OS X are proprietary to Apple, allowing it to ensure a smooth, integrated experience. Apple brings consistency to the quality of end-user experiences while simultaneously giving enormous flexibility to developers.

The iPhone has become a means to experience not only its many functions, but also the joy of innovation itself, by making it easy for developers to incorporate location- and motion-sensitive functionalities, audio and animation, information access, content sharing, and enticing look and feel of user interfaces. Developers experience what iPhone/iPod Touch end users would experience. Apple gave developers the exact same SDK tools Apple uses internally, whose components were designed by Apple with the experience of the end user in mind. What is also less publicized is Apple's effort to bring selected developers inside Apple through live meetings and a dedicated SDK website. Through these platforms, Apple encourages developers to share their development experiences with the firm and with the community of other developers. By giving developers the ability to "visually compare" the performance of different parts of the mobile application, and by sharing this information with Apple's internal teams, the company learns about the performance of applications early on. Apple followed suit when launching the iPad in 2010. In conjunction with the launch, the company released a new, iPad-compatible version of the SDK; an iPad programming guide for third-party software developers; iPad code templates for developers to build on; and an iPad Simulator that showed developers how their apps would look on the new device's larger screen. The iPhone Developer Program, which enables developers to conduct testing and upload their apps, was immediately expanded to include the iPad.

Apple continues to learn from its interactions with developers, enhancing its strategic capital through the wealth of insights obtained by analyzing user experiences and functionalities of popular applications. By engaging in a dialogue with developers around these insights, Apples expanded the SDK in spring 2010, launching iOS4 with more than 1,500 APIs (Application Programming Interfaces) and a new iAd service that allows developers to generate advertising revenue—which is split with Apple on a 40 to 60 percent basis. Developers, in return, submitted more than 15,000 apps per week, with one developer of the iPad app The Elements earning more in sales on the first day than from its past five years of Google ads on periodictable.com, and that's not counting new iAd revenues.

Apple also generates insights about new value innovation opportunities with selected business customers that it brings inside the enterprise, learning how they want to use the iPhone in their own downstream co-creation with consumers. A case in point is Johnson & Johnson and its co-development with Apple of its iPhone-based engagement platform, the LifeScan glucose monitor system. Imagine a young teenage girl who is a diabetic. She has to track her blood glucose and give herself insulin injections. Using the new J&J system, she does not have to guess how much insulin she has to take before her meal. She can instead go into the meal builder app on her iPhone, pick the type of food she wants to eat, and use the app to estimate how many carbohydrates she will be taking in. The app then calculates the insulin dose she needs. She can also view all of her previous readings and thus track her condition. In addition, she can communicate with parents, caretakers, doctors, and other diabetics, sending both her glucose numbers and a message on the iPhone. Thus, the iPhone is a "meta platform" for innovation co-creation, as Apple continues to open it up to partners and expand it into entirely new opportunity spaces.

Further, by giving users the ability to rate applications and share their experiences directly with the application developers (through the App Store), Apple bridges the gap between the developers' thinking about the user experience and the actual thinking of users about their experiences. The mastery of Apple lies in bridging the "downstream" experience co-creation (the iPhone/iPad as an engagement platform for end users) with the "upstream" experience co-creation (the iPhone/iPad SDK as an engagement platform for developers and Apple's partners). As Jobs said, the software is indeed the user experience with "technology" as a seamless integration of hardware and software, intersecting with the "liberal arts" and humanity, as he often puts it.

While software is central to enabling new experiences, IT is central to enabling large-scale engagement platforms. As business and management processes have become embedded in IT, global IT service and consulting companies like Infosys and IBM have risen to the challenge (and opportunity) of helping enterprises build the next-generation technology capabilities for co-creative innovation. We conclude this chapter with their examples.

IT as Enabling Innovation Co-Creation at Infosys

Infosys of India is well known for its expertise in IT services, amassing $4.7 billion in revenues in 2009, the majority from large companies outside India. Infosys maintains an internal R&D arm, Software Engineering Technology Labs (known as SETLabs), whose goal is to anticipate technology evolution and its impact on business. In 2006, the vice president and head of SETLabs, Subu Goparaju, began recognizing a need for innovation co-creation. Several clients had approached Infosys seeking help to identify and pursue new innovation opportunities and to augment the capabilities of their organizations to keep up with the breakneck pace of IT change. Kris Gopalakrishnan, the current CEO of Infosys who was then COO, encouraged SETLabs to engage the sales and delivery constituencies within Infosys on the topic of co-creation. Goparaju set up an Innovation Lab within SETLabs to focus specifically on co-creation.[13]

The Innovation Lab team immersed itself deeply in co-creation research, practices, and strategies, and created a model for innovation co-creation that shifts the core tasks of brainstorming and problem solving outward: beyond individual proposals to co-creative interactions, beyond features and processes to engagement experiences, and beyond the networks of a particular firm to a wider community of co-creation. Infosys believes that organizations adopting this model of innovation co-creation can generate faster, smarter, cheaper, and more effective innovations.

The Infosys model contains five key pillars that bring innovation co-creation to fruition. The first pillar entails *access to contextual knowledge and information.* Because next-generation innovations now occur predominantly at the intersection of different cultures, domains, and technologies, Infosys has found it important for innovators to have access to a diverse set of technologies and disciplines that create insights into industry trends and emerging business models, rather than relying on expertise in a single domain. When innovators lack access to contextual knowledge and information, Infosys has noticed that their innovation process tends to be slow, expensive, and "trailing edge."

More often than not, such diverse competencies do not reside within a single department or even within a single organization, so these competencies need to be brought together from different parts of the organization and from beyond organizational boundaries (i.e., external experts and partners). This is the second pillar of innovation co-creation: a *collaborative network of experts and partners.* In reality, timely access and sharing of knowledge is too infrequently achieved in organizations. Expert knowledge and information is typically in silos within organizations. Co-creative innovation, in contrast, is about including more stakeholders, especially those who can bring and debate new points of view, share technological breakthroughs, and identify "next" practices. Bringing together capabilities of different stakeholders from around the world and beyond the boundaries of an organization, with different interests and diverse motivations, to co-create on a single integrated platform dramatically changes the paradigm of how innovations are generated—and with it, the technology-enabling environments required.

The third pillar of innovation co-creation is *integrated methodologies and tools*. This involves collaborative and communicative tools for idea generation, simulation, and evaluation of innovations. But this pillar is not so much about the variety of tools as it is the challenge of focusing on the engagement experience of innovators, i.e., enabling easy access to these tools and helping them apply the most appropriate methods in a given context. The fourth pillar is *engaging events and experiences*. This involves various mind-stretching exercises for divergent thinking, experimentation, learning and enhancing creativity, and making the innovation experience exciting and fun.

The combination of these four pillars expands the practice of innovation to a wide range of people within and outside organizations. The four pillars revolve around the central fifth pillar, *an integrated and co-creative technology platform* that provides various collaborative, visualization, communication, and information tools for enabling Infosys and its clients to co-create valuable experiences with *their* customers and stakeholders.

One such client is a large banking organization in North America that sought to enhance its innovation capabilities during the 2008 downturn. Infosys set up what it calls "co-creation workouts" between the Infosys client account teams and Infosys partners, and also between Infosys consultants and the client's internal stakeholders (from both the IT and business sides). These workouts are live engagement platforms that are central to the client's co-creation experience with Infosys. Infosys and its client first came together to share new ideas, knowledge, insights, and perspectives that are relevant to the client's business domain. Once the objectives of innovation were settled, the five pillars model provided a platform through which the client, Infosys, and other invited participants could co-create. (Infosys and its client agreed on the governance process and rules of engagement for different participants with different rights and roles.) Infosys provided various tools (e.g., collaborative workflows and social networking) to facilitate productive and creative interactions among the platform participants. As innovative ideas were generated, Infosys helped all parties visualize the experience of new, cutting-edge technologies and services (e.g., mobile banking services).

More than a hundred new ideas were generated in this fashion, cutting across the experiences of opening an account, transactions, funds transfer, and small business services, in some cases enabling new types of co-creative experiences for bank customers. One idea, for instance, was an easy-to-understand yet comprehensive representation of an individual's financial health through an indicator that constantly monitors banking transactions and contains alerts about certain events (such as hitting a specific balance). Customers can set the alerts, and they can edit and personalize their individual health indicators with fine-grained transaction details. Another idea that emerged was for the bank to set up a social network on which customers could invite family members, and those with whom they chose to share information, in order to work collectively on financial decisions. A related idea was linkages between joint accounts and community members—for example, allowing parents to approve children's transactions on a "watch list" created through parents' mobile phones. For B2B customers, a strategic idea was to enhance their ability to offer new services to existing clients: for example, helping business consultants build cost statements and invoices with data that a client provided them.

While these ideas by themselves may be interesting, what is more important is that they are the outcome of what Goparaju refers to as an "innovation co-creation capability." He notes that the goal of Infosys is to co-create a unique engagement platform with each client organization and its participating innovators, and then help the client build the IT capabilities that underlie the realization of the ideas that emerge from the innovation co-creation process.

Generating New Business Opportunities at IBM and Shell

IBM has been in the forefront of tapping diverse talent to create value and innovation capabilities with its clients.[14] In 2001, the company conducted a worldwide internal brainstorming conversation called World Jam. Employees from around the globe logged in to a webpage to discuss ten urgent issues, such as how to retain valuable employees and how to work faster without compromising quality, and over the space of three days they made more than 6,000 posts in an online forum that allowed them to see and comment on multiple conversations at once. Participation was much higher than some IBM managers predicted, and the discussion was rich.[15] In 2003, an internal Values Jam followed, in which more than 22,000 employees debated and rewrote the company statement of values. This Jam resulted in free-flowing, candid discussions over three days that were subsequently mined with text analysis software. What emerged was a set of values that represented and engaged IBMers. Other Jams have since followed, engaging people worldwide—from both inside and outside IBM—on important issues such as the problems of rapid urbanization. Through these Jams, IBM employees, partners, customers, families, and friends have helped identify new opportunities and emerging trends. Clients have also taken advantage of the web-based conversation platform and analytics that IBM developed to conduct their own internal Jams.

In addition to these global brainstorming discussions, IBM also conducts more focused sessions for co-innovation. Through the Global Innovation Outlook (GIO) program, IBM facilitates one-on-one interviews, focused roundtables, and wide-ranging global conversations with thought leaders on topics of interest—everything from the future of water politics, to the role of Africa in global business, to issues of security in society. Executives around the world read the reports for insights into how the world is changing.

Following its advertising campaign for a Smarter Planet, IBM convened a series of conversations on how to build "smarter cities," exploring how progressive cities are modernizing and spurring economic development. The discussions sparked new thinking and meaningful action across the entire ecosystem of a city—from mayors to CEOs of private companies to citizens. Conversations initiated at the Smarter Cities events have led to partnerships like the one formed with Dubuque, Iowa, in 2009, to make it the first "smarter" sustainable American city and an international model of sustainability for communities of fewer than 200,000 residents. Similar IBM initiatives include smart energy systems, more efficient transportation and decongestion systems, and analytics for public safety and data visualization. As noted by CEO Samuel J. Palmisano, "Smarter infrastructure has measurably greater economic and societal leverage than traditional infrastructure."[16]

The IBM program that drives perhaps the deepest co-creative conversations with clients is Innovation Discovery. This process brings together the best and brightest minds from both a client's internal organization and from IBM's extended network, to discuss breakthrough innovations. IBM developed the Innovation Discovery process to work with clients to discover and explore new growth areas, and then bring its vast technology and industry expertise to bear on making the emergent ideas real. Participants from IBM include IBM Fellows, Distinguished Engineers, senior researchers, industry leaders, and other top subject matter experts from across the company, as well as business unit executives and people drawn from other innovation programs. On the client side, the participants typically include five to seven executives representing different parts of the organization, such as innovation, business groups, technology functions, marketing and other customer-facing functions, and IT. Through a variety of virtual and face-to-face sessions, these people collaborate to co-create insights into new business solutions, whether focused on technology, a new business model, a breakthrough service, or more complex global innovation opportunities involving multiple stakeholders.

The Innovation Discovery process has five phases. In the first, both sides discuss the client's business needs and strategic priorities and learn about each other's capabilities. In the second phase, the teams identify areas to explore and plan collaborative working sessions that focus deeply on new opportunities. They can draw on IBM's extended resource network—IBM experts who are not part of the Innovation Discovery team—for broader input. In the third phase, new growth opportunities are fleshed out. In phase four, the teams determine the business potential of new growth opportunities, set priorities, lay out roles and responsibilities, and develop action plans. The final phase is about supporting these plans, enabling teams to navigate challenges as they arise and committing to their success.

IBM customizes the Innovation Discovery process for each client, ensuring that they get access to the breadth of its business and technology expertise in the industries and innovations that most interest them. Jade Nguyen Strattner, director of Client Experience at IBM and founder of Innovation Discovery, says that her team has collaborated with IBMers in more than thirty countries to conduct engagements for nearly one hundred clients, exploring innovations in customer experience, business analytics and optimization, growth in new markets, and other areas. For example, Innovation Discovery has helped accelerate a leading U.S. car rental company's ability to improve its customer experience, identify new services by which a government agency can improve the lives of citizens and the vitality of small businesses in its province, develop new business models for telemedicine, and harness the power of internal communities to create value for a global energy company.

Royal Dutch Shell and IBM used the Innovation Discovery process to explore how they could jointly drive innovation and use each company's expertise to create competitive advantage in several grand challenges. The result is an approach that Shell considers a leading method of innovation from among all of its suppliers, both IT and non-IT. (IBM is one of Shell's key IT application suppliers.)

At the beginning of the process, these two large organizations realized they needed more clarity on the difference between collaborative initiatives and traditional client-supplier relationships. They outlined several parameters that needed to be defined to facilitate up-front, open, and transparent discussions. This framework for collaboration included:

- Types of collaboration: What challenges are appropriate for collaborative research?
- Requirements: Investment and resources needed for collaboration.
- Commitments: Time and focus given to projects.
- Outcomes: Terms of IP ownership, commercialization, and joint go-to-market plans.

For example, collaborative research is a good approach where no solution exists for an industry challenge or where there is only a partial solution that lacks key technology components. For Shell and IBM, this meant selecting challenges where the solution requires domain expertise from Shell (e.g., subsurface and reservoir engineering) and technical expertise from IBM (e.g., computer modeling, analytics, and computer simulation). The partners agreed that they would both own new intellectual property created through the collaborative research, and furthermore, that the results of their work can be used by Shell in their operations, while IBM is able to commercialize the related technologies.

For Shell and IBM, Innovation Discovery and the collaboration framework has deepened the relationship between the two companies. Shell has incorporated the results of the Innovation Discovery process throughout its operations, and IBM has gained opportunities to bring research to bear on specific industry challenges. Shell's Downstream VP and CIO, Arjen Dorland, says, "Innovation Discovery enabled us to look at real business challenges in new, innovative ways. The experience invigorated us to pursue a more collaborative relationship with IBM."

94

In summary, innovation co-creation is about enabling "co-creative interactions in innovation" among individuals and driving the underlying management processes in co-creative fashion. This applies equally to whether the innovation outcomes are operational, product-service oriented, or new business models. The first three examples featured in this chapter progressed from companies using talent outside the enterprise as part of their core business models (Camiseteria), to established companies leveraging talent outside in modest fashion to bring customers inside the product development process (Wacoal), to wider co-creation of innovation with multiple communities (Orange). Mozilla and InnoCentive showed how platform providers that have open business models must also engage their employees, their clients, and their clients' customers to make innovation a more co-creative process. With the example of Apple's SDK initiative, we showed how development platforms could be linked with a customer platform to create an ever-widening flow of innovation. Finally, we discussed how vital the expertise in marshalling enterprise IT capabilities is in maximizing co-creative innovation potential, and how companies can enlist the specialization of IT services firms (e.g., Infosys and IBM) in building that expertise.

Taken together, the examples in this chapter illustrate how enterprises can successfully co-create innovation, making participants' interactions with the enterprise more "multisided" and their experiences more meaningful. In the next chapter, we discuss how enterprises can expand the scope and scale of interactions across the entire business network—from customers, distribution, and sales channels to partners, vendors, and suppliers—by applying the core principle of co-creation.

Chapter 4

Engaging People Among Business Networks

Propelled by rapid advances in tools for collaboration, information networking, and communication, enterprises are developing new styles of business networks. These networks let different players in the value chain come together—often through a nodal company that provides the leadership and facilitates execution—to create, improve, and deliver new product and service offerings. Members of the networks share risks while combining competencies to create new innovations that each player could not achieve separately. Some of these enterprises are even connecting the interactions of their customers across their business networks. Making these interactions co-creative provides new pathways to expand mutual value in business networks.

In this chapter, we discuss how to reap the benefits of co-creation by expanding interactions among people in business networks.[1] Here again, the core principle of co-creation—engaging people to create valuable experiences together while enhancing network economics—is at play. That is, success will come from using the experiences of each network member, to foster collaboration and communication through the various engagement platforms that enable contextualized interactions across the business network.

The examples covered in this chapter are:

- **Brother,** the Japanese sewing machine maker, which illustrates how companies (even established ones, not just Web 2.0 companies) can build networks of customers and business partners for the benefit of all participants.
- **GE Healthcare,** in the diagnostic imaging business, which demonstrates how companies can engage networks of small businesses. By becoming a "B-2-smallB" nodal company, GE Healthcare facilitates the delivery of advice for small businesses.
- **Toyota Scion,** which exemplifies how linking customer communities with networks of suppliers, channel partners, and media agencies can generate a unique brand with a distinctive, powerful culture.
- **Crushpad,** an innovative winemaker, which illustrates the value of opening up each link in a traditionally closed industry activity chain and engaging a vast network of customers, business partners, and suppliers.

Engaging Dealers in the Network at Brother

Brother Industries Ltd., which recently celebrated the one hundredth anniversary of its sewing machine manufacturing business,[2] exemplifies the value of engaging a business network involving retailers and end customers. In 2008, it was the leader for sewing machines on its home Japanese market, with a 33 percent share measured in units sold, and was the runner-up globally to Singer, with a 20 percent share of the worldwide market. The United States was a different story. As a latecomer to the U.S. home sewing machine market, and without access to U.S. dealer channels to sell its high-end machines, Brother had to focus on low-end machines sold through mass-merchandise channels such as Walmart.

This strategy allowed the company to enter the U.S. market successfully, but Brother discovered that the market was saturated and offered little growth potential. With the beachhead established at the low end of the market, Brother started wondering how it could develop a more lucrative, higher-end business that would help it penetrate the specialty dealer channel. Brother's first step was to design embroidery sewing machines suitable for this dealer channel. These machines were priced from $1,000 to 2,000, with higher-end computerized models such as the Innov-is 4000D going up to $5,000. The embroidery machines were lightweight and portable, with variable speed control and a wide selection of built-in stitches. Sales of the 4000D model proved higher than Brother expected at first, but these early sales slowed down as competitors started offering their own high-end machines. Internet channel competition further eroded margins.

Brother sought a new approach to increase its sales. In 2006, designers and engineers from Japan traveled to the United States to visit "superusers" of the company's machines. Immersive market research with these enthusiasts revealed that the existing machines were too small—in particular, the arm was too short for big projects such as quilted tapestries. Most of the enthusiasts were older women who had difficulty seeing the detail of thread tensions and needle holes; some of them used magnifiers. Most revealing, they often went online to share their passion with fellow enthusiasts, showing off specific projects and learning from one another's sewing experiences. Furthermore, while Brother had been providing "amateur-style" patterns and "family-style" patterns such as Disney and Nickelodeon characters, the superusers were exchanging professional-style patterns and customizing their designs.

In 2007, Brother began developing a new high-end machine, code-named the X1, for these enthusiastic "crafters." This machine had the world's longest arm at 10 inches, a built-in camera that captured the point of sewing, the world's biggest color touch control panel, digital connectivity through a USB port, and a web-enabled library of embroidery patterns that could be downloaded directly into the machine. The company also launched a social networking website dedicated to sewing and quilting hobbyists where customers could share their sewing experiences, including photos of their projects.

A core insight—and therefore one of the key selling points for such an expensive machine—was that Brother could help consumers learn more about sewing, which suggested that it include dealers and craft shops in its market development initiative. The company began sending educators to dealers to teach them how to make projects with crafter hobbyists, and also began adding to the resources it offered craft shops. Until then, specialty stores had been viewed as a place where products could be displayed and an occasional craft magazine could be picked up, but not as a place for learning and exchange. Brother realized that craft shops can be community- and education-based engagement platforms for enthusiasts and their friends, and that working with them was a great way to to enhance offerings and reach new customers. For instance, the company learned together with these craft shops that many young homemakers wanted to learn about sewing but did not have enough time or know where to begin.

Customers can now engage in meaningful conversations with knowledgeable and skillful dealer-salespeople about products and projects. They can also take training classes at the shops, regardless of the brand of machines they own. Brother is also experimenting with the retail space as a communal platform. Online customers have access to design software that allows them to make custom designs, share their designs with the community, and engage in conversations with other enthusiasts about their designs. Brother is in the process of enabling the community to bring their experiences offline, tapping into the power of live interactions through the craft shops.

Brother has also reoriented its marketing and sales organization to support its co-creative initiatives. In the past, Brother's marketing—especially the market research function—was heavily Japan-centered and consequently struggled to understand market patterns in the United States. But for the development of the X1 machine, the company set up a marketing division in the United States, and Japan-based product engineers now closely communicate with their American counterparts. Salespeople have also shifted from the mass channel to the dealer channel, and devote a significant amount of their efforts to finding capable local dealers who can accommodate the hobbyists. The X1 machine is to be sold only by Brother-certified dealers who agree to develop the ability to train customers and engage them through in-store quilting and sewing clubs. An important element of the approach is that it is not a hard sell. Customers can bring their own sewing and quilting machines to the stores, whether or not they bought them there.

Some dealers have been reluctant to take part because the new activities are time-consuming and do not necessarily lead to direct sales. To overcome this short-term bias, Brother invites dealers to its training facility, where the focus is not only on the product but also on how to create sewing projects. With support from the educators who conduct in-shop seminars and demonstrations for customers, dealers are beginning to see the potential for sales growth. Brother has also changed the content of its semiannual dealer meetings, which used to be primarily focused on entertainment but are now training-oriented, featuring product and project education as well as business education. Interestingly, dealers now willingly pay a registration fee for the meetings because they see the value.

Linking Small Businesses with Partners at GE Healthcare

Large companies wishing to sell to smaller companies can build a business network if they're willing to co-create with them to fulfill the smaller organizations' needs, such as infrastructure, access to capital, and market knowledge. GE Healthcare provides an example. One of its fastest-growing customer segments is small outpatient imaging centers (OICs), to which GE sells imaging machines and diagnostic services. There are more than 6,000 OICs in the United States, which are owned by over 2,500 different parent companies—

a very fragmented market of small businesses, but one that generates about 40 percent of GE's diagnostic imaging business. They were therefore felt to hold great promise for a co-creation effort.

GE Healthcare's then general manager for OIC Marketing, Rob Kulis, approached the authors to help develop a new business model through which the firm would have more dialogue with its customers and develop more collaboration. To get started, Kulis organized several co-creative workshops with OIC customers, from physicians to center managers. Rather than tell them what GE Healthcare planned to do, he began by inviting participants into an open dialogue, following a brief interactive presentation on the co-creation movement and on GE Healthcare's aspirations in co-creating value with them. Kulis engaged everyone in a candid discussion around several exploratory themes, including health insurance changes, improved imaging technology, and the increasing popularity of imaging for a range of medical uses. He also emphasized to participants that the dialogue need not revolve around GE-selected themes, as had been the case in the past.

OIC customers discussed their needs in securing legal, financial, staffing, and planning resources to support and expand their facilities and stay competitive. The OIC owners faced increasing costs, stiff competition, and legal changes such as the Deficit Reduction Act of 2005 (DRA), which had reduced Medicare/Medicaid payouts for certain imaging procedures. The DRA affected the profitability of OICs, and in some cases meant that the companies would at best break even on investments made in the latest imaging technology. The result was a consolidated marketplace, tighter capital markets, and a longer wait for revenue and return on investment. To survive, OICs faced restructuring in the core functions of their business:

1. *Business planning and finance.* Many people in the OIC business did not have prior experience in running such a business, as they typically had worked as physicians in hospitals where they had not been involved in business planning and financial operations or in the actual building of OIC facili-

ties. So GE decided to offer assistance in business planning that would allow for financing facilities and equipment in ways that preserved capital and maximized cash flow.

2. *Technology and capital planning.* OICs also needed to select equipment to align better with market demographics and demand, train technical staff to use that equipment to the fullest, and make full use of IT tools.

3. *Marketing and growth promotion.* OICs had to market their services aggressively by making referrals easy for physician practices and publicizing that their exams were quick, pleasant, and comfortable for patients.

4. *Process improvement and operating efficiency.* OICs had to streamline their workflow for maximum throughput, and improve their cash flow by clearing up account receivables, collecting and processing payments quickly, managing reimbursements effectively, and applying strong purchasing discipline.

Kulis recognized that putting together a business network that would help OICs with these core functions would reap great rewards—for both them and GE. He and his team envisioned that such a network would provide advice, consulting, and solutions for the myriad business problems the OICs faced. In 2007, Kulis launched a web-based platform consisting of a comprehensive network of product and service vendors in finance, legal services, information systems, imaging center design and building services, marketing and communications, and business services. GE Healthcare evaluated the vendor partners based on market needs matched with a vendor's specific capabilities, knowledge, presence in that market, and responsiveness. The vendors who joined the network were contractually obligated to meet certain levels of service and quality standards rather than receiving payment for affiliation. Kulis believed that creating customer value was more important to the long-term growth prospects of the network (and GE Healthcare) than any moderate royalty fees that might have been generated. GE Healthcare not only gave OICs access to this network but also provided educational content, access to industry conferences and webcasts, and a peer-to-peer network for sharing best practices.

After consulting with OICs, Kulis offered two levels of service. The first was the nonmembership level, which was open and free of charge to any OIC registering on the portal. The second service level was the membership level, costing $20,000 annually and targeting the top 20 percent of GE Healthcare's OIC clients. For centers that committed to using a certain amount of content, participating in the best practice–sharing community, and providing ongoing feedback through blogs, the membership fee was waived. The membership level provided everything in the nonmembership level plus access to an Ask an Expert platform, where clients could submit questions to any vendor partner in the network, gain access to vendor partner white papers and intellectual property, and get more extensive educational content. In addition, webcasts and tuition for special conferences were included in the fee.

During the first fifteen months of the program, GE Healthcare invested about $2 million and reaped the reward of registering over 1,500 clients as nonmembers and 100 of the top 20 percent of clients as members. Ultimately the program has improved customers' equipment purchasing and thereby strengthened GE Healthcare's business (revenue figures are not public). For example, if an OIC is expanding and needs to locate good properties, the faster it can solve that problem, the faster it will need equipment for the new locations. Additionally, by providing customers with objective advice through the vendor network, GE Healthcare enhanced its position in the minds of customers, which improved customer loyalty and ultimately led to less competitive buying situations for GE Healthcare's equipment, services, and solutions.

Connecting Consumers and Stakeholders at Toyota Scion

Toyota's Scion brand illustrates the power of connecting consumers, channel partners, media agencies, and suppliers. The Scion story began in 1998 at a Toyota Motor Corp. executive committee meeting. A chief engineer played a loud music video showing images of a boxy, low-slung vehicle in an urban setting. His message: If Toyota hoped to win over Generation Y and the next generation of car buyers by 2020, it had to revamp both its product and its thinking. He was calling for a radical approach to automotive innovation.[3]

Five years later, in 2003, Toyota launched the Scion line in the United States with two models: the xA, a stout, subcompact hatchback; and the xB, a boxy, five-door wagon. The xA and xB were lightly modified versions of two Toyota-brand Japanese domestic models. A year later, Toyota rolled out the tC, a small coupe with a sportier look, created exclusively for North America. In 2007, the xA was replaced with the xD model, designed for the Scion brand and not borrowed from another Toyota brand or market.

From the start, Toyota's strategy was to appeal to the youth market, hooking them as long-term customers who would transition into buying its bestselling Toyota and Lexus models. Toyota's first effort to connect with Gen Y in the late '90s, dubbed Genesis, was not so successful. Genesis tried to play off the main Toyota brand using conventional marketing strategies and techniques. The lesson Toyota learned from Genesis was to give Gen Y its own brand. Scion's marketers understood that the young generation had different norms than older buyers—in their expectations of cars, their approach to consumption, the tendency to scrutinize everything closely, the demand for freedom of choice, and the desire to coalesce socially. It was a collaborative generation that communicated instantly, dissolving the distinction between the real and virtual and seeking a two-sided involvement with the brands that were anchors of meaning in their lives.

Scion also understood that Generation Y sought self-expression and that they used their cars to express their personalities. For that reason, Scion embraced the hot-rodding aftermarket, where enthusiasts hacked powertrains, modified the bodies of their cars, and personalized their vehicles to suit their own tastes. These young drivers spent as much time accessorizing, customizing, decorating, and cleaning their cars as they spent riding in them. They also showed a desire to belong to close-knit communities, and they attended rallies, shows, and cross-country events. Scion strategists had studied closely the growing "tuner" aftermarket of enthusiasts, mainly twenty-something males, who spent more than $4 billion a year dressing up and boosting the look and performance of their vehicles. Scion's goal was to bring this aftermarket inside the carmaker.[4] From the start, Scion models were highly customizable, with options like fancy wheel covers and an array of audio upgrades, to name just a few.

The company appealed to young buyers in other ways, too. No-haggle pricing in hip showrooms was designed to make the purchase process easier, as were financing and loan applications on the internet. Buyers could create their own cars virtually, showing the company the exact design they wanted, down to the floor mats and the leather around the stick shift. Scion soon found that two-thirds of buyers had configured their cars online before walking into a dealership.

Toyota's goal in marketing Scion was to ignite love and passion for the brand and let the community spread the word. To become the Gen Y vehicle of choice, Scion launched viral marketing campaigns that included word-of-mouth efforts, with the goal of engendering a Scion subculture. Cars were only a part of the identity; concerts, CDs of emerging musicians, art installations, a film contest, and basketball tournaments all created an awareness of the new brand. These events eschewed the traditional hard-sell approach and instead let people simply take part in the activities. Scion marketing extended to the virtual world Second Life, where it became the first carmaker to open a dealership—on which, as on Scion's website, users could personalize their cars.

Another unconventional marketing effort was Scion Speak, a social-networking engagement platform that allowed Scion owners to meet and communicate with each other in both the online and real worlds. Scion Speak was introduced in stealth mode months before the official launch. On this platform, Scion owners could design their own personal crests online, using a virtual language of hundreds of design symbols to communicate what kind of music they were into and where they were from—all developed in collaboration with the Scion community and graffiti artists that brought them to life. The personalized crests could be made into window decals or actually painted onto the car, uploaded to Facebook or MySpace, or emailed to a social network of fans. As one Scion enthusiast put it, "It's more than just a car, it's a community and an outlet for you to be creative."[5]

Scott Goodson, creative director of Strawberry Frog, the creative agency behind ScionSpeak.com, said, "We did something most brands wouldn't dream of doing: We handed it all over to our consumers. We furnished them with tools. We let them play with those tools. We let them talk about it online and spread the word, months before the official campaign launched. We let them take pride in it. Then—and only then—did we open the floodgates and launch Scion Speak campaign. The point is, you don't create an authentic social media campaign. The culture does."[6]

Aware that the average Scion buyer spent around $1,000 on accessories, the company also opened up its manufacturing to parts and accessories makers. Scion developed a process with the Specialty Equipment Market Association (SEMA) to transfer technology from Toyota's development side to aftermarket manufacturers who wanted to develop products for Scion vehicles, such as performance wheels, chrome exhaust pipes, and light panels. For instance, SEMA members could access design files of engine, bodies, and suspension systems three to six months before the introduction of new models. The goal was to encourage the development of a co-creative ecosystem for Scion, as Apple has so successfully done.

Scion had sold more than 600,000 vehicles by the end of the 2008 and claimed the youngest median age, 31, of customers in the auto industry. This success slowed in 2009, however, as Toyota and Scion sales fell more sharply than those of many automakers in the Great Recession. Scion announced plans to reinvent the brand

anew, as it did in 2003, with edgier designs and more rapid introduction of new models.

The Essence of Co-Creative Ecosystems at Crushpad

Crushpad is a custom winemaking company founded in 2004 in
San Francisco. The company's business architecture consists of
several linked engagement platforms through which individuals or
businesses can work with Crushpad staff and affiliated businesses
to make their own wine. Crushpad is at the center of a network
of suppliers, partners, investors, employees, and consumers. The
company's customers include wine enthusiasts and amateur winemakers, professional winemakers, wine retailers, wine bars, and
restaurateurs.

From the start, Crushpad had two incarnations: a physical facility in San Francisco where grapes are processed and fermented,
and a community website where people make decisions about the
winemaking and track progress. Customers are encouraged to visit
Crushpad both in person and online as frequently as they can, in
order to participate actively in the full experience of winemaking
and understand all aspects of it. To facilitate this participation, the
company has broken down the process of winemaking into five
steps—creating a plan, growing and monitoring the grapes, picking and processing the grapes, aging the wine, and labeling the
bottles—with more than thirty specifications. Customers can engage as much or as little as they wish at any point along the way in
this decision making. The minimum order is for 25 cases, or 300
bottles, which can be either picked up or delivered.

In 2007, more than 5,000 Crushpad clients, a diverse bunch
ranging from men and women in their twenties to seventies, including lawyers, doctors, Silicon Valley techies, and financial types,
made 1,400 barrels—35,000 cases—of 650 wines. Most first-tim-
ers make the minimum, one barrel, and persuade several friends
to share the $7,500 cost ($25 per bottle) in exchange for cases of

the eventual 25. (Prices range from $5,700 for a white blend to $15,000 for a "cult cabernet.") Crushpad's success led to it opening a second physical location in Bordeaux, France, in 2009.

There are seven major engagement platforms in Crushpad's co-creative ecosystem:

1. *A wine-definition platform* engages individuals—acting for themselves or on behalf of their business—around two key questions: What varietal do I want to make? and What style of wine do I want to make? (E.g., a big, fruit-forward wine or a more reserved, subtle wine.) Crushpad suggests that one of the easiest ways to start as a customer is to say, "I'd like to make a wine like X, but different in the following ways." Crushpad's Winemaker's Minute video podcasts demystify winemaking and explain its art and science in a straightforward way.

2. *A vineyard-selection platform* involves people in two key questions: What location is conducive to growing the preferred varietal? And which vineyard should I choose? Video podcasts provide behind-the-scenes looks at prominent West Coast vineyards and in-the-field tutorials from top vineyard managers. Customers can buy small lots of grapes from high-end vineyards through Crushpad or they can purchase their grapes on their own.

3. *A wine-harvest platform* then engages individuals and small businesses around the critical question of when to pick. This is when the customer, acting as a winemaker, starts to determine what goes into the bottle. The key issue is ripeness, and Crushpad provides analytical tools and methods to determine ripeness (e.g., measuring the sugars, acidity, and pH) and physiological maturity (e.g., visible characteristics such as skin and stem color, skin and pulp texture, seed color, berry flavor, and the ease with which the berry can be pulled off the stem). Crushpad experts give advice on climate considerations (in cooler climates pick grapes when sugars reach

an acceptable weight, and in warmer climates before acidity falls too low) and hang time (longer hang time will usually drive more physiological ripeness, but in warmer climates this comes at the risk of higher alcohol and lower acidity, which can leave a wine tasting "hot" and "flabby" and also expose it to greater risk of weather-related problems).

Crushpad engages customers to help determine their wine style (which will inform the desired ripeness) and manage risk, and then collaborates with the growers to determine how to select a picking day together. The company provides a high level of transparency throughout, with winery webcams called the Crushpad Cam and instant messaging with knowledgeable employees at Crushpad, as well as facilitating social interactions with fellow customers.

Through Crushpad's online social network, Crushnet .com, and the Crushpad Cam, customers can monitor the activities at the vineyard. Videos capture the picking and sorting process, which are streamed live to the web. And after the fruit is delivered to the winery, customers can come into Crushpad's state-of-the art, 34,000-square-foot winery and help destem, crush, ferment, and press the grapes. Video also monitors the activity in the winery, allowing customers to chat live with those working the crush.

4. A *wine-aging platform* engages customers in decisions about the type of cask to age the wine in and how long to age it, as well as whether to allow, encourage, or block malolactic fermentation (a secondary fermentation that happens naturally), and when to remove the lees, which are the solids left after fermentation that fall to the bottom of the barrel during aging. As this process proceeds, Crushpad encourages customers to take part in tastings and in making blending decisions, and to participate in racking wines from barrel to barrel.

5. A *bottling, packaging, and labeling platform* allows private and business customers to choose the type of bottle and bot-

tle closure, and to design the label. Most people have a more difficult time making packaging decisions than with the actual winemaking decisions, so Crushpad provides access to a packaging team that helps customers work through their ideas.

6. For professional winemaking customers, Crushpad offers its *commerce engagement platform*, which assists in the seeding of start-up companies and offers a fulfillment infrastructure. Crushpad also handles the regulatory paperwork and shipping and provides the analytical tools and templates to develop business plans. Leonard Stecklow, an executive for a Boston-based financial company, provides an example of this emerging population of wine entrepreneurs. Stecklow and a partner sold fifteen cases of their 2005 Nola Syrah wine to two of New Orleans's best-known restaurants, Commander's Palace and NOLA. "It cost us $14.50 a bottle to make and we sold to the distributor for $29.50," Stecklow said.[7] By linking customers like Stecklow to its supplier network, Crushpad has also garnered tremendous response from growers.

7. *Crushnet offers an ongoing social community platform* for individuals and winemaking groups wanting to share their experiences of winemaking and exchange tips. Vineyards are also part of this engagement platform, so customers can have ongoing conversations with growers. The Crushnet social networking site is replete with social interaction tools, including both public and private blogs for groups making wine together. One such group is the Juice Crew, a group of wine-loving strangers brought together by a few bloggers, which wanted to make a barrel of Super Tuscan–style red wine. The platform also features user-generated videos, allows photo posts, and hosts many forums.

A key reason for Crushpad's success is the flexibility it allows participants in choosing the extent to which they want to participate at any given stage of the process. Crushpad provides a glimpse into the essence of true co-creation: *enabling individuals to engage anywhere in the ecosystem, at whatever level of involvement they desire, at whatever stage of the process.* The individuals and businesses who become involved with Crushpad do so gradually, progressively inserting themselves more and more in the wine decision-making process and expanding the scope of their co-creation. In that sense, Crushpad is a hands-on platform architecture where one learns how to make wine. This element of learning, in addition to choice, is key to the value of the experience that any given engagement platform will offer.

In summary, focusing on the experience of all parties and building effective platforms to create value together, provide the foundation for organizations that seek to build, manage, and expand the growth of business networks. The best co-creation experience is enabled when co-creators can engage with the entire business network, as we saw with GE Healthcare, for example. This requires not only linking upstream with downstream engagement platforms, but also opening up management processes inside the enterprise, representing a transformational challenge in human terms (as we saw with Brother) or technology terms, (as exemplified by Crushpad). The experience of other parties in the network besides the customer is equally crucial; for example, Toyota's Scion strategy would not have worked if the firm had not been able to get dealers excited about the co-creation approach.

In the next chapter, we discuss how to expand stakeholder relationships to build social ecosystems involving the varying motivations and perspectives of different types of stakeholders, such as nonprofit, nongovernmental, and civic organizations and individuals at the bottom of the economic pyramid.

Chapter 5

Building Social Ecosystems

Social responsibility in business has gained momentum, and companies are playing a more active role in tackling economic development, environmental protection, and other social issues. This movement has required many companies to work more closely with governmental organizations, nonprofits, civic groups, and consumers. A recent *Economist* survey noted that while "doing well by doing good" has become a fashionable mantra, few large companies can afford to ignore corporate social responsibility (CSR). The survey concluded that done well, CSR "is not some separate activity that companies do on the side, a corner of corporate life reserved for virtue: it is just good business.[1] Co-creation is a means of ensuring that your company does social responsibility right.

But it is more than that, too. Co-creation takes CSR a significant step forward because all stakeholders have a say in it and benefit from outcomes. Co-creation increases the *social legitimacy* of enterprises while simultaneously expanding business value. Further, it goes beyond CSR to transform the *very business of busi-*

ness by bringing together various stakeholders in what might be called "social ecosystems." Co-creation taps into the knowledge of participants in the social ecosystem to create a freer flow of information, engage people more wholeheartedly, and enable richer, fuller stakeholder interactions (e.g., donors who can provide not only financial capital to charities but also education and business expertise). The human experience not only becomes more meaningful for everybody, but in the process business capabilities are deepened, making them more sustainable. In the end, the economics of the entire ecosystem are changed, creating economic benefits for all parties.

In this chapter, we describe several ways through which enterprises are building social ecosystems and putting social responsibility to work in new ways: through social innovation and economic development with new types of customers (e.g., those at the bottom of the economic pyramid); private enterprises engaging with public and social enterprises; and civic organizations engaging with social workers, entrepreneurs, and philanthropists.

The examples covered in this chapter are:

- **ITC e-Choupal,** originally a trader of agricultural commodities, which has singlehandedly reorganized and reshaped the Indian agricultural market, helping farmers better choose their crops and sell their products. This leads to an economic lift for all parties in the network.
- The Chilean bank **BEME,** which has co-developed with micro-entrepreneurs a comprehensive offering of business and personal loans that fit their unique cash flow patterns.
- The electric power and automation manufacturer **ABB,** which worked with Indian villagers, the government, and nongovernmental organizations (NGOs) to bring solar power units to a remote area.
- Finally, **Ashoka,** a global social entrepreneurship organization, which shows how connections between donors and recipients of assistance can be made more co-creative.

Deepening Economic Development at ITC e-Choupal

When it comes to the building of a social ecosystem, ITC e-Choupal is a world leader in the for-profit sector. ITC Ltd. is an Indian conglomerate with multiple activities. Of interest to us is ITC's agribusiness division, which buys, processes, and sells agricultural products to customers around the world. View this as commodity trading, comparable to what Cargill or ADM (Archer Daniels Midland) do. The company has also partnered with a number of manufacturers to sell farm equipment, fertilizer, and other agricultural inputs to farmers, as well as consumer goods, health care, and microfinance services.[2] This activity is comparable to what a cooperative or a national distributor or dealer of agricultural products would do in Western markets. As a result, ITC's agribusiness division is both a customer of agricultural "outputs" and a supplier of "inputs" for Indian farmers.

ITC created the e-Choupal program in 2000, with the goal of improving its position in the global commodities export market, especially for soybeans, and to source high-quality agricultural raw material for the company's newly launched packaged-brands foods business. The management of the agribusiness division realized that the way to improve the firm's position was to lift the economic performance of the entire system, most notably that of the farmers.

The word *choupal* means "meeting place" in Hindi. There are in fact three different engagement platforms provided by ITC e-Choupal, each deploying a different mix of physical and virtual tools and engaging an ever-expanding set of players in the agriculture ecosystem.

The first engagement platform is at the village level. It consists of kiosks with internet access, managed by an ITC-trained local farmer called a *sanchalak*. These kiosks are typically located within walking distance of five to six villages, and farmers gather there to discuss issues with one another and with the sanchalak. They also make use of the internet as well as other resources, and provide:

- Information in the local language on the daily weather forecast, prices of various crops, and agricultural news

- Knowledge and advice about farming methods and soil testing specific to each crop and region
- An email facility to connect with scientists at agricultural universities and ITC's expert network, as well as fellow farmers who may have dealt with similar crop challenges
- The ability to purchase seeds, fertilizers, pesticides, and a host of other products and services, ranging from insurance policies to tractors and toothpastes (more than 160 companies are partners in the ITC network)
- Access to land records, health and education services, nongovernmental organizations (NGOs) working for cattle breed improvement and water harvesting, and self-help groups (e.g., groups that facilitate the saving of farmers' income, and consequently access to loans)

The sanchalaks have become trustworthy agents of change. Every sanchalak takes an oath before the community that he will serve their best interests without discrimination. He also agrees to a social contract that he will spend part of his income on community welfare. One sanchalak, Akhilesh Singh, says, "Farmers consult me on all critical decisions, and I am the repository of their transactions through e-Choupal. My status in the nearby villages has gone up."[3] The incomes of farmers have also increased as a result of working with better seeds, better herbicides, and securing higher prices for their crops (particularly as a result of lifting the quality of their crops to meet ITC's more demanding quality levels).

The second e-Choupal engagement platform consists of facilities located 25 to 30 kilometers from the villages, where farmers take their tractor-loads of grain. Each of these hubs serves about forty to fifty choupals. ITC's hubs give farmers an alternative option to going to the *mandi,* the traditional, government-mandated marketplace. Mandis are notoriously inefficient marketplaces where farmers frequently are cheated in weight and price and are not necessarily paid in full on the same day, in spite of government regulation to that effect. By contrast, the e-Choupal hubs employ electronic weighing, conduct objective quality testing, ensure spot payment, and provide rest-stop services. In 2004, these hub operations were expanded to include retail stores called Choupal Saagar, which offer about 7,000 square feet of space and provide a wide range of agricultural inputs and consumer goods.

By 2008, ITC had developed about 150 hubs, serving over 6,500 e-Choupals in 40,000 villages and reaching more than 4 million farmers. The stated goal was to scale up to 20,000 e-Choupals, 100,000 villages, and 10 million farmers by 2013. ITC chairman Yogi Deveshwar says, "From that scale, nobody will be able to undo it. It is a daunting task for a single company. We have taken one major step in the journey of a thousand miles."[4]

The third engagement platform consists of a growing network of companies eager to tap into India's rural markets. ITC acts a nodal company—pulling together the resources, products, and services of many different suppliers of "farmer input" and buyers of "farmer output"; injecting a lot of agricultural expertise into the system; and utilizing its scale to drive down cost. For agricultural inputs sold through Choupal Saagar, for example, ITC is able to aggregate demand across several villages and deal directly with manufacturers in its network, giving it strong buying power to drive down product prices. ITC has built a new social ecosystem in India's villages that connects the community of farmers, agricultural suppliers, government research centers, NGOs, and consumers to global markets.

But ITC is also pursuing its own economic self-interest with e-Choupal. Since the launch of e-Choupal, profits have multiplied five times, to $20 million. On the cost side, ITC has dramatically improved its procurement efficiency. It has reduced its transactions costs by 25 to 30 percent on average by eliminating some of the handling costs involved in the traditional mandi system (including transportation, labor, bagging, and commissions).

There is also a strong revenue gain. ITC can now better control the quality of its procurement, bypassing the mandis and driving quality up by creating higher standards. As a result, the company's food division has been able to produce higher-quality products without higher costs, thereby driving more sales. A case in point is the Aashirvaad brand, which became one of India's largest-selling wheat flours within just two years of its launch. In other cases, ITC has been able to create a new market where there was none. For example, ITC's food division was able to launch ready-to-cook instant pasta at the very low price of rupees (Rs) 15 for an 83-gram packet, when the only other similar product was an import priced at Rs 85. ITC also generates new revenues from commissions from partner companies on all products and services sold through its retail platform. And ITC enhances its revenue base by providing a menu of service options to its customers downstream in the value chain, based on lot size, packing, delivery point, storage, option to cancel, quality segregation, credit terms, and pricing. These options differentiate ITC from other commodity players.

Growth has also come in the form of new products and services resulting from "soft" insights provided by the new system. For instance, ITC has gained a more granular understanding of the interaction between soil types, seeds, and fertilizers, which it has used to promote new hybrid seeds, fertilizers, and tilling techniques that help farmers save money in seed, land preparation, plowing time, or water usage, while also helping them maximize crop yield. The knowledge gained from farmers has allowed ITC to provide soil-testing services at its labs and build a data warehouse of soil properties in the villages where it operates. This data is now used by agricultural input companies to generate better products and services for farmers.

ITC has driven the design of new weather insurance products for farmers, with new pricing structures reflecting more accurately the impact of rainfall and temperature changes on individual crop yields. The firm communicates this data to individual farmers through the sanchalaks, using a mobile technology platform that enhances e-Choupal scalability. This allows ITC to create an analytics database. E-Choupal also benefits from ideas generated by frontline retail employees interacting with customers at the Choupal Saagar retail stores and tractor hire and repair services.

ITC also strives to introduce new production techniques that encourage rural people to "stay on the farm" rather than go to cities in search of minimum-wage work. The company created demonstration farms to showcase production and harvesting techniques (e.g., irrigation, plant beds, and intercropping) for improving the quantity and quality of crops and for testing new crop varieties. The sanchalaks identify lead farmers who use the new techniques, publicize events, and disseminate best practices in their communities. ITC is building a vast network of global resource partners that includes Nunhems, which offers hybrid seeds; Bayer, with expertise in crop science and use of fertilizers and pesticides; International Development Enterprises, India, for drip irrigation technologies; the Central Institute for Medicinal and Aromatic Plants and agricultural universities for best practices; and Well Grow, an internal ITC unit that supplies neem-based fertilizers. In supporting the farm demonstration engagement platform, this network has created "entrepreneurial hubs" that move farmers from subsistence farming to more professional standards of agriculture, thereby improving their standard of living. ITC understands that every village, every sanchalak, and every farmer is different, with unique needs, motivations, and desires for growth.

ITC has also identified several potential new businesses for rural communities, including an employment exchange for rural youth with a focus on employability skill-building, rural tourism, and biomass-based energy. ITC created this employment exchange after learning that it is becoming more difficult for Indian farmers to support a family on agriculture alone. In the e-Choupal areas, about 90 percent of twenty-one- to thirty-year-olds are looking for job opportunities outside agriculture yet wish to remain local. At the same time, some businesses are expanding in the rural areas of India and are looking for skilled rural employees. ITC designed the employment exchange platform in partnership with Monster.com to match up the supply and demand for rural skills; they not only match job openings with applicants but also offer training and career advice. The sanchalaks play an important role in verifying the identity of job applicants, providing the traceability and integrity that employers look for. To minimize corruption, however, sanchalaks have no impact over the employment decision.

The growth of the retail distribution outlets of ITC—the Choupal Saagars—has caused a redefinition of the role of sanchalaks and triggered the creation of a new job: the samyojaks. Sanchalaks have predominantly farming and agricultural skills, as opposed to inventory management or distribution skills, which made them increasingly ill-suited to retail goods and services on a growing scale. Sanchalaks themselves were expressing reluctance to being seen in their villages as mercantile people selling products and collecting money. In the new model, ITC has set up *samyojaks,* whose role is to manage the inventory in the Choupal Saagars and serve as wholesalers between ITC headquarters and independent rural retailers—typically villagers who generate additional incomes for themselves by acting as local distributors. Many of those samyojaks had inventory management experience gained in the old mandis. The sanchalaks are now reserved for a more consultative role, acting as facilitators without experiencing social alienation in their villages. Sanchalaks introduce rural retailers to the samyojaks where needed and help in partnering with banks within ITC's business network to assess the credit risk for each retailer. As a result, ITC engages partner manufacturers, sanchalaks, samyojaks, retailers, and farmers together, thereby co-creating mutual value in "win more—win more" fashion.

The co-creative thinking from ITC e-Choupal has also spread more widely within ITC's other businesses, including the company's paperboards business. Chairman Deveshwar spearheads a farm forestry initiative to mobilize subsistence farmers and tribal people to plant trees in local wastelands—a strategy requiring substantial investment, a longer gestation than is typical, and considerable senior management attention to manage market uncertainty and business risks. ITC has also invested extensively in R&D to create clonal tree saplings that are disease-resistant and grow faster in harsh conditions, which makes the growing of pulpwood species on degraded wasteland sustainable and offers a continuous source of income for growers. These buyers are free to sell to buyers other than ITC, similar to the e-Choupal model. In the process of changing the lumber supply chain in this manner, ITC is also transforming its paper business into a significant producer of environmentally friendly, chlorine-free paper and paperboard.

Engaging Micro-Entrepreneurs at BEME

In the 1990s, Chile's state-owned bank, BancoEstado, began searching for a solution to the difficulties faced by the country's micro-entrepreneurs, who were marginalized by a financial system that denied them access to capital.[5] In 1996, the bank established a subsidiary, BancoEstado Microempresas (BEME), with the mission to promote equal access to funding for all Chileans, with a particular focus on lower-income groups. The idea was for the bank to improve the country's economic health and generate profit for itself.

BEME defines micro-entrepreneurs as businesses with annual net incomes of up to $84,000. These micro-entrepreneurs come from the manufacturing, business, and service sectors, but also include independent professionals and small business traders. In 1998, BEME set up a Customers' Committee comprising micro-traders and businesses with varying income levels, in industries as diverse as transportation, agriculture, fishing, and technical and professional services. BEME also invited unions to form "working boards" to discuss the bank's programs and policies, strengthen their relationship with them, and gain cooperation. The Customers' Committee and BEME together discussed the need to shift the bank's approach from an internal focus on microcredit products to the required external focus on microfinancing needs. As a result, BEME decided to engage into co-creation with micro-entrepreneurs, in effect expanding its offering.

This new focus led BEME to co-develop numerous product innovations "by micro-entrepreneurs for micro-entrepreneurs." This required a transformation of the role of BEME salespeople, who had to move away from their desks—physically and metaphorically—and begin visiting customers at their places of business or in their homes. The bank worked, for example, with people whose business involves collecting used cardboard for recycling purposes. It found that their main issue was finding a suitable three-wheeled cycle with the necessary stability to carry the cardboard. Acting as a middleman on behalf of these micro-entrepreneurs, BEME helped them approach vendors who could design the new tricycle, supported the development of the agreements with them, and provided financing to buy the tricycles. For small grocery store owners, BEME facilitated the co-development of merchandising displays to enhance the look of the small grocery stores, again providing financing to buy the displays.

Within two years, BEME co-created more than twenty-five products with micro-entrepreneurs, all involving microfinancing. The transformation required of its internal processes proved massive. For example, the bank had to match the cash-flow patterns of its clientele. People driving school buses were allowed to forgo payments in the summer, since they had no earnings during those months. Even the bank's schedule had to adapt to that of micro-entrepreneurs: those working in outdoor markets were off on Mondays each week, for instance, so BEME offered special services and discounts for them on that day.

BEME takes such a holistic view of micro-entrepreneurs that it's even willing to finance their personal needs beyond the business. The bank provides personal loans for everything from education and housing to medical and life insurance, thereby linking their business and personal needs in an integrated relationship traditionally reserved for more affluent customers. These personal microloans follow the same lending rules as business loans and are based on estimated capital, the nature of the expense or investment made, and repayment capacity.

The bank has been very successful in reaching people traditionally left out of the financial system. As a result, BEME's customer base has grown to more than 360,000, with an annual growth rate of 19 percent over five years. The bank has issued more than $500 million in loans, with an annual growth rate exceeding 40 percent. Although traditional banks view micro-entrepreneurs as high-risk, BEME's savvy in identifying the true risk involved has led the bank to limit its default rate to a spectacular 1.4 percent.

Generating Environmental and Social Impact at ABB

The stated corporate vision of ABB, the Switzerland-based leader in power and automation technologies, is to help its customers use electrical power more efficiently and increase industrial productivity while lowering their environmental impact. ABB seeks to balance economic success with environmental stewardship, to the benefit of all its stakeholders. Like many other global organizations, ABB uses the guidelines of the Global Reporting Initiative (GRI), an independent organization that developed a sustainability reporting framework, in tracking and disclosing its sustainability initiatives and indicators.[6] Michel Demaré, CFO of ABB, says, "We want our employees to share a broader vision of the company's role in society, our responsibilities, and accountabilities to all stakeholders— not only to investors and customers, but also to their colleagues and local communities."[7]

This goal took shape in the desert areas of Rajasthan in northwest India, where ABB's Indian unit created an Access to Electricity initiative for several villages and households that were not connected to the power grid. The dwellings there are very scattered, and power requirements are low. But these desert areas have an average of 325 sunny days each year. ABB recognized that Rajasthan presented a unique opportunity for electricity generation through solar photovoltaic (SPV) panels, which convert solar energy into electricity stored in a battery bank.

With the help of an Indian NGO, ABB gained access to village members, including the village council, and provided them with a pilot SPV unit. The company was aware that villagers would have to view the SPVs as affordable enablers of income generation in order to be convinced of their value. The company was also sensitive to the fact that villagers would want to be involved in the process of formulating the program, says S. Karun, head of Sustainability for ABB India.

Through discussions with villagers, ABB understood they would be willing to make a one-off investment of about $125 toward the system (a third of the SPV lighting system price). The concept was to get them to experience how electricity would improve their lives and discover how it could help them earn more money. The average annual income of a family in these villages is around Rs 30,000 (about $750). A lighting system comprising a small (40WP) SPV panel, a low-maintenance 12-volt battery, a charge controller, and three compact fluorescent lamps would cost about Rs 15,000 (around $375) per system, and it could run household appliances.

ABB entered into a private-public partnership with the government of Rajasthan, agreeing that the SPVs would be paid for in three equal parts: by the house owner, the government's Rajasthan Renewable Energy Corporation, and ABB. The company engaged villagers, NGO members, the state government, the supplier of the SPV systems, and a local organization for installation and maintenance of the systems in crafting the program. In 2006–08, ABB deployed the system to approximately 1,100 households, touching about 6,000 people in seven villages in Rajasthan's interior.

The program has reaped substantial rewards for all parties. The main sources of income in the villages have traditionally been carpet weaving, animal husbandry, carpentry, basket weaving, shoemaking, and tailoring, and villagers had always had to stop working at sunset. Electrification has allowed them to work longer hours and increase their output. They can also take orders more easily through mobile phones that the electricity has made available. The program has spawned a new business in the villages, the maintenance and repair of SPVs. ABB has trained SPV service technicians and now offers annual maintenance contracts at the nominal cost of less than a dollar a month.

Giving villagers a financial stake in the SPV units is what makes the program sustainable. Adam Roscoe, head of sustainability for ABB Group, commented after a visit to the remote villages that "in [ABB's] other Access to Electricity models around the world, systems provided free were not maintained, whereas the ABB model gives the householder real ownership, and their investment in the equipment gives them an interest in maintaining it, thus enhancing the long-term sustainability of the model."[8]

By improving the economic outlook in the villages, the new system has also reduced migration to cities, a growing problem in India because of urban overcrowding. There has also been an increase in the daily attendance of children in schools by about 18 percent, including more female students, as evening studies and educational support have become available. The employment opportunities for local youth have risen through better education. The average income of many households, particularly those involved in weaving and tailoring, has increased by about 20 percent. Almost all households now have a mobile phone, and women can cook at their leisure, since they no longer have to finish food preparation before sunset. There's even more social interaction in the village community now that people don't have to rush to complete their work before dark. As a result of their newfound empowerment, the Rajasthan villagers have also now become more actively involved in furthering the development of the villages while retaining their communal culture.

Empowering the Nonprofit Citizen Sector at Ashoka

The not-for-profit sector plays a particular role in the creation and management of social ecosystems. These organizations serve poor people around the world who lack access to adequate products and services in areas such as health care, housing, water, sanitation, and nutrition. Many of them are also discovering the power of co-creation. One of these is Ashoka, a nonprofit organization based in Washington, D.C.

Ashoka operates in seventy countries and supports the work of what it calls "social entrepreneurs," i.e., people who apply entrepreneurial principles to social problems and organize initiative resulting in social change.[9] Ashoka's role is to identify these social entrepreneurs and fund their plans, typically for a period of three years. Through this funding, Ashoka aims to foster the growth and professionalism of the "citizen sector," its term for nonprofits and NGOs. Bill Drayton founded Ashoka in 1981 with the goal of elevating the citizen sector to the competitive equal of the business sector. "The citizen sector is halving the gap between its productivity level and that of business every ten to twelve years," he says.

Ashoka's approach to selecting its social entrepreneurs—called Ashoka Fellows—is rigorous and multifaceted. They must have a "knockout idea" with broad social impact. Ashoka tries to evaluate each candidate's idea carefully, including how it will be executed and the results it will produce in terms of social change. Most important, Fellows must show entrepreneurial qualities. Ashoka says it "is looking for the Andrew Carnegies, Henry Fords, and Steve Jobses of the citizen sector."[10]

Ashoka engages its Fellows in an active partnership rather than treat them as passive recipients of funding, as many nonprofits do. Ashoka maintains close communication with the Fellows around the world, checks with them regularly on key metrics of success, helps with network building, and brings in professional consultants to provide pro bono consulting services. The Global Fellowship is an online network of all current and former Fellows. They use the network to connect with other Fellows who may deal with similar issues, making them part of a larger group with a shared mission and vision. For its part, Ashoka learns every day from its exposure to a wide variety of ideas from Fellows and consultants.

Beyond simply funding its Fellows, Ashoka aims to scale up its Fellows' ideas and build a powerful network around emerging best practices. The organization looks for commonalities across Fellows' individual programs and sets up multiparty conversations. In early 2010, for example, Ashoka united nine Fellows in Latin America in the Latin American Collaboration on Building Integrity Systems, where they came up with policy recommendations to eliminate government and corporate corruption. Recognizing that these best practices increasingly apply globally, Ashoka also created the Globalizer program to help Fellows whose social entrepreneurial ideas are inherently transnational, and therefore globally scalable. The Globalizer program catalyzes the Fellows' plans through a newly developed online network and an "accelerator panel" that brings together leading entrepreneurs from the business and nonprofit sectors to support the chosen Fellow. The panels also develop metrics by which to gauge the program's progress.

Ashoka's web-based engagement platform, Changemakers.com, brings the Ashoka ethos to a wider audience. Changemakers is an online community of people interested in social innovation. Rather than focusing on a few selected Fellows, Changemakers is open to all—thus, its motto, "Everyone a Changemaker." People discuss issues, share stories, and join groups (oriented topically or geographically) on the site. They can also participate in the many "collaborative competitions" that Ashoka sponsors on the site, in collaboration with other nonprofits and for-profit organizations. Each competition focuses on a different social issue, with submissions invited every three months. All entries are posted online for the community to view and critique. At the end of each competition, a panel of judges chooses three finalists. The online community then votes for the winner, which is funded with cash prizes ranging from $1,000 to $25,000.

For example, through this platform Ashoka launched the Global Water Challenge (GWC) in 2008 to discover and support entrepreneurs with groundbreaking approaches to the world's water and sanitation challenges. The contest was to identify proven concepts that could be scaled up and disseminated by connecting innovators with global investors. More than one hundred submissions poured in from thirty-five countries. One such initiative came from Sudan, where an innovator had launched a bartering system to exchange a local natural resource for water treatment equipment that radically reduced waterborne diseases. In another instance, a Nigerian entrepreneur created cheap, clean, and sustainable energy from human waste.

The role of co-creation has been steadily spreading beyond business circles into the social arena over the last two decades. Some companies have realized that their business ambitions were best served by setting up entire social ecosystems that would co-create economic value with all players in the value chain, as ITC e-Choupal has done with farmers and BEME with micro-entrepreneurs. Some companies have understood that they could create new markets out of whole cloth, as ABB has done in India. Over the same period, the not-for-profit sector has mushroomed from a small and fragmented area to one of the fastest-growing organizational sectors. Co-creation has unlocked a great deal of latent potential in this sector, as Ashoka demonstrates. These examples illustrate that co-creation is a continuous and evolving journey that mobilizes an ever-expanding universe of stakeholders and relationships in the social ecosystem.

In the next chapter, we discuss how co-creative design of engagement platforms serves as a springboard for the continuous expansion of co-creation opportunities.

Chapter 6

Designing Engagement Platforms

In applying co-creation to their own enterprises, managers often wonder where to start. In part two of this book, we will suggest an orderly development of co-creation capabilities that starts with employees inside the organization and gradually moves out to customers, suppliers, and partners. But beyond this general movement, there are no natural entry points for co-creation, since any external-facing process can potentially be transformed into co-creative engagement. In the end, co-creative enterprises open up many processes to co-creation, and by the time they are done the sequence they use becomes quite irrelevant.

The way to get started is by designing an engagement platform with some chosen individuals somewhere in the system and then evolve the design of the platform with the people who engage with it. The idea is to start simple and keep the design of the platform loose enough so that it can evolve as a function of people's observed engagement. Engagement platforms, particularly in the early stages, are like sandboxes where people collectively design with the organization their future modes of interactions.

Devising an engagement platform (such as a website) involves experimentation and learning—and usually some missteps. It is nearly impossible to build a co-creative platform that ensures participants a perfect experience right out of the gate. Platforms evolve in trial-and-error increments, with the roles of co-creators often changing significantly over time. This is the fundamental point of this chapter: the *design* of engagement platforms evolves as a function of the co-creative process, through ongoing interactions among co-creators, expanding the space of experiences, the scope and scale of interactions, platform linkages, and stakeholder relationships in the ecosystem.

The examples covered in his chapter are a bit different from those in the rest of this book. They include our analysis of how companies well on their way to co-creation could take additional steps to strengthen their engagement and collaboration with customers and other stakeholders, to keep interactions alive, and make the human experience the *true focus* of their co-creation. A natural tendency, even for organizations initially successful at co-creation, is to make their engagement platforms progressively more firm-centric and forget that the experience of customers and other participants is what made them successful in the first place.

Although co-creative design applies equally for suppliers, partners, and employees, we will motivate it with customer engagement platforms. The examples include:

- **TiVo,** which initially missed out on the need of its customers to co-create and then rapidly attempted to catch up, yet still could do more
- **AmazonFresh,** where we discuss how co-creative design principles can be used by Amazon as it forays into the online grocery business
- **Google,** where we imagine how its enterprise search offerings could go beyond the firm's well-established user-testing and product evaluation interactions
- **Jabil Circuit,** an electronic manufacturing services company, where we imagine how an existing engagement platform

could be taken to a new level of business value co-creation in a production environment

- **Dassault Systèmes,** the French design software developer, which is shaping its future on the power of experience visualization and value discovery in enabling real-time co-creation between design professionals and customers.

Expanding the Space of Experiences

TiVo began life as a digital video recorder for television and has since evolved into a network of related services. People typically have hundreds of TV channels available, and TiVo allows them to search their TV listings, set recording options, and automatically record shows (using different parameters, including titles, genres, and actors). Yet millions of viewers still have trouble finding and recording programming they like. It seems that what TiVo records is not always what they like to watch.

As cable, satellite, and other providers of digital boxes started to catch up, TiVo had to evolve the design of its platform continuously to stay competitive. TiVo began providing live, on-screen recommendations of shows its customers are likely to enjoy. It brought in partners such as Amazon.com, YouTube, Netflix, and Disney. It provided detailed information and reviews for each TV show or movie. Customers could download new content instantly. TiVo also allowed its users to hit a thumbs-up button while watching a commercial for a TV show, flagging it for later recording, removing the tedium of having to remember the name of the show, the channel, or the time. Users could also share their own content with other TiVo platform users, including photos, videos, and channels.

These moves represent a significant step toward co-creation, yet TiVo could do more. For instance, it learns about its user preferences for content by asking people to rate what they watch but suffers some limits in doing so: for example, it does not keep track of multiple users in a household (e.g., parents versus children), leading to mixed recommendations. Nor does TiVo offer multiple playlists or ways of organizing them better. Users have to page down long lists in its video-on-demand service. While different units, say, in a living room and bedroom, can be networked, TiVo physically copies content from one unit to another and does not allow streaming. As a result, disks can become full quickly. The proprietary TiVo format makes it hard for people to transfer and watch content on other devices. TiVo could make experiences more contextualized, more personalized, and more integrated with other media experiences. More than 160,000 enthusiasts actively participate in discussion forums on TiVo's website, where they have generated more than 5.5 million posts. Their passion is evident. TiVo could step in and structure the dialogue more forcefully among its fans on such an active website. In particular, the company could more actively leverage its willing customer base, through co-creation, and evolve the design of its website and offerings.

Expanding the Scope and Scale of Interactions

Online grocery shopping is making a comeback after its implosion during the dot-com bust, when companies like Webvan scaled up much faster than their consumer base. Now, with more than a billion people shopping on the web, online grocery shopping is taking off. Amazon, the leading online retailer, is getting in on the action.

In 2007, Amazon launched a pilot initiative in Seattle called AmazonFresh, which delivers groceries to customers' homes.[1] Amazon knows how to provide a rich customer experience online, which has been a major factor in the company's rapid growth and the great loyalty customers have demonstrated from the start. Amazon has had its share of stumbles, such as not allowing users to search their order histories (and thereby make easier repeat purchases) for a long time, or allowing users to mix and match addresses and credit cards easily. The company had to undertake a substantial redesign of its website in 2007 as pages became too crowded and items became hard to find, as a result of many groups within the company adding their own cool (or not so cool) features. In general, however, Amazon has done a great job of successfully managing the back-end complexity of operations, logistics, and IT infrastructure needed to support online retailing. AmazonFresh shows the same qualities when it comes to customer experience, but the service has yet to provide a truly co-creative engagement platform.

AmazonFresh has gotten several important things right. When people log onto the website, they can search or browse for available groceries much like in a traditional store. They can filter items through criteria such as "vegetarian" or "gluten-free." Once new users have added the first items to their shopping carts, they are presented with a quick, easy-to-follow service setup tutorial, requiring only one screen and a couple of minutes. The site allows users to select delivery options, most frequently on the same day or next day, and to ensure that the time desired for delivery is indeed workable.

AmazonFresh has instituted several behind-the-scenes processes that facilitate smooth, reliable fulfillment. For starters, the company projects demand for its inventory within a two-week window. It works with suppliers to build the needed inventory, receives goods into the fulfillment center, and stocks the shelves. Once stocked, items appear on the website, and customers can purchase only what is available. AmazonFresh runs daily checks to ensure perishables are well within expiration dates. It also pays careful attention to product recalls. AmazonFresh helps people build their shopping lists on the website throughout the week, as they run out of items and think of new things they want. When customers are ready to order, they can return to the website, hit the gateway page (which often features specials), select their existing shopping list, and quickly add other needed items to their shopping cart. They also have the option to duplicate previous purchases, a simple but highly useful feature for those of us who keep rewriting the same list every time we go to a physical grocery store. AmazonFresh emails recommendations on certain items to previous buyers. Once the company receives an order, it picks and packs it, adjusts inventory levels, then notifies the customer that the order is on the way and delivers it. AmazonFresh's co-creation strategy focuses on both the "first mile" of the customer experience—customers building a running grocery list at home, for example—and on the "last mile"—i.e., the store or delivery experience, which is the way grocery stores have traditionally competed. The website offers a more engaging way to plan one's grocery purchases, and the company works hard on the delivery experience. For example, drivers wear clean booties over their shoes so that they can bring crates of food directly into the customer's kitchen without tracking dirt in, as well.

Although AmazonFresh is an impressive platform in many respects, the company has not yet tapped the full range of opportunities suggested by its interactivity. Online grocery shoppers often worry about the quality of fruits and vegetables, since they cannot directly assess them by touching, smelling, or handling the products. Imagine how much more engaged AmazonFresh shoppers would be if they could observe the product being packed or interact with packers as they're preparing their grocery bag (recall the Crushpad example in chapter 4). The platform also currently lacks product reviews and blog tools for communication among shoppers, in spite of Americans' increasing interest in food and cooking. These tools would allow shoppers to share their experiences of certain foods, swap recipes, or exchange grocery lists, for example. They could also share their diet experiences and form support communities, which AmazonFresh could supplement by providing information about product nutrition and ingredients.

Some of these ideas (and many more) originated with an AmazonFresh manager and a designer exposed to the core principle of co-creation. For millions of consumers, Amazon has earned and deserves its global reputation for its ferocious focus on customer experience and for how it engages customers in co-creating that experience. Amazon can push this engagement even further. It can garner new insights from dialogue with customers about their actual experiences, particularly if the dialogue is initiated in real time (for example, through instant communication tools). The breadth of customer experiences transcends any company's view of customer experiences. By bringing customer experiences deeply into company processes through a process of co-creative innovation, AmazonFresh would learn faster from its customers, increase the likelihood of meeting customers' expectations, reduce costs (e.g., associated with refunds), and minimize negative word of mouth. Co-creative design would expand the existing experience mind-set of designers inside the company, by enabling them to better interpret customer insights they are exposed to and make design changes that enhance the AmazonFresh experience overall.

Expanding Platform Linkages

Even ever-inventive Google hasn't yet tapped into the full potential of co-creation. Of course, it has embraced several co-creative approaches to innovation, such as tapping a worldwide network of friends of its employees to help the company's software designers create new web services. Google employees send out early mock-ups of web services to their friends and ask them to comment on those designs. Marissa Mayer, Google's vice president of Search Product and User Experience, says of the network, "They're co-creating products. They're not writing software code, but are offering a huge amount of insight to shape the products."[2] Further, by using open APIs in its software, Google invites the worldwide community of software developers to co-design new mash-up applications and services based on Google's core system. For example, this is how Google Maps works. Google follows the same approach with its Android platform, which provides an open approach to enabling mobile telecom services.

But merely providing open platforms to employees and customers does not necessarily mean that people's experiences in using the platforms are co-creative. They must be proactively designed that way. Consider Google's enterprise search platform offering. Enterprise search helps workers retrieve information that lies within company databases but can be quite hard to find.[3] In spite of its obvious benefits, enterprise search technology has failed to evolve as quickly as external consumer web search technology, commanding only about 10 percent of the overall search market in 2007.

Back in 2002, Google entered the enterprise search market with two devices: the Google Search Appliance and Google Mini, with the key difference between the two offerings residing in the amount and types of information that can be searched, the capacity for user load, and the cost. The devices are marketed as plug-and-play—i.e., they're easy to set up, integrate well into a company's IT infrastructure, and are ready to use—but they do require a fair amount of IT skill in hardware and software. Many companies turn to an external systems integrator for installation. Google supports users with online manuals, presentations, and expert call center staff. Google lists over 9,000 firms as customers for these enterprise search services, including major firms such as Boeing and American Express, leading educational institutions such as the University of Michigan, and government organizations such as the California Department of Transportation, as well as numerous small and medium-sized businesses. Google's customers are supported by a large partner network including systems integrators (SIs); IT consulting companies, which help design enterprise search strategy and solutions; and independent software vendors (ISVs).

Thus far, Google has taken a feature-based approach to the enterprise search business, focusing on factors such as ease of setup and maintenance, cost, the amount of information that needs to be searched, and speed. Two of these features involve a relatively straightforward installation and a sparse administrative interface.

But the company could take a substantial leap forward through co-creation. For example, Google could dramatically improve its offerings by considering the daily experience of the in-house IT person trying to help company employees use the search tools. The software can be configured by IT staffers for URLs, directories to crawl, and security settings, but it ignores the complex interactions

135

the IT person has with users in the different business units or out-side the company. IT departments get involved with executives, compliance officers, salespeople, and many other employees, as well as with external partners such as SIs and IT consultants (e.g., Ac-centure, Deloitte, or Infosys), ISVs (SAP, Siebel), and Google itself. These interactions span multiple phases, including evaluation, pur-chasing, deployment, setup, configuration, maintenance, and inte-gration with the IT infrastructure and other enterprise applications.

Inevitably, each business unit will have different information needs, data storage policies, and data types. For example, an em-ployee in the procurement department may need to search for all past contracts with a certain vendor, while a salesperson may need to search for a particular customer in a customer list. One can-not expect an IT person to know all the URLs, file systems, and information sources that need to be searched and indexed within each business unit. Security and compliance issues will likely also vary from department to department and among levels of employ-ees. For instance, the policy documents within an HR department should be accessible to all employees, but employee performance records should be accessible only to people who have been granted the necessary authority.

Google hasn't tailored its search offerings to this level of detail, though. After a search appliance is set up and configured, users must perform searches within the confines of the general security policies and authorization levels set by the administrator in the cus-tomer organization. Based on our interactions with users and other descriptions of user experiences in the blogosphere, the inability of users to configure searches specifically for their business unit is quite frustrating. Another area in which users want more flexibility is in fine-tuning the search results. Users would like to order results by what is most relevant to them. Although Google has added to its enterprise search software a self-learning algorithm that analyzes employee clicks to improve the relevance of search results, the re-sults by and large still cannot be contextualized.

By giving end users the flexibility to build their own search experiences, Google in return would get data on their interactions with the system. Further, by giving its partners—SIs, consultants, and ISVs—access to user search data and technical know-how about its relevance algorithm (yet keeping certain aspects proprietary), Google could gain from co-creators' expertise, while also generating additional value for both itself and its partners. These changes would appear seamless to end users but enhance their search experience and improve productivity within the customer organization. Ultimately, this would also allow Google to co-create unique value more efficiently with the legions of small businesses through search experiences that are contextualized to each business or individual.

Expanding Stakeholder Relationships in the Ecosystem

Jabil Circuit has evolved from its original position as an arm's-length contract manufacturer and is now tapping into the power of collaborative interaction, yet it could still do a lot more from a co-creative standpoint. Jabil further illustrates that the co-creation principle can be applied at highly operational levels within an ecosystem.[4]

Contract manufacturing traces its roots to the mid-1970s, when several companies began printed circuit board assembly. Today, the electronics manufacturing services (EMS) industry offers numerous manufacturing services, including product design, supply chain management, global distribution and logistics, and repair services. Typically, their business customers, the so-called original equipment manufacturers (OEMs), retain ownership of product designs and brand names while also pursuing aggressive cost reductions and profit improvements. As electronic product life cycles shorten, fast time-to-market has become increasingly critical for EMS companies.

The contract manufacturing industry grew to more than $300 billion in revenue in 2009. It is dominated by Tier 1 companies (revenues exceeding $1 billion), including Flextronics International (which acquired Solectron), Celestica, Sanmina-SCI, and Jabil Circuit. These five companies alone account for more than half of the total market revenues. The smaller contract manufacturers (Tier 2, with revenues between $250 million and $1 billion, and Tier 3, with revenues less than $250 million) have traditionally carved out niches by providing great customer service and quality management.

In the conventional ecosystem of electronics, a big EMS company has thousands of components suppliers on one side and hundreds of customers on the other side. It is difficult for suppliers to have much bargaining power, as electronic components have largely become commoditized. Most OEMs retain some in-house manufacturing experience, which gives them a clear picture of the cost and profitability of EMS companies. This allows them to dictate prices and puts extreme pressure on the EMS companies to streamline the services they offer. OEM customers gain additional bargaining power over EMS companies from their ownership of brand names, product designs, and marketing channels.

Facing these competitive pressures, EMS companies have recognized they cannot survive by limiting themselves to the traditional manufacturing services. Over the last decade, EMS companies have moved toward fulfilling almost every aspect of the manufacturing supply chain. They have become integral partners in the product development cycle by adding expertise in areas such as front-end design, full system assembly, repair and warranty service, and logistics. As a result, the points of interaction between EMS and OEM companies have changed. The main interactions used to take place at the end of the value chain, when EMS companies provided the finished products. But as the EMS companies have gotten more involved in R&D, repair and warranty service, and logistics, their interactions with their customers now take place much earlier in the process and can involve any point in the system.

Jabil Circuit, based in St. Peterburg, Florida, offers manufacturing and supply chain solutions to electronics and technology companies across a broad range of industries, including automotive, computing and storage, consumer, defense and aerospace, instrumentation and medical equipment, telecommunications, and networking products and peripherals. Jabil's customers include world-class OEMs such as Nokia, Philips, Cisco, IBM, HP, and Intel. In 2008, Jabil's revenues were just over $12 billion.

A decade ago, Jabil's relationship with one of its major customers was limited to the manufacturing of sub-assemblies for just a few products. Today, the customer partnership spans the entire supply chain. Jabil's design centers provide full product design, while its global network of manufacturing operations satisfies cost, speed, and market demands. The partnership now encompasses all service areas in each geographic area that Jabil serves. Offering more services in more locations has enabled Jabil to accomplish one of its key goals: building strong relationships with industry-leading electronic products companies. Jabil's design competency is becoming more and more important to its business, as well as building more flexibility into its manufacturing and supply chain to satisfy customers' ever-changing demands.

As successful as it already is, Jabil could augment its use of co-creation in many ways to expand stakeholder relationships. In production planning, for example, OEM customers typically email or fax purchase orders to Jabil three weeks in advance of the required delivery date. If there are any questions regarding the parts or manufacturing processes, Jabil's manufacturing personnel will raise these issues with customers through the business unit manager, again by sending emails or faxes. If a customer needs to change the delivery time—which is quite common for EMS firms—it sends a request to Jabil, which responds yes or no based on its capacity, utilization rate, and status of current planning, all things into which the customer has little transparency. If Jabil has already started building the products or has purchased the parts, it will deny the customer's request. If the customer wants to move up the delivery dates, it usually needs to pay a premium, and there's still no guarantee about the new requested delivery. If there are any manufacturing problems, such as supplier quality, supplier on-time delivery, manufacturing quality, or design quality problems, Jabil typically informs the customer three days before the promised delivery date via emails or phone calls, leaving the customer to adjust its delivery time to its customers, retailers, or distributors on very short notice. Thus, the customer typically has little flexibility in the timing of building and delivering its products.

To correct these issues, Jabil could design a web-based production engagement platform so customers could view its current preparation status, the production schedule, and the current manufacturing utilization and capacity. Through the website, customers could also see other customers' schedules (anonymously). Such a system would improve customers' visibility into Jabil's productivity, quality, and capacity, allowing them to better prepare for potential difficult situations. Jabil's customers would also be able to see other customers' experience with Jabil and their production schedules. Customers could get involved earlier in any issues that could potentially delay delivery. If demand increases for a customer, it could look into the firm's current utilization rate and bid for the available capacity. Jabil could go so far as to create customer communities, connected through the web forum, through which customers could negotiate anonymously exchanges of slots (with or without a premium price) or purchase slots from other customers.

In summary, as the TiVo, Amazon, Google, and Jabil illustrations suggest, *co-creative* design thinking can continuously expand value creation opportunities (see Figure 6-1).

Figure 6-1:The Expanding Universe of Co-Creation Opportunites

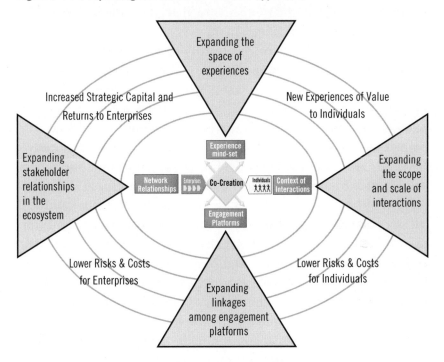

The New Frontier of Co-Creative Design

Co-creative design requires visualization. Without it, the experience tends to be dry, analytical, and "left-brained." Think of the difference between looking at a blueprint of your house—which is what an architect would typically offer you—and receiving photos of your house as it is being built. Or better yet, imagine being able to watch a filmed video of your house, or even being given the ability to turn on cameras and direct them remotely where you want in the house as it is being built. Which process—blueprint sharing versus photos and videos—is most likely to engender a good experience for you, if you consider yourself a co-designer of the house? The main difference lies in the emotional engagement that visualization allows, enabling the co-creator to "feel the design." Through

141

visualization, design and innovation becomes right-brained and emotional, unleashing an experience that goes much beyond the structural aspects of the innovation.

It is inherently hard for co-creators to visualize what they are getting without design transparency. Moreover, co-creators may "kind of know" what they want, while the enterprise "kind of knows" what co-creators want, but misalignment happens easily without the experience of real-time visualization and dialogue. The co-creation experiences can be disappointing, and the company's costs go up to address that—as do the risks to future business in the age of the empowered individual. Addressing this critical challenge requires understanding how humans make choices and feel satisfaction with those choices. We are wired to think in simple images about what we want in a particular choice or interaction. The emergence and selection of details challenges the brain to adjust, to create new maps and images to accommodate the changes being made in the process of visualization. Observing and participating in the creation of a unique experience we have chosen allows the brain to adapt, consider, and integrate the actualization of what we imagined. That is the power of providing design transparency and access in the co-creation process. And its success grows out of a dialogue designed for "co-discovery," as interactions unfold among co-creators and the enterprise. All co-creators must have simultaneous access to innovative tools that enable them to articulate, explore, and discover what's of value together.

As communications and information technologies advance, three-dimensional visualization, simulation, and prototyping tools are enabling technology firms to provide a higher quality of engagement with customers. One of the most interesting firms in this area is Dassault Systèmes of France, which advocates a resolutely experiential view of design software. Dassault is the global leader in what is now called product life cycle management software (PLM); the term reflects the fact that the tools of design go beyond computer-aided design and extend to the production, distribution, maintenance, and eventual disposition of products.

The CEO of Dassault Systèmes, Bernard Charlès, advocates a live, interactive view of design where customers can co-create in real time with designers through the use of highly visual software that simulates the future experience of the product. Dassault originated in the more analytical world of automotive and aerospace design; its CATIA software can be found in all major car and aircraft companies in the world. Under Charlès, however, the company has been transforming itself into what one might call a "customer experience transformation partner" that helps customers and designers jointly visualize the future customer experience. To get there, the company has augmented its capabilities over time, first acquiring a company called Virtools whose know-how is closer to video games than engineering design, then spearheading a community of designers called 3DVIA, which offers free design objects for download. It has also created an entity called 3Dswym—this stands for "three-dimensional see what you mean"—which allows customers to co-create designs of consumer products and visualize them online. 3Dswym reflects a collaboration between Dassault and Publicis, a top global advertising and communications agency, an effort to combine the rich, analytical heritage of product design tools with the visual and imaginative power of an advertising agency. Dassault also acquired the PLM business of IBM, Dassault's longtime partner, and is doggedly pursuing its goal of transforming the company—not to mention the entire PLM industry—toward enabling a better visualization of the customer experience.

Charlès is a soft-spoken man but is relentless about the transformative power of co-creation. He has the advantage of having a $1.8 billion software company at his fingertips. Although Charlès's world is business-to-business rather than a consumer world, his ambition is comparable to that of Steve Jobs taking on the computer industry and refocusing it single-handedly on the human experience rather than on bits and bytes. Indeed, as Dassault has branched out beyond aerospace and automotive clients into fashion and consumer electronics and even physical architecture (e.g., architect Frank Gehry uses Dassault software to model his buildings), the company is also opening up its innovation and design possibilities to the next generation of talent. Dassault uses online and social media to encourage young people to experiment with its tools online and to nurture design communities. For instance, people can create 3D models of characters to embed into their Facebook pages (and eventually into games that they will create), and they can build 3D models of the exterior of their homes and embed them into Microsoft's Virtual Earth (similar to Google Earth). With the success of movies such as *Avatar 3D* (the highest grossing film of all time) and the ongoing movement toward 3D experiences and virtual and augmented reality in films, on television, and on the web, Charlès vision is nothing short of the "democratization of design," as he puts it.[5]

There is a significant price to pay, however. Co-creative design requires a profound transformation of the company expert's role and experience, from an exquisite specialist largely protected from the vicissitudes of customer feedback to a fully exposed co-creator interacting continuously with a community of passionate customers. This is not for everyone. Not all designers are comfortable moving out of their protective ivory towers or willing to acknowledge that untrained customers can contribute on a par with the highly trained professionals that they are. Many companies have found that customer co-creation in design is more limited by the willingness of designers to engage than by their ability to attract customer co-creators. When it comes to co-creative design, the challenge is larger inside than outside.

Many enterprises may not be comfortable with co-creative design. Whether designing a product, a meeting process, a website, a physical place, or any other type of engagement platform, designers in firms typically like to focus on an end point. Witness the emphasis among designers on user need, user interface, and user experience. The problem with these end points is they require a highly provider-centric process that imposes the provider's narrow view of design and gauges the participant's response within that narrow process. In this way of thinking, the designer is an expert who designs for the user.[6]

Co-creative design, in contrast, starts with people as seeking desirable and meaningful experiences. They often cannot articulate beforehand what these experiences are, because they have by definition never "experienced" them. People typically discover what is meaningful to them through visualization and dialogue. Thus, the enterprise must give them tools that help them on these fronts (and thereby help the enterprise). The eventual design of the engagement platform will need to incorporate both the "lived" experiences of participants and their imaginative skills, stimulated by the tools and knowledge provided by company designers. In co-creative design, the company designer and co-creator interact collaboratively and creatively in two-sided fashion (through transparency, dialogue, and access) in contrast to the conventional sequential back-and-forth of design testing and feedback.

Such co-creative design thinking extends all the way to the strategic architecture of organizations and their management processes. How to begin the journey of transforming your enterprise's management processes through co-creation, and build the capabilities to reap the benefits of a full-fledged co-creative enterprise, is the subject of part two of this book.

PART TWO
MANAGEMENT CO-CREATION

Chapter 7

Transforming the Enterprise Through Co-Creation

Any enterprise seeking to co-create with its customers and multiple stakeholders needs to apply this new mind-set to the nature of engagement between management and all co-creators *inside* the enterprise. But bringing about such transformational change requires challenging and mutating the "DNA" of the organization. It is not uncommon for institutions to invest a huge sum of money and resources over a few months into "driving change" and yet be quite unsuccessful. One of the key reasons for failure is that the change process itself is not co-created. Managers typically assume that if a particular predefined change process is used, then a solution will emerge. What is hard to change is the dominant mind-set of organizations, including the way individuals view each other, their collective beliefs, culture, and assumptions. After decades of experience with organizational change management, it has become abundantly clear that successful change management is best achieved through *engagement of those affected by change.*

How to transform the organization through co-creation is described in detail in this chapter.

Co-Creative Transformation at La Poste's Retail Division

La Poste Retail is the division of the French Postal Service that manages its 17,000 post offices and distributes the products of its mail, express package, and Postal Bank divisions. Toward the end of 2007, the senior sales and marketing officer of the French Postal Network, Marc Zemmour, executive vice president in charge of sales and a seasoned veteran of many administrations at La Poste, and a key member of his team, Fabien Monsallier, the chief strategy officer, a manager who loves to experiment with new approaches, decided to launch an exploratory effort in co-creation.[1] They had reached the conclusion that engaging employees more actively in improving services was vital. The service had been steadily losing sales because of the rapidly decreasing volume of mail (about 5 percent annually), being replaced by online communication, and the sales decrease had been offset only marginally by growth in the package business. In spite of great efforts to develop additional services, the distribution division had also continued to lose sales, and post offices were being closed. Four successive CEOs had failed to steady the ship.

Like many postal services, La Poste Retail has been the butt of many jokes about the patience required to endure long lines and the lack of motivation of post office employees. Zemmour and Monsallier believed that the absence of a customer orientation at La Poste Retail was central to the division's problems. The history of La Poste Retail was one of top-down command-and-control management. La Poste still used the term *brigade* to describe teams of tellers and was organized into seven hierarchical levels. Zemmour and Monsallier made a pitch for a new managerial approach based on co-creation. In order to test whether a co-creative approach would work at La Poste, they approached the Center-East region, one of

150

the six large regional areas of La Poste Retail, headquartered in Lyon. The region comprises a network of 4,000 branches and employs close to 7,000 people. Julien Tétu, who manages the region, volunteered to pilot the project.

The three of them quickly assembled a steering committee of senior executives to prepare the ground for the large-scale transformation they had in mind. It took a bit of diplomacy to get going, given La Poste's history of social conflict "This is probably our last chance at a turnaround," Tétu asserted. One of the people Tétu drew into the co-creation adventure early on was Béatrice Tourette, former auditor turned marketing and communications person for the Central-East region. Tourette brought the discipline of process to the project, relying on her remarkable intelligence of what motivates people to change.

Piloting the Approach in Lyon

The team quickly settled on three locations for the pilot co-creation effort: the heart of downtown Lyon, the suburbs, and a small countryside town, chosen in order to tap into the experiences of three primary groups of customers: regular, or "mass market," customers; professionals, such as small office or home office self-employed people; and low-income people, often immigrants living in tough urban neighborhoods. The team reasoned that the three locations would give them a representative sample of customers.

As is often the case with experimental approaches, solutions progressively emerged from overcoming some early obstacles. The team learned from some mistakes made in organizing the early workshops, which saved a lot of time later on. Influenced by more traditional market research techniques, the team's original intent was to focus on customers as the primary generators of insights for the transformation, and only bring in La Poste people to "listen to the customer." They were promptly reminded that employees wanted to do a lot more than listen and had to be involved on an equal footing with customers. This was driven home to them in the early workshops, particularly through what became known as "the

151

Georgette episode," from the name of a particularly articulate post office employee in a small town, who expressed in no uncertain terms that if there was going to be any co-creation, she was going to be part of it.

Here's how it happened. In each of the three locations, the group was following the same sequence of three workshops. Day one involved a co-creation workshop with teller employees only (Georgette and her colleagues), to understand their experience and interactions with customers (externally) and the postal hierarchy (internally). On the first part of day two, customers joined teller employees to share their respective experiences in the post office (Georgette, her colleagues, and their local customers). In the second part of day two, the co-creation team conducted working sessions with the post office managers to debrief what they had learned with the employees of the post office and their customers.

Georgette was the most vocal. She felt massively disengaged, unrecognized, frustrated. Her younger colleagues were visibly upset by her massive display of negativity, particularly given the presence of a camera capturing the moment. "Why don't they give me early retirement now?" she said. "I only have two years to go. I get no recognition from anybody for my forty-year career at La Poste. My boss is nice enough but ineffective. Headquarter guys set up sales quotas that are so unrealistic, I know on January 2 that I'll never reach them. Sometimes I don't even understand these goals, like how I am supposed to be incented for helping La Poste become a leader in providing banking advice? I never receive any credit for that, as far as I can see." There were a few redeeming features to her job that she grudgingly acknowledged, like the ability to spend her whole life working in the little town she'd chosen to live in, the friendship with her colleagues from the post office, and job security. All in all, this was a pretty depressing day for members of the co-creation team.

However, the next morning with customers, Georgette seemed a new woman. Customers knew her as a local celebrity painter and loved her. To them, *she* was La Poste. They were full of questions about how the post office works. Georgette was the one explaining why they did things the way they did. Ideas were flying across the room. Her mood was upbeat and her enthusiasm infectious.

Working through it, they came to see that Georgette's "Dr. Jekyll and Mr. Hyde" behavior was a function of whom she was dealing with: she told a mostly negative story in dealing with the internal hierarchy of La Poste, yet a much more upbeat one in dealing with external customers. This helped the team appreciate how important customer contact and anchoring in the local community were in the teller experience. Tétu summarized it in the following fashion: "Evidently, the key is to re-create trust between teller employees and managers. We must leverage what's positive and energizing for them, namely the relationship with the customers. It is upon this relation that we must build the team in each post office."

Unfortunately, post office managers were not present in the early workshops with employees and customers, with the process bringing them in only at the end in a separate debrief session. Somehow, the more traditional employee focus-group thinking had again seeped in, and it was feared that the presence of post office managers would inhibit the free flow of insights from their subordinates. From there on, the team understood they had to err on the side of inclusion and invited post office managers from the beginning. In spite of similar reservations, members of the regional and top management teams of La Poste were also progressively included in those workshops, getting steadily better at co-creating new ideas with their junior colleagues, rather than trying to manage them in overly directive fashion. Some workshops involved putting five hierarchical levels in the same room, something La Poste Retail had never done before.

Of course, not all pain inflicted onto teller employees came from the inside. Some customers were also pretty good at dishing it out, particularly in the more urban post offices. Security was a big concern because French post offices are also banks and are occasionally held up, primarily in tough neighborhoods. Less dramatically, but a

153

threat nonetheless, customers agitated by a long wait occasionally abused some teller employees verbally. Tellers were also disturbed by common customer complaints about letters or packages that had not been delivered even though they were at home when the mail person came by. The mail and package delivery people, it was discovered, occasionally failed to ring because they felt unsafe going inside certain buildings.

After conducting three waves of co-creation workshops in the Lyon area in three months, the team had assembled a pretty clear picture of the experience of the four players they wanted to focus on: customer, teller employee, post office manager, and "the hierarchy." It now understood how these different actors interacted with each other, and what experience came out of it. They were ready to roll.

Developing a Nationwide Approach

The Lyon co-creation workshops had created some buzz within La Poste. Fabien Monsallier and Julien Tétu realized they needed to broaden the leadership coalition and "go national." This meant moving in two directions: engage the newly arrived CEO of La Poste in the effort, and convince Tétu's regional colleagues to join in. Tétu invited Jacques Rapoport, the new CEO of La Poste, to come to Lyon and learn about the co-creation project. Rapoport endorsed it with enthusiasm because he believed something deep had to change about each post office in France.

This project fitted nicely with the early steps he had in mind to transform the retail network of La Poste: establish some basic service standards for big post offices; begin to transform the traditionally partitioned post office building, with its long wait line; and create open spaces with individual service islands, such that it "explodes" the traditional wait line. The service standards that were defined included, among others, a maximum allowable wait time for simple operations (less than 5 minutes), an average allowable time required to claim a package or a registered letter (less than 8 minutes); a maximum time allowed to respond to a complaint (48 hours); and the guarantee that all tellers will be open if the wait time exceeds 10 minutes, to demonstrate the "all hands on deck" readiness of each local team.

Rapoport also launched a giant renovation program for the 1,000 largest post offices, which were in dire need of it. In these new facilities, the giant dividing line between teller employees and customers was replaced by service islands spread across the space. Some greeters now welcome customers, and customers and employees stand next to each other without separation, while automated machines provide easy access to basic products.

Although such an investment suggests a major financial bet, Tétu believed that the battle with competitors would not be waged on the size of the investment, but on the door-to-door mobilization of each post office employee around customers.

"Our network is not a technical or mechanical network. It is one hundred percent human. The quality of our service depends entirely on the men and women who welcome and serve our customers. Our service quality is directly proportional to the competences, the intelligence, and the daily motivation of these men and women. To change the physical nature of these post offices or simply apply new service standards won't change a thing unless teller employees personally participate in this adventure from the start. We need them to *co-create this change* with us."

Tétu and Tourette then developed a co-creation process that was sufficiently simple to be understood by all, which included gamelike modules aimed at facilitating an easy, team-based co-creation in all offices. They proposed to structure the program around four "co-creation areas" that had been identified in the regional workshops, each of them representing a key part of the customer experience, either because it was negative, or because it was essential. They convinced the CEO to construct the co-creation approach around these four experience areas:

- Accessibility: How can we be accessible when customers need us?

- Customer care: How can we ensure that customers come into an easy-to-understand space where they feel welcome?
- Service efficiency: How can we guarantee that we efficiently provide customers what they need, whether it includes information, receiving a service, or securing an appointment?
- Quality of advice: How can we make sure that our customers feel properly cared for and receive a personalized answer, whether they are in the postal operations or in the banking part of the post office?

The co-creation approach was meant to engage each post office employee in improving the four customer experience areas, either individually or as a team. The problem had now been stated clearly, and the ambition linked to each topic set, thereby challenging each individual to co-create a personal response.

In March 2008, Tétu and Tourette launched a two-year program, called Welcome to the Post Office, that touched 707 districts of the Center-East region. They put in place a robust rollout process, which included ready-to-use tools supported by a task force recruited among La Poste's internal consultants. By the summer of 2008, more than 1,200 people had engaged in the co-creative process.

Based on this early success, the CEO Jacques Rapoport challenged the five other regions to put in place a similar participative process in their region. The method developed by the Center-East region was "suggested, but not imposed."

Paris Catches Fire

Michel Garnier, head of the Paris region, was the first to declare his interest. Garnier is a man who speaks with modesty of the spectacular results he's achieved at the helm of his region. He started by figuring out how much help he could receive from his Lyon colleagues if he was to launch a co-creation project in Paris. Of course, he decided to co-create the deployment of the approach, borrowing the tools developed by the Center-East region but granting everyone a license to modify them to encourage appropriation at all levels.

Tourette invested some of her own time to facilitate the migration of the relevant know-how, utilizing the Lyon center of excellence she had established.

On May 2, 2008, at the Arab World Institute in Paris, Michel Garnier launched the first wave of the new Welcome to La Poste of the Greater Paris Region in the presence of one hundred post office managers. He immediately stated his ambition to reorganize through co-creation the 571 districts of the region in two years. To do so, in addition to his management team and his area managers, he mobilized his sales managers, the project managers of the regional support teams, the organization specialists, and the internal consultants who had been earmarked for the program, as well as regional human resources people and many others.

Through this program, the management of the region also designed and implemented a new retail format in the Paris post offices by adapting to the region the main features of the proposed nationwide program. The final model used by the greater Parisian region was also influenced by an initiative developed a few years earlier in the region and originally called Breaking the Teller Line, thereby illustrating the profound change that was to take place by getting rid of the bulletproof glass of yesteryear. This concept was also briefly known as Opening the Teller Line, before becoming what it is today, i.e., the new Customer Service Space.

Michel Garnier remembers a second key date: September 24, 2008, at 3:00 pm, to be precise. On that day, Jacques Rapoport, CEO of La Poste Retail, visited the post office of his childhood at La Reine Blanche (literally, the White Queen) which had just been renovated in the new Customer Service Space format, and had a revelation he describes as "quasi-mystical." This vision never left him after that, motivating him throughout the transformation and thereby illustrating once again that the personal experience of top managers plays a key role in large-scale change.

On December 1, 2008, at the post office of Le Marais, also just renovated through the Customer Service Space format, the first official communication on the Welcome to the La Poste of the Greater

157

Parisian Region program took place, featuring the new opening hours that had post offices open until 8:00 p.m. On that day, Garnier also presented the project for the renovation of the Louvre post office, another landmark site in Paris. When he'd agreed to consider the renovation of the Louvre post office, Rapoport had begun to talk about a "complete renovation of all Paris post offices." Garnier had mentally discounted the possibility, knowing the challenge this would represent. But on that day, Garnier received a phone call from Jacques Rapoport, who was on vacation in Bangkok, confirming the desire he had expressed earlier to give the region the mandate to "redo all of Paris in a year." During the Bangkok call, and impressed by the enthusiastic engagement of Parisian post office employees for the co-creation approach, Rapoport also decided to concentrate one-third of the nationwide investment budget onto the city of Paris. Later, more than half of the national investment budget of La Poste ended up being dedicated to Paris.

Paris as a Giant Construction Site

The transformation project required an enormous real estate component to realize the new space allocation model, which put customers at the center of that space, where they had direct contact with teller employees who were now freely moving about. Thirty million euros were dedicated to this renovation, and 132 post offices were entirely redesigned. Nothing of this magnitude had ever taken place in the French Postal System. All bulletproof windows disappeared, except for one, kept for its museum value.

In record time, the management of the region had to analyze requirements, do the work required by zoning laws, establish specs, select contractors, agree on contracts, and manage suppliers, not to mention relocate huge numbers of personnel and machines during the renovation. "We knew this would not be a quiet and lazy river," Garnier says, in his metaphoric style. "But it turned out to be a tsunami."

Closing post offices for renovation required perfect coordination of the project management sequence, so that customers could still find an open post office near their home or work during the renovation. This meant meeting strict deadlines and sacrificing vacation and weekends.

Garnier refers to the work accomplished in the renovation of the 132 post offices in the new Customer Service format as having "trampled habits and accelerated time" for La Poste. But the adventure is far from over: 253 post offices remain to be transformed in the greater Paris region as of this writing.

Teller Employees Out of Their Cages

But the real estate component is only a small part of the story, compared to the human effort involved. The management of the region had trained internal consultants as change agents to aid the deployment of the co-creation approach of the Welcome to La Poste program. But the region's management had also insisted on massively mobilizing the line personnel in its post offices to engage teller employees deeply in the process, with the help of their management, rather than overrely on internal consultants. In that spirit, all teller employees received a short training and were asked to interview customers in the public hall of the post office, armed with a simple questionnaire. It was as if they were receiving some basic principles of skydiving one minute, and the next thing they knew, they were jumping out of the airplane.

For many teller employees in Paris, this was a frightful experience, something they'd never done before, and for a few, something they wished they'd never do again. Some did a great job, and others did not. Some exchanges with customers were very rich, while others were perfunctory. But all tried, and there turned out to be great power in the sheer number of people involved. Teller employees gave each other courage and took the plunge, usually working in groups of two, in a sweeping process where each of them became market researcher and process consultant in one fell swoop.

One customer became so excited that within twenty-four hours of the workshop, she'd fired off four emails to her post office team and polled three neighbors on how to improve the post office. Much to their surprise, employees discovered many customers were passionate about La Poste and wanted to contribute. The management of La Poste originally had thought that community involvement was reserved for big consumer brands like Nike and Apple. They discovered La Poste could also unleash passion and a huge mobilization of energy.

After each exploratory encounter with customers, teller employees were invited to gather and reflect on what they'd learned. They'd never talked about these things together before, particularly in the presence of their direct supervisors and post office managers. They were a bit uncomfortable at first, but rapidly got going. Some ideas were "sent upstairs" because they extended beyond the local post office. Other ideas could be implemented right here and now. The excitement had become palpable.

Changing Opening Hours in Co-Creation with Employees

In Paris, as in Lyon, the new opening hours—until 8:00 p.m. during the week and on Saturdays—is the most visible form of the change at La Poste Retail. This transformation resulted from the engagement created by the regional management of La Poste around the question that was posed to employees: how should they make each post office more "accessible" for customers?

Julien Tétu, as pioneer of the transformation in the Center-East region, explains that the key was to move from a "confrontational" logic, where managers used to spend one month building an organization model on their own, then three months trying to impose it onto employees, to a "co-construction" logic where they spend three months co-creating a new organizational model within the joint team of managers and employees, then one month translating it into schedules and work cycles.

Of course, post office managers are not able to accommodate every desire of postal employees, but collectively both parties have achieved a better balance between employee and company constraints. Because employees are now acutely aware of customer desires and La Poste's economic constraints, they started shifting some of their personal aspirations to the benefit of the collective interest during the co-creation process.

One of the long-standing frustrations of La Poste management had been its perception that unions were resisting the opening of post offices on Saturdays, in spite of the fact that customers had it high on their list of requests. In the end, it turned out many employees had nothing against working on Saturdays, provided they were granted the right to have a flexible schedule during the rest of the week. In other words, La Poste discovered a new paradigm of productivity: operational efficiency comes from the ability to engage employees around a "win more–win more" solution to the scheduling issue.

Meanwhile, new dynamics had developed in some post offices. The dialogue between employees and customers in the public halls of the post office generated another idea: why wouldn't we engage customers in the discussion of opening hours jointly with postal employees and management? At La Poste Retail, as in most postal services around the world, opening hours had historically been set by headquarters. During customer discussions, another expectation emerged: customers would love it if the local post office could adapt its opening hours to the market days of their village, town, or city neighborhood. Shopping for fresh food and other necessities at open-air markets is a staple of French social life. Because these markets start as early as 7:00 a.m. two or three times a week, some customers wanted the local post office to open at 7:00 a.m. on those days, allowing them to shop at the market and do their post office business at the same time.

In the traditional design, La Poste Retail could not afford to allow co-created opening hours at the local level, since it could not physically keep track of the specifics of every open-air market day in each village, small town, or city block. By default, it had defined a standard schedule that best matched what it perceived to be the needs of customers and the constraints set by regulation and union negotiations pertaining to its workforce. The schedule it had come up with was the best countrywide compromise it could devise and "sell" to the national unions.

The most remarkable achievement of this transformation is that many new post office schedules resulted in a net extension of opening hours at a constant manpower level, something the management of La Poste Retail had wanted to do for years but had never dared include as a negotiation item with the unions. Because teller employees and customers had established this need for longer opening hours together, it evolved naturally. Today, La Poste Retail remains in listening mode, curious to engage its employees in new *co-created human resource practices.*

An Engagement Platform to Co-Create Between Local and National Levels

While the live co-creation process was occurring in the post offices, the management of La Poste Retail resolved that some problems could not be properly addressed at the local level because they involve nationwide processes or issues. To address these issues, the firm's management decided to develop an internet-based exchange and innovation platform for post office employees. The idea was to allow all employees to express their views on problems needing to be solved or suggestions that may contribute to the improvement of the four previously mentioned customer experience areas: access, customer care, service, and advice.

The intent behind the internet development is to offer employees a global vision of all co-creation initiatives under way and to invite them to participate in those initiatives through the site. Six months after its launch, 1,578 suggestions had been published, unleashing a participative wave where each suggestion was hotly debated among employees: over the first six months, 12,873 comments had been posted, with 9,772 votes on suggestions!

La Poste also set up a telephone-based platform to allow customers to describe what they considered as "irritants." To ensure that these items got addressed by the organization, Jacques Rapoport nicknamed his monthly executive committee meeting "the committee of irritants": regional and national executives discover with him the most popular suggestions, decide with him on what should be implemented, and follow up on implementation. Many significant improvements have been implemented through this process: replacement of equipment deemed inefficient or obsolete, modification leading to better access to automated machines, or changes in the IT system to allow customers to save time at the teller.

By allowing employees and managers to elevate problems that could not be dealt with at their individual level to management, La Poste has unleashed the four powers of co-creation. The experience of customers has improved because they can now get what they need much faster or more readily, including the reduction of wait time at the post office and the ability to bypass the post office altogether for some operations. The experience of employees and managers has also improved as they now have better relations with their clients and save time in back-office operations. La Poste Retail also benefits as an institution: back-office costs have dropped, maintenance costs have been reduced because equipment and machinery are serviced more effectively, and La Poste now continuously learns from its customers since they are better engaged through the live and internet co-creation processes.

Spectacular Results

In November 2009, Jacques Rapoport proudly reported that the Paris region had reduced its average wait time by 60 percent over a year, while at the national level the 1,000 largest post offices had reduced theirs by 50 percent. Only 42 percent of people were able to drop a registered letter in less than 5 minutes in September 2008, but 74 percent were able to do so by October 2009. For the 1,000 largest post offices in France, this number was up to 85 percent (86 percent in Paris). For more complex operations such as depositing or wiring money, only 65 percent of customers were able to carry out their operation in less than 10 minutes in September 2008, but by October 2009 this same number had gone up to 82 percent.

The most spectacular customer service results were achieved in the regions that embraced co-creation. The Center-East region, while historically a strong commercial performer, had been dead last among regions in terms of quality: only 40 percent of its post offices had met the national quality standards. A year and a half after launching the co-creation effort, the region was tied for first place. The other two regions that embraced co-creation—the greater Parisian region and the Southern region—also made spectacular progress. Regions that stayed away from co-creation have not exhibited any noticeable progress.

Finally, 95 percent of customers declared themselves satisfied with the service of La Poste Retail in the offices that had been renovated. There is no comparable benchmark from a year earlier for these specific post offices, but La Poste was a notorious laggard in all comparative benchmarking studies involving retail places or banks.

About 92 percent of customers found it easy to know how to navigate the new layout, and 93 percent were pleased with the new level of service. La Poste does not publish the results of its employee surveys, but the engagement of its employees is also rising rapidly, particularly in all post offices that have embarked on the co-creation journey. The correlation between employee satisfaction and customer satisfaction is intuitively evident to all who have participated in the effort.

Fabien Monsallier sums up the transformation in the following fashion: "Management set some clear direction, then made a significant commitment of capital for the renovation. After that, we got out of the way and let employees and customers reinvent the model at the local level. That's about it." When asked where La Poste might go next, he takes a deep breath, taking time to enjoy what's already been accomplished. "There's much more we can do in the co-creation area," he adds. "We've just scratched the surface when it comes to customers and employees coming up with new offerings or changing the way we operate. We've only just begun."

The New View of Organizational Transformation

In summary, as the La Poste example shows, any enterprise can start and sustain co-creative transformation. The paths to transformation are many, representing a strategic choice to be made by each organization depending upon its prevailing culture, management outlook, initiatives, aspirations, and leadership. Success is a function of the active involvement of managers and employees at all levels. The key point is this: *Leaders must co-create the transformation path.*

Of course, companies have been transforming for years, following numerous waves of process reengineering and change management techniques. All these approaches have advocated some form of mobilization, ranging from the benign need for "buy-in through involvement" to the larger-scale mobilization process of some corporate transformation models. So what does co-creation bring to the world of transformation?

The answer lies in the role of stakeholders (individuals) in the change process. In co-creation, all stakeholders, especially customers and employees, are an integral part of the creativity in the transformation process and its design, because it is in his/her own self-interest to do so. As co-creators, they gain a better experience and better economics through the new co-created interactions. This type of involvement means the change process is itself co-created between the company and its stakeholders, and does not proceed from some corporate blueprint of that change. As a result, the transformation process cannot be designed *a priori,* an occasionally threatening reality for corporate change agents who have been schooled for years in the structured change processes of quality, reengineering, or change models. This requires them to let customers, employees, and other key stakeholders co-create the transformation path.

Another major difference lies in the fact that the starting point of the co-created design is the individual's experience, rather than the firm's processes. Most traditional transformation models start with a process architecture of the firm and ask themselves: what does the customer want from each process? The "process customer" is then interviewed through some research on what they expect in terms of outcome from the process offered by the firm—for example, what

165

lead time do you consider acceptable from our order fulfillment process, or what features should we embed in our design process for our new product? This is a company-centric way of attempting transformation. It will improve the company's performance, but its innovation potential will be far lower than if the company imagines a new customer experience *with* its customers, then devises with them the new interactions required.

Of course, the greatest difference of all lies in the ultimate goal of the transformation, which is to allow the customer to co-create his/her own experience with the firm, not only in the change process, but also in the eventual day-to-day experience of the firm's products and services that will result. The best way to get there is to use a co-created approach to transformation. If you build it with them, they're already there.

A good starting point of the transformation is with company people already in contact with customers in their day-to-day lives, since they contribute most directly to the experience. These can be salespeople, customer service agents in a physical place or remotely located in call centers, store personnel in retail industries, or technical application or applied engineering people in business-to-business worlds. The idea is to identify people at the point of contact with customers, team them up with their immediate customers to initiate the co-creation, then see whether their existing interaction can be broadened to other neighboring interactions, or lead to deeper forays into the customer system or the company organization.

Successful co-creation efforts have both a top-down and a bottom-up component. In the top-down component, the senior management team develops a high-level view of what is to be achieved, and then facilitates and guides the transformation process. This process is itself often the result of an internal co-creation effort involving the members of the management team. The bottom-up component of the transformation process is critical to the transformation to becoming a co-creative enterprise. The art of co-creation lies in simultaneously identifying innovative ideas and the people willing to mobilize themselves around them, both inside and outside the company. The faster the company can scale up this process, the more likely it is to get a truly transformative result. Ideas do matter, but the energy of self-selected groups of customers and employees providing the passion and energy to pursue them is even more important. In co-creation, the analytical value of an idea is inextricably linked to the human energy that powers it.

How to lead the organizational transformation to put the "human" back in resources, co-create productive and meaningful employee and managerial experiences, and regain the lost soul of the enterprise through redesign of managerial decision making, is the subject of the next chapter.

Chapter 8

Leading the Co-Creative Enterprise

As we saw in the previous chapter, in truly co-creative enterprises, priorities cannot simply be dictated from the top. Leaders in those organizations relinquish the conventional institution-centered "cascade and align" view of management to move to an individual-centered "engage and co-create" view. To make this possible, organizations establish engagement platforms for employees that allow them to debate, discuss, and establish priorities and to participate in the transformation process. Co-creative enterprises have the capacity to amplify weak signals pertaining to problems or new ideas, to figure out a way to experiment on the fringes, and to generate sparks in all parts of the organization.

This does not mean, though, that senior management doesn't have to guide the process. On the contrary, senior managers play a critical role in guiding the organizational processes for co-creation. They may do so by building a constantly evolving organizational design around growth projects (as illustrated by Cisco in this chapter), through the personal leadership style of the CEO (as shown by HCL, the Indian technology services company), or through a formal performance management system (as adopted by ERM, the Anglo-American environmental consulting services company).

Management Makeover at Cisco

Way back in 1993, John Chambers, CEO of Cisco, declared that his enterprise was going to "change the way the world works, lives, plays, and learns." What he saw coming was that "the network was capable of changing everything—*all of life's experiences* beyond just work."[1] Chambers recognized the evolution of worldwide computer networks as a major "market transition," which he defines as subtle but profound disruptive shifts that "begin many years before the market grasps their significance."[2] He believes that business is entering the next generation of new productivity and growth, enabled by Web 2.0 collaboration and networking technologies, and says that "only those companies that build collaboration into their DNA by tapping into the collective expertise of all employees—instead of just a few select leaders at the top—will succeed, as more and more market transitions occur at once."[3] What Chambers calls "the human network effect" means that "the future is about collaboration and teamwork and making decisions with a replicable process that offers scale, speed, and flexibility."[4] Remarkably for a technology company CEO, Chambers understands that networks are about people enabled by technology, not the other way around.

The network revolution is well under way internally at Cisco, where employee usage of online discussion forums is up 1,600 percent from mid-2008 to mid-2009; WebEx use is up 3,900 percent over the same period; and use of CVISION, a YouTube-style internal video sharing system where employees can upload videos, audio clips, or photos, is up 3,100 percent, with 54,000 out of 66,000 employees taking part. The most popular content on CVISION is team updates and product and sales information.

But Cisco has gone much further in transforming itself into a truly co-creative enterprise. For Chambers, technology-enabled engagement platforms can be used to transform the "management of management." Cisco has launched an internal reorganization that attempts to overcome the conventional silos found in a large organization by involving many more employees in the company's governance. This massive management makeover spreads the company's strategizing and decision making toward ad hoc groups involving as many as 750 executives, a far wider strategic management base than in most large, established organizations. There are three levels of these teams: "councils" are established where Cisco believes it has a $10 billion opportunity, "boards" are created for $1 billion opportunities, and "working groups" are formed for more tactical initiatives related to a board or council. As Chambers has explained, "Working groups are accountable to boards, boards to councils, and councils to the operating committee, which consists of two dozen or so senior leaders at Cisco. Each person on a board, council, or working group has the authority to speak on behalf of their entire organization, allowing decisions to be made in real time, with all who may be affected by the decision sitting in one room."[5]

The goal of the new structure is to enable Cisco to move rapidly on opportunities that span the capabilities of the company rather than just respond by silo or function, and ultimately get more products to market faster. Each plan has an owner who makes a commitment to his or her peers and is measured on the results. Chambers extols, "The boards and councils have been able to innovate with tremendous speed. Fifteen minutes and one week to get a plan that used to take six months!"[6] For example, a vice president convened a board of sports fans to brainstorm how Cisco might enter the sports business. The outcome was Stadium Vision, a new product that allows stadiums to coordinate the display of game information, video, and advertisements on multiple screens. Other councils and boards have resulted in Web 2.0 offerings and a new financial incentive system for employees.

By having to work together in the boards and councils, leaders of Cisco business units who formerly competed for resources and power now share responsibility for one another's success. The groups have also given Cisco a deeper pool of managers who can act like mini CEOs and COOs. Cisco is now extending the new management structure to its key initiatives for customers and partners, such as the Commerce Transformation program, which seeks to reduce the complexity of the IT systems that Cisco customers, partners, and sales representatives must use in working with the company. Cisco's IT infrastructure included more than 400 applications (many of them supporting products and services that the company had acquired), leading to a complex and inflexible interface for placing and tracking orders, renewing maintenance agreements, evaluating leasing options, and configuring products. Ad hoc councils comprising business and IT leaders from different functional groups were given the responsibility for planning the Commerce Transformation road map.

One of the first projects undertaken was the Partner Deal Registration (PDR) application, which gives partners secure access to Cisco pricing and business process services. Before PDR was developed, Cisco employees had to help partners manually through the company firewall. Six months after the rollout of PDR in early 2008, it had attracted more than 9,000 partner-users from around the world, who processed 37,000 deals worth $1.2 billion on the system. By mid-2009, there were close to 20,000 partner-users on the platform, and 56,000 deals worth $3.92 billion had been processed.[7]

Enterprise 3.0

Cisco refers to the next phase in its strategy as Enterprise 3.0, in which joint partnerships with customers are enabled by the company's collaboration tools, along with Web 2.0 technologies such as blogs, wikis, and social networking models for collaboration. An example is Cisco's I-Prize initiative, which has opened up the company's innovation management process to its customers, business partners, and the general public. Anyone can contribute ideas around chosen innovation themes, with prizes, grants, and seed capital being awarded for winning ideas. The program began when

Cisco's emerging technologies business group offered to fund and take to market the best ideas thought up by employees. The company's emerging technologies group created the I-Zone, an internal, web-based workspace (built around a hosted service called BrightIdea.com) for employees to submit ideas and discuss them with others. To increase the quantity of ideas, Cisco soon opened the platform to nonemployees and announced the $250,000 I-Prize. The benefit to Cisco was the opportunity to develop and market a new business based on the winning idea, which was a plan submitted in 2008 by two German computer science students and a Russian systems engineer to improve energy efficiency over power lines by using Cisco's Internet Protocol technology. Buoyed by this success, Cisco announced a second $250,000 I-Prize in 2009 for ideas around "the future of work," "the connected life," "new ways to learn," or "the future of entertainment."

Internally, Cisco has embraced social networking for business, with its employees blogging and using social networking tools they have made themselves—in many cases even exceeding the function of commercially available wikis, YouTubes, and Facebooks. On the customer-facing side, employees view Cisco.com as a forum for engaging customers around their questions and fostering interactive discussions with partners. Cisco piloted this approach with its top customers in 2009 and is now rolling it out across the broader customer base.

Cisco has managed risk and return effectively through four downturns, in 1993, 1997, 2001, and 2003, each time emerging stronger in terms of percentage of the industry's market cap and market share. In the deepest downturn of all, the Great Recession of 2008–2009, Cisco's management transformation enabled it to remain highly profitable throughout, and in fact look for opportunities rather than retrench. Its boards and councils were working on thirty new projects at the start of 2010, with major projects on security and surveillance and on remote health care rolled out at the deepest part of the recession. "We are the most aggressive we have been in our history, in the middle of what everyone thought was the height of the downturn," Chambers has said.[8] By pulling customers, partners, deeper levels of employees, and even outsiders into its management processes, Cisco is removing a portion of the risk that new ideas will lead down a blind alley. One of the great benefits of the new corporate structure for Cisco customers is that the business units now take direction from one of the boards or councils when introducing or withdrawing a product. This check-in prevents a seemingly good decision from being made in isolation, which could actually be a bad decision if, say, large clients depend on a particular product to solve a complex business problem.[9]

The transformation of Cisco's management structure has not all been smooth sailing. When Chambers started to focus Cisco on collaboration between the senior staff, some people found it exceedingly hard to change, and about 20 percent of executives left the company. For one thing, compensation had previously been based on market share, but under the new system, executive pay is based on the company's overall performance. Teamwork is now an aspect of employees' performance reviews. Chambers has said publicly that he had to make changes to leadership in order to get the selfless interaction he was trying to achieve. The benefits of decentralized management have become clearer over time. For example, as Nick Watson, vice president of strategic accounts at Cisco notes, "when Cisco made its first-ever funding request a few years back, the banks reviewing the company noted that its organizational structure was a distinct competitive differentiator."

As Chambers has said, "In 2001, we were like most high-tech companies, with one or two primary products that were really important to us. All decisions came to the top ten people in the company, and we drove things back down from there."[10] Today, Cisco is powered by thousands of leaders. It points the way for even a large global business to operate as a distributed management system, *where leadership is inclusive, management processes are collaborative, and organizational change is an ongoing, co-creative process.*

Organizational Design Around Employee Experiences at HCL

As enterprises embrace the concept of engaging their employees through co-creative organizational processes, they begin to see the positive effects of reduced dependence on top-down processes. HCL (Hindustan Computers Limited) is an example of such a transformation involving deep employee engagement, built around the unique model of leadership practiced by Vineet Nayar, its charismatic CEO.

Founded in 1976 by Shiv Nadar, widely regarded as an industry visionary and pioneer, HCL is one of only three computer hardware companies of the 1970s that still exist today, along with IBM and Apple. But HCL has had its difficulties. In the 1990s, HCL slipped behind, as it delayed getting into software and services. In 1998, Nadar reorganized the company into two components: the India-facing HCL Infosystems, a company focused on hardware and software integration, and HCL Technologies, a global IT services company. By 2004, though, Nadar realized that HCL Technologies needed more groundbreaking changes to succeed in the face of increasingly fierce competition. Nadar appointed Vineet Nayar, who had demonstrated unique leadership capabilities, as president of HCL Technologies in 2005.

Nayar immediately started on a transformation of HCL. He had perceived that in order to thrive, the company needed to improve the way it interacted with customers, and that this would best begin with employees first. He formulated a multipronged turnaround strategy, with the rejuvenation of the job experience and empowerment of employees at its core.

When one of the authors met Nayar in 2008, it became evident that he viewed his organization as "pivoting" around the interactions that his employees have with his customers—the "zone of value" for a people-intensive service business such as his, as he put it.[11] Nayar believes in what he calls "inverting the management pyramid," starting with frontline employees. Employee engagement is often defined in terms of fulfilling the needs of an employee, for everything from compensation and benefits to the working space. Nayar says that companies must also address "the aspirational needs of an employee." You do this by starting with the assumption that every employee has professional and career aspirations, and is also looking for a larger cause, one that could be fulfilled by a satisfying engagement experience with colleagues in the organization and its customers and stakeholders. Says Nayar, "People and their tacit knowledge are your most important asset."

Co-Creating Employee Experiences

While it may seem at first contrary to conventional wisdom to put "employees first," what Nayar really means is that the co-creation of employee experiences is essential to sustaining the continuous transformation of large, high-turnover services organizations. HCL needed to introduce a new experience for customer-facing employees, whose sales and service delivery actions directly influence customers, and to the employees who support them.

Nayar, who became CEO in 2007, was intent on transitioning from rigid command-and-control to a management approach that enables enriched employee experiences in all interactions, whether with customers, partners, stakeholders, or fellow employees. Nayar speaks of the "inverse accountability of the CEO to the employee" and of a "culture of transparency." His first initiative was dubbed Mirror, Mirror. It invited employees to look into the mirror and candidly discuss their daily experiences in the organization. It was aimed at learning from employees and communicating with them. Nayar also set up a communications and marketing team of about thirty young people, called Young Sparks, reinforcing their inherent desire to win. He sought a brand mantra that captured his desire to change the employee experience. And so the Employees First, Customers Second (EFCS) tagline was born to capture this inside-out transformational process. Using an intranet-based technology platform, Nayar then launched a program called U&I (for You the Employee, and I the CEO) to engage in open dialogue with his employees and begin engendering "trust, transparency, and management accountability." Any employee can log in to the intranet site and pose a question to Nayar that can be read by everyone in the company.

This engagement platform opened the floodgates. Questions poured in, about 400 per month. Nayar personally responded to many of them, emailing his thoughts and inviting responses to be publicly posted. In addition, weekly polls gave a sense of how employees felt about various issues. Nayar also created a blog where he shares his strategic thoughts with the entire organization. He engages in frequent dialogues with employees through videoconferences, and he launched Directions—live, town hall–style meetings where employees can speak candidly. The presence of these multiple engagement platforms created what Nayar refers to as a "common language and shared vision and actions across the company." Soon he was beginning to change how employees experienced the company and how they got work done.

The Smart Services Desk initiative is one outcome. This ticket-based system allows employees to flag anything they think requires action in the company, from "my seat is not working" to "my compensation is off-kilter" to "issues with my boss." These tickets can be "closed" only by the employees themselves, who can watch what actions are being taken for resolution. Employees feel empowered to initiate and accept or reject problem resolution, thus contributing to transparency and empowerment.

As part of his drive for management accountability to employees, Nayar told HCL's executive management council that he would post his own 360-degree feedback process online, so it could be viewed by the entire organization. (This system allows all employees to rate the performance of their boss, their boss's boss, and any three other peer managers they choose, on about eighteen questions, using a five-point scale.) Initially, employees learned that Nayar was seen as good at motivating employees and committed to team building but a little shaky in execution and getting things done on time. Eventually many managers followed his example of public ratings. Today, employees at HCL can see not only the ratings of their bosses, but also those of their peers.[12]

Nayar notes that the need for restructuring the office of the CEO is even more critical today. In 2009, following the global slowdown in the economy, he said, "It is now time for the organizational structure to become flat. Rather than directing from the top, or leading from the front, CEOs need to assume the role of a coworker and adopt more effective collaborative techniques. In short, responsibility and accountability will need to flow both top to bottom and bottom to top. As companies realize the important role frontline employees play in the everyday business of customers, they are increasingly making employees the bishops of this game, and they are going to drive change in the global market."[13]

Such cultural transformations are a long-term process, of course. HCL's commitment to engaging employees is ongoing. Anoop Tiwari, head of human resources, says that the new employee experience cuts across all types of interactions of employees in the organization. He points to new initiatives like Unstructure, a new engagement platform being designed to spark the creativity of "intrapreneurs" inside HCL by connecting them with mentors from beyond the walls of the organization. These mentors, who include global thought leaders, engage with HCL employees on topics such as "How to get every single employee to impact customer experience?" "How to cater to the needs and dynamics of Gen Y?" and "How can social technologies energize the business ecosystem?" Such discussions recognize that the employees collectively are the main source of the company's future intellectual capital.

The Challenge of Growth at ERM

We have now seen two organizational processes aimed at engaging employees into co-creation with their firm. We showed how Cisco builds a constantly changing, organizational structure around its growth projects. We also saw how HCL's CEO works on involving employees in a constant process of dialogue with the organization.

We now turn to a third organizational process: building a

177

co-creative performance management system, demonstrated by Environmental Resources Management (ERM), a very successful global environmental consulting services firm with roots that go back thirty-eight years.[14] Though headquartered in the United Kingdom, it has 137 offices in 39 countries, employing about 3,300 staff members and generating $695 million in global revenues. ERM helps its large corporate and government clients identify and manage their environmental and related risks. The firm's services range from traditional remediation services for environmental managers in the chemicals, oil, or gas industries to sophisticated liability risk assessments done for C-level executives. The firm is an old-fashioned partnership, with 350 partners scattered all over the world, 40 of them in regional or practice leadership roles—but it is also backed by a private equity firm recruited to finance its growth.

The ambition for growth at ERM is particularly strong given the leveraged model established when a private equity partner was added. ERM's economic model is predicated on the assumption of moderate to high growth in revenue and profit over the next few years. If growth goals are met, the value of the firm will increase substantially. ERM may then bring in a new investor or become publicly listed, allowing the private equity partner to exit the business at a significant value gain while also generating value for ERM partners. Conversely, the failure to grow will result in little or no value increase for ERM partners, with most of the proceeds of the sale accruing to the private equity firm and a few co-investor partners who took the financial risk in the first place.

Late in 2005, Pete Regan, then CEO, and John Alexander, his newly appointed COO (now CEO), became concerned that in spite of the firm's obvious imperative to grow, the 40 partners might be overly focused on short-term profit and insufficiently attentive to growth. While initially puzzled that their colleagues did not rally around the growth objectives, given the equity opportunity, Regan and Alexander realized it was hard for partners to visualize this future and somewhat hypothetical value increase.

The entire history of ERM is one of excellence at the office level. Each office is known as an operating company (or OpCo) and is managed by a powerful head who controls resources and activity in his or her "territory." Recruiting and talent development are done at the office level, essentially following an apprenticeship model where junior members of the firm try to emulate the office's partners. Most offices have a unique "feel" about them and reflect the personality of the office head and two to three of the more senior partners.

The strength of the office-based heritage of operational excellence at ERM had also become its Achilles' heel, however. As is often the case in professional services, some of the OpCos had become isolated baronies that pushed back on corporate mandates for growth or any suggestion that they partner with other entities involving resources outside their office. Office heads tended to protect both their clients and their staff, often preventing either from accessing other capabilities of the firm. Partners in each office could live well by being operationally excellent year after year, focusing on delivery of existing services for clients. Bonuses would remain high as long as office heads did not increase costs by hiring or promoting any new partners who might take time to generate revenue. As a result, the firm was not growing.

Each office already used a performance scorecard. In spite of its official denomination as a "balanced scorecard," ERM's version focused predominantly on financial and operational metrics (revenue and profit), with a smattering of people measures (e.g., staff turnover, safety, and health record). Regan and Alexander realized that whatever else they would attempt to do for growth, they had to preserve the strength of the firm in operational excellence. As a result, they decided to make operational excellence the first theme of their new strategy map. They also concluded that there was nothing wrong with the existing scorecard, as long as it was viewed for what it was, i.e., an operational scorecard rather than a driver of growth.

"It is not an either/or situation between profit and growth," Alexander said. "We need both. What we need is a mechanism that rewards operational excellence *and* encourages growth at the same time."

Setting the Direction for Growth

"How about building something like a strategic scorecard" Regan suggested. "We could have two scorecards. The first would reward operational excellence in the form of an end-of-year cash bonus, like what we have now. The second one might grant new shares to partners, allowing them to receive some new tangible rewards for working on growth. The value of those shares is potentially high if we hit our growth targets. This would capture their attention and would rebalance the agenda between operational excellence and strategic growth."

Late in 2005, Regan and Alexander assembled the firm's senior management in Houston to lay out the growth agenda and start devising how shares would be allocated to individuals. Together, they decided to add three new growth themes to the solidly established theme of operational excellence (along with another supporting theme around people). The growth themes were:

- Service excellence
- Key client management
- New innovative services

The first of the three growth themes, service excellence, was defined by the team as the ability to meet customer expectations. As a consulting firm employing scientists and engineers, ERM had historically been less focused on client satisfaction than on technically delivering what it had committed to. As a result, clients would often praise the quality of the work but occasionally complain about the tardiness of some studies or the lack of responsiveness exhibited by certain offices to requests for additional information. The challenge for ERM management was to motivate the office heads to engage with the service excellence team it had created and encourage them to adopt these service best practices inside their offices.

The second growth theme, key client management, had to do with the global nature of ERM's large clients. ERM increasingly works with large global companies that have large process or discrete manufacturing facilities, such as Coca-Cola, Dow Chemical, and Royal Dutch Shell. These companies expect ERM to provide the same level of service in all parts of the world, whether in Europe, the United States, Asia, or Latin America, thereby creating a challenge for the highly decentralized office-based structure of the firm. To address this challenge, ERM initiated a Key Client Director program (KCD), for which it identified global leaders for selected large accounts to coordinate and integrate all business development and delivery initiatives for a client. The main challenge for KCDs was to orchestrate the collaboration of several local offices in selling and delivering globally.

The third and final growth theme had to do with the delivery of new innovative services, including the migration of services from office to office. ERM's Key Service Directors (KSDs) act as practice leaders or subject matter experts in designing and delivering new services. Their role is to act as thought leaders in practices such as Environmental and Social Impact Assessment for new development projects, or Corporate Assurance, which helps companies design and implement programs and management structures to consistently meet environmental health and safety standards and regulations. The service directors' challenge was to penetrate the inner sanctum of regional offices and motivate them to develop new service capabilities beyond their existing comfort zone, which typically had to start with the recruiting of a new partner who would spearhead the new practice in the office. Therein lay the rub, since the new partner would potentially put at risk the steady flow of bonuses for the existing partners.

The management team put together a blueprint of each growth theme, connecting strategic objectives via the capabilities they wanted to build, processes tied to each theme, client outcomes they wanted to generate, and financial results they hoped to see.

"This is as far as we should go in laying out direction," said

Alexander. From that point, he wanted to turn over the scorecard-building process to the forty regional and practice leader partners and have them generate their personal scorecards, based on the blueprint that had been developed. Every office head had to tell how they would partner with the service excellence team, the Key Service Directors, and the Key Client Directors, to grow beyond the office traditional perimeter. The reverse also needed to happen. The service excellence team, the KSDs, and the KCDs had to engage with the office heads and agree with them on what they would accomplish together.

Co-Creating Individual Scorecards

The two executives laid out a three-part engagement process involving three global meetings over a one-year period. They kicked off the personal scorecard process in Ascot (in the U.K.) in February 2006. They used their scheduled Rio de Janeiro global meeting to take stock of progress in May 2006. The process then culminated with a Basking Ridge, New Jersey, meeting in November 2006, where each personal scorecard was finalized. This timetable allowed rollout of the new performance management process for 2007, including the potential granting of new shares for each partner linked to achievement against their strategic scorecard.

Through this process, each of the forty individual senior partners found himself or herself invited to *co-create a personal strategic scorecard* with relevant colleagues. The growth themes originally developed in Houston had been further fleshed out in the first Ascot meeting (albeit still in high-level terms). Each partner now had to identify the specific individuals with whom he would have to engage to make these growth themes a reality. This required developing common goals with colleagues across the complex ERM matrix of geographies, services, and global clients. The performance management system was no longer a soft litany of desirable behaviors. It was a strategic scorecard with teeth, potentially leading to the co-creation of significant wealth for all parties.

The head of the Midwest OpCo, to take one example, identified five constituencies with whom he would have to engage to drive the growth agenda of the firm. For simplicity's sake, let us focus on three major constituencies he decided to address (together, they represented 70 percent of his strategic scorecard). He reasoned that his first growth ambition should be to engage his Midwest partner colleagues differently than in the past, coaxing them into accepting new hires and nudging them toward taking greater risk. He suggested 40 percent of his share allocation should go toward the accomplishment of this new goal. He also suggested that 20 percent of his growth points be allocated toward new services within the Midwest, which required partnering with two specifically identified Key Service Directors in the M&A and Remediation and Consulting Management practices. He proposed that another 15 percent of his shares go toward inter-OpCo collaboration, i.e., "signing up" to sell and deliver in partnership with three other U.S. office heads who happened to have either prospects or projects in the Midwest, or were interested in developing business in their geography with large Midwest-headquartered corporations.

Instead of the sterile battles of previous years, where functional leaders would complain about lack of access inside the offices, and office heads would complain about the high cost, weak client skills, and lack of accountability of functional heads, the newly co-created performance system invited all parties to agree on joint goals. Most important, each side stood to gain from doing what also happened to be the right thing for the firm.

Once different parties identified a key axis of co-creation linking them, they went on to agree on the specific performance goals that would define success in that interaction and how each goal would tie to the various growth themes that had been identified. For example, the head of the Midwest office identified the specific way through which he would foster growth with his Midwest partners by encouraging them to hire new blood and by setting more ambitious revenue growth targets for the office as a whole (the people theme). He set revenue goals in the two specific practice-based programs in partnership with the two sponsoring KCDs who could commit resources to help him get there (new innovative services theme). He set common goals with three of his OpCo head colleagues in the United States on business development and project delivery service targets (service excellence theme).

In the final workshop in Basking Ridge, the flip-chart sheets of all forty senior partner scorecards were posted on a wall, with each partner invited to look at his colleagues' scorecards and work out any discrepancy. One of the key principles used was reciprocity, i.e., if partner A had partner B prominently featured on his strategic scorecard, presumably partner B should also have partner A on his own scorecard. There were a few alignment issues to be worked out at the last minute, but by and large, partners had co-created their own interlocking agendas long before the meeting, making the final workshop more a celebration of the new growth agenda than a confrontational working session. The ERM leadership team had managed to reconcile operational excellence and growth objectives through co-creation.

Perhaps the best way to sum up the results is to quote from Regan's Chairman's Report from August 2008: "2007 was a year of exceptional performance and continuing change at ERM. We achieved our highest-ever growth in the past year, growing earnings by 23 percent and revenue by 19 percent. These were delivered in conjunction with strong operating cash flow, which was in excess of 100 percent of operating profit."

Regan goes on to say in the corporate report: "Throughout the financial year, we have continued to undertake a number of actions to invest in the future growth of the business. These have ranged from reshaping our regional management teams to focusing on areas of increasing client demand such as climate change, compliance assurance, and impact assessment and planning. In total, operating profit grew faster than net revenues, and the impact of this positive operational gearing raised our operating margin to above 13 percent."

Buoyed by a strong economy, the performance of the company remained exemplary in the two years after the introduction of the co-created scorecard. In fiscal year 2008, net revenues grew another 23 percent (assisted by a shift in foreign exchange rates) with earnings before interest and tax up by 26 percent. ERM even managed to continue growing in fiscal year 2009 in spite of the worldwide recession, with revenues increasing 9 percent in constant currency and earnings before interest and tax up by 6 percent.

When leaders engage employees and harness human energy, management processes become more co-creative. Both managers and employees win when each side understands the value of engaging the value co-creator on the other side, using internal platforms that facilitate active, explicit dialogue between them, and allowing response in real time to their changing needs and expectations. *Becoming a co-creative enterprise ultimately requires enabling new linkages among employees (i.e., internal co-creation), customers (community co-creation), and partners (network co-creation).* A key role of senior management, and leaders at all levels, is to enable these linkages and accelerate the migration toward a co-creative enterprise.

In this chapter, we saw how three different organizations have fostered the engagement of employees in co-creating with their firm. With Cisco, we saw the power of designing a rapidly shifting project-based structure that mobilizes the energy of the entire organization. With HCL, we saw the value of a CEO intent on challenging his entire organization to co-create with him, senior managers, and one another. And with ERM, we saw the power of a formal performance management process that invites individuals to develop their own scorecards by working with their peers.

In the next chapter, we discuss how to move beyond processes to co-creative engagement in operations, which is at the heart of an effective functioning of the co-creative enterprise.

Chapter 9

Going Beyond Processes to Co-Creative Engagement

Managers in co-creative enterprises go beyond processes to enabling engagement platforms. The biggest hurdle for most organizations is enabling all parties to participate more easily and with more impact by allowing a two-way flow of engagement, rather than by simply streamlining sequential processes and thus straitjacketing outcomes.

Our traditional representation of processes tells only half the story of what goes on in reality. The half story is told from the vantage point of providers, who typically design their processes set by the customers of those processes—internal or external. Once customer specifications are gathered, the provider designs and executes the process against those specifications.

This assumes that value is created by the provider's process and is passively received by a process customer in the form of a predictable and repeatable experience that matches the customer's needs. It is as if a tango were conducted from the perspective of only one of two dancers, limiting the experience of the second to answering the question: "How would you like for me to dance for you?" Once this has been specified, the second dancer then becomes a rag doll following the first dancer's moves on the dance floor, before finally being asked: "Did I deliver on the moves you requested from me?"

The missing half of this story is the one that would be expressed from the vantage point of process customers, if they were asked to do more than simply state their needs. Increasingly, process customers not only want their specifications to be met, but they want the provider's process to respond in real time to *their own process of engagement*. They want the provider's process not to be a mindless solo dance, but to accommodate their own moves. In this view, what has to be designed is an interaction comprising a double flow of processes, one coming from the provider and one from the customer. Now, both people are dancing, and the process customer is invited to initiate some moves on their own. The quality of the experience is no longer judged through the eyes of a rag doll evaluating her partner's moves, but from the perspective of how much fun both parties have dancing together.

In this co-creative engagement, process customers are no longer passive—i.e., they do not limit themselves to stating needs and requiring specifications—but they're actively involved and participate in the design and delivery of their own experience. This mode of thinking opens the door to *a new philosophy of operations* where the role of companies is no longer to design processes in the traditional sense, but to set up platforms where the producer's and the customer's process meet to co-create a unique experience for both parties every time they interact. The company's role is no longer solely to stage the dance of the second partner and deliver it with Six Sigma precision, but to provide the engagement platform—the dance floor, the music, and the rules of engagement—that will enable the best possible dancing experience for both partners at the lowest cost.

In this chapter, we discuss how to jump-start this transformation toward co-creative engagement. We discuss the detailed example of

Predica, owned by the French banking giant Crédit Agricole, and how it transformed its new product management process to one of co-creative engagement.

Instituting Co-Creative New Product Management at Predica

Crédit Agricole is one of the leading banking groups in Europe. It is also Europe's second-largest banking network. Crédit Agricole is at its core a retail bank that also sells asset management, investment banking, and insurance products. Predica, one of its divisions, designs life insurance products and manages sales through the Crédit Agricole and LCL retail banking network. It is a big business in its own right, with sales of about €20 billion. In 2007, Isabelle Steinmann, head of Product Development at Predica, who also manages a team of about seven product managers specializing in various Predica products, was tasked by Jean-Yves Hocher, then CEO of Predica, with developing and launching a new product. It was to be partly a unit-linked life insurance product—i.e., a life insurance policy whose yield is partially indexed on a series of mutual funds, rather than on the stable but low return provided by more conservative euro-denominated bonds (the investment in mutual funds is made in increments or "units," hence the name). The product was targeted for younger customers and was meant to act as the first step in teaching young people how to save money for the future.[1]

Hocher, who had started his career on the retail banking side of Crédit Agricole, had risen to become head of one of the regional banks of the group; Crédit Agricole is a federation of thirty-nine regional banks in France. Hocher started with two simple ideas. First, he believed Predica needed an entry vehicle to attract young people who'd never saved a penny in their lives. Second, he was intent on getting these young people to discover the potential upside of a securities-indexed product, while still protecting the core of their investment. Being an astute financier, he also knew that such a product would allow Predica to escape the reserve requirements of euro-denominated products and would be more profitable for Predica. While Steinmann agreed with the intent, she wasn't sure how to overcome the challenge of getting the mass of consumers to understand the relatively complex functioning of these products.

As she also headed the Competitive Intelligence Department of Predica, Steinmann was familiar with unit-linked products already on the market. The most notable of these competitive offerings was from ING Direct, the online division of the large Dutch financial services company. ING Direct had made a splash in the industry by conquering 5 percent of the French market, thereby demonstrating the willingness of some customers to use the web to invest in a reasonably complex savings product. Hocher posed a direct question to Predica's product development team: "How do we out-innovate an innovator like ING?"

An obvious place to start was with the minimum investment threshold. Whereas ING required several thousand euros to get started, Predica's product could be made more affordable. Steinmann thought the new product should also be simple and more flexible. So, following Hocher's lead, Steinmann outlined a value proposition for the new product—dubbed Cap Découverte (Cape Discovery)—as follows:

- The product should be *very affordable*. How about offering a subscription process requiring an investment of only 20 euros a month (minimum)?
- It should have *low fees*. How about 2 percent? ING offered 0 percent in fees, but the Crédit Agricole branches somehow had to be compensated for the service they provided through their advisors.
- The product should be *simple*. How about just two mutual funds options (instead of thirty or more for ING)?
- Payments should be *flexible*, i.e., customers could interrupt at any time, increase or decrease the amount as a function of how their financial life was going.

These looked like reasonable starting points, but Steinmann was not sure how to get the product to stand out. Of course, the branches of Crédit Agricole provided a powerful distribution machine for Predica products. One limitation, however, was that Predica did not sell its products directly; it supplied them to the regional banks, which in turn trained their branch advisors to sell them to customers. Although Predica "trained the trainers," the regional banks ultimately decided on the product launch strategy. And branch advisors were swamped with products promoted by the various product divisions of the group, from simple checking or savings account products, credit card, real estate loans, consumer loans, or other investment products. "How do I get advisors excited about Cap Découverte when they handle close to two hundred different products?" she wondered.

Over the ensuing weeks, as the conversation rolled back and forth among the product development group, the senior management of the firm, and the actuaries who were developing the product, Steinmann began to see the value of a novel co-creation process in designing and rolling out the new offering—one where decisions would not be made by the usual handful of experts, but by a much larger collective of Predica employees and customers. Steinmann also recognized her role as head of Product Development would have to change in order to facilitate this process. In particular, she reasoned, the way to make Cap Découverte stand out in the minds of end customers and retail advisors—especially the junior advisors most likely to be selling the new product in the branches of Crédit Agricole—would be to engage them in the design of the selling-buying experience, and perhaps the design of the product itself.

A Complex Set of Characters in the Product Development Story

Predica developed a protocol for launching the co-creation initiative. This began with the identification of all the parties playing a role in the product development process. They are the people whose experience the co-creation process tries to improve, by allowing them to engage with one another differently. Co-creation starts with people, not with analytical steps in a process, so the first step is to figure out who should be involved.

Steinmann got a little discouraged when she realized as many as ten actors played a role in the product development process (including herself). Somehow, she would have to co-opt all of them in one form or other. As the *product manager* in charge of the Cap Découverte launch, she sat quite far back from the customer who would eventually buy the product. In fact, only two populations were even further removed than Steinmann from the end customer:

- The *Actuarial, Financial, and Compliance Department* was where the financial and legal integrity of new products got tested, ensuring that Predica would make money with the proposed design and guaranteeing that all regulatory requirements were met.
- *Predica's top management*—Jean-Yves Hocher and his team—played a key role in vetting new product design, introducing new offerings to the regional banks' top managers, and valuing them in the context of the firm's overall strategy. As one would expect, Predica's top management had life-or-death power over the design of a key new product like Cap Découverte.

To reach the end customer who would eventually buy the new product, six other players had key roles:

- The Predica *Communications Department* controlled the resources dedicated to customer-facing communications and advertising, which meant they could boost or slow down new products that competed for their promotion funds.
- *Predica salespeople* handled the day-to-day contacts between the regional banks and Crédit Agricole. They were an institutional sales force that called on the regional banks and on the retail branch advisors to foster interest in Predica products. They could convey more or less enthusiasm for a new prod-

uct and greatly influence its success. They also developed all the sales support material used by retail branch advisors.

- The *regional bank top management* had the power to take or turn down the new Predica product. Each bank was an independent entity, so bargaining power in the Crédit Agricole system was in favor of the regional banks, not the product divisions like Predica.

- *Branch managers* were also critical because they set the performance goals for branch advisors. If branch managers were not on board with a new product like Cap Découverte, they would set goals that lowered the product in the advisors' lists of priorities, and Cap Découverte's goose would be cooked.

- Each of the thirty-nine regional banks also had an *insurance specialist* who advocated within the branches in his region for insurance and Predica products. Because each bank is itself a large organization, the insurance specialists acted as product managers within the regional banks, orchestrating all insurance training and support for the retail branch advisors and playing a particularly important role at launch time.

- *Retail branch advisors* were obviously key players at the end of the chain since they interacted with the end customers. Crédit Agricole employed about 40,000 bank advisors in the branches, and about 60 percent of them were the junior advisors Steinmann wanted to focus on, as they tended to be the face of the bank for young people starting their financial life.

- Finally, there was the *end customer* or buyer of the product.

Steinmann realized her job would be to get this complex group of participants to agree on both a product design and a launch process for Cap Découverte. She also knew from previous launch experiences that the process could be painful, pitting her as "the product expert" against constituencies who all had a good reason to not like her design. She was ready for a new approach.

The View from the Product Manager's Bridge

To look at the world from her own vantage point as product manager, Steinmann and her team tried to identify the limitations of their own interactions with other actors in the chain. Product managers had the largest number of interactions with other parties, justifying their role as the orchestrator of the co-creative effort, as shown in **Figure 9-1.** It struck the team, however, that the product manager interacted with a lot of people but usually touched only one or at best two other players at a time. In other words, the product manager interacted with others in short sequential processes rather than as the facilitator of longer streams of interactions involving multiple players. As a result, the product manager was placed in the difficult role of being either an expert who arbitrated between conflicting demands or a traffic cop who encouraged better coordination between the warring factions—without ever getting them to look at the same picture in the same room at the same time.

Figure 9-1: The Predica Product Manager's Interaction Map

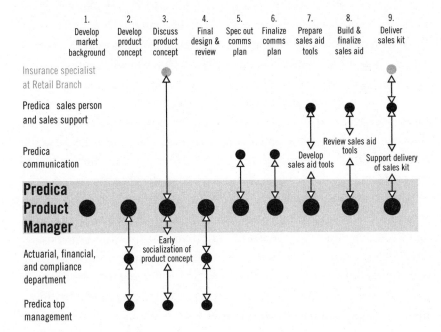

What was missing was a joint engagement platform, where all the parties could see the design of the whole new-product elephant and participate in building it together. Steinmann pointed out that her interactions with market experts and external sources often suggested product features—for example, little or no loading fees—that differed greatly from the demands from actuarial people, for whom generating fees was an integral part of the financial model. While there is an inherent conflict between customer desires for affordable products and company requirements for profits, Steinmann imagined that if both parties could look at a live model of the product she would maintain, it would result in a better-integrated, co-created design. This later became the simple product design and product launch platform now used by Predica, a simple shared representation of the latest design and launch process for the product at any given time, offered in one place and visible by all.

Along the way, they also attacked some narrower but irksome issues buried in the product management interactions. For example, the team examined more closely how the print materials used to explain the product to the customer were being developed, as well as the support material provided to the sales staff. The participants agreed that their current back-and-forth process of developing both the customer-facing communications package and the advisor-facing support material was suboptimal because it did not create mutual transparency for the product manager, the external agency developing the communications package, and the external agency developing the sales support package. As a result, the product manager was frustrated because she had no ability to influence the design of either package. Similarly, the two external agencies were often rebuffed in their desire to meet the product designer and hear the intent of the product "from the horse's mouth." The product team also concluded that the two external agencies should have a way to make their designs transparent to each other, since the advisor tools and the end-customer communications package should have a common look and feel. There again, the solution proved fairly obvious once the culprit interactions were identified: build a simple advertising and communication collaborative process that creates transparency and reusability of graphic objects across the various promotion packages being developed and provides the ability for coaching by the product manager toward a more common look and feel.

Examining the span of its interactions with other protagonists further, the product development team recognized a major short-coming: Steinmann worked little with either retail branch advisors or customers during product design, except for an occasional focus group. She lamented that her interactions stopped at the point of delivery of the sales tool to the retail bank's insurance specialist.

The View from the Branch Advisor's Bridge

The team then decided to turn the table and see what the world looked like from the vantage of the *retail branch advisor*. They real-ized that advisors, like frontline employees in other businesses, are split between *two* fronts: they spend part of their time working with customers and another part dealing with other bank employees, as shown in **Figure 9-2**. The employee-facing interactions caused them frustration similar to that of the product manager, in that the advi-sors never had access to the actual developers of the training and sales tools but typically got a filtered version from the insurance specialists instead. What lay upstream of the insurance specialist was as opaque to the retail branch advisor as the world of retail branch advisors was to Steinmann.

Figure 9-2: The Retail Branch Advisor's Interaction Map

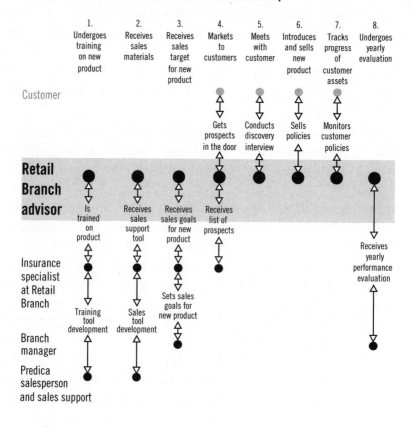

From the retail branch advisor's perspective, it also struck the product development team that advisors were quite isolated. All of their customer interactions were one-on-one discussions. The team reflected it must not be terribly comfortable for a young advisor, two or three years into her professional career, to go head-to-head with customers on products as complex as life insurance without any support from colleagues at the bank or Predica experts. Yet the advisors were held accountable for strict sales goals, which occasionally incented them to venture into uncomfortable sales pitches.

In contemplating the quality of interactions, another key point struck the team: once customers had purchased a product, there were no more interactions. Thereafter, customers could seek out their advisors with questions about products, but for the most part, the bank's contact consisted of sending them statements and managing routine customer service issues such as a change of address and change of beneficiaries. Steinmann realized the company could provide more value to the customer both before and after the purchase of a product.

The Predica team quickly identified two other areas of interaction for improvement: in the retail branch advisor's participation in the design of her own training and sales tool development, and in the delivery of the salespeople's communication and support packages. "The product manager suffers from the lack of access to the retail branch advisor, and the retail branch advisor deplores the lack of contact with Predica people," the product development team reflected. "Somewhere in there must be a way to build an engagement platform that links these two populations and unleashes powerful co-creation forces."

As the former general manager of a Crédit Agricole Regional Bank turned head of Predica, Hocher was excited about the prospect of involving both retail branch advisors and their customers in the new co-creation process, and he supported the team in moving to the next step, which involved launching co-creation workshops in the field, with the ultimate intent of conceiving new engagement platforms linking players together better.

Winning the Hearts of Branch Advisors

Steinmann looked for a retail bank among the thirty-nine in the Crédit Agricole network willing to experiment with co-creation and launch the workshop process. The Centre-Loire Regional Bank volunteered to be the pilot case, and offered the Predica product management team a first workshop with about twenty advisors in Bourges, a small town known for its medieval history and spring festival. The advisors group comprised mostly junior employees, supplemented with two midmarket advisors, one private client advisor for high-net-worth individuals, and one branch manager.

The day played out as a systematic and lively exploration of what a retail branch advisor does, fleshing out the nature of their customer interactions as well as their interactions involving other bank employees. They videotaped the proceedings of a co-creation workshop and later played back the results, hoping to uncover emotional responses that could become the rallying cry for the co-creation effort. The branch manager, somewhat defensively, explained the legal and fiduciary limitations in involving young, inexperienced advisors with risky financial products. He was instantaneously counteracted by a group of young female advisors who told him in no uncertain terms that one had to start somewhere, that the new product was an opportunity to learn, and that they wanted to be involved with it.

"We'll learn together," one of the young advisors said. "We'll figure it out together within each branch. We'll support each other." Thus a spontaneous community of passionate young advisors was born. The older private client advisor, who worked in the same branch as a couple of the junior advisors, offered herself as a coach in teaching how securities work. The community was getting stronger already. The film of this moment became widely circulated within Predica and popularized under the name *Les Demoiselles de Bourges* ("The Damsels of Bourges"), a take-off on a well-known French movie called *Les Demoiselles de Rochefort*. The film captures the moment where the Predica product manager grasps that if an engaged community of entry-level retail branch advisors could be built around the new Predica product, they'd do a much better job of selling.

The co-creation workshops with the young advisors sought to develop a broad view of the advisors, not merely as recipients of Predica's processes. Predica aimed to engage customers in a generative discussion of their "expanded life"—whether the company happened to be involved in that life or not. The team made clear that they sought a permanent process of co-creative engagement with advisors, not a one-off focus group as with traditional market research. In most cases, the traditional Predica process managed by the sales force engaged just a tiny sliver of the advisor's life: she was mostly a "channel" to sell more products. If Predica could capitalize on the greater aspiration of the young advisor to grow profession-ally, a whole world could open before them. But how could Predica devise an engagement platform that does that? Steinmann reflected that a web-based co-creation platform would provide an efficient means to scale up the workshop process and allow for larger-scale co-creation among the multiple constituencies involved.

Determined to fan this spark of co-creation into a flame, the Predica team started conceptualizing how it could build a platform that would help the community of young advisors capitalize on the new Predica product. The team subsequently developed a web-based platform prototype where bank advisors could learn about finance, securities, and life insurance, share their experiences of selling the Cap Découverte product, and provide feedback to Predica on cus-tomers' reactions to the product. The site has suffered through the ebbs and flows of Crédit Agricole's and Predica's overall IT funding cycle but is now gaining stature in the firm.

A throwaway remark by one of the "Demoiselles de Bourges," captured on camera at one of the workshops, caught Steinmann's attention. "By the way, our customers will learn with us," the junior advisor had said. "After all, the customers we want to attract with this product are very much like us—young, trying to learn how to save. We'll do it together." Steinmann wondered whether Predica should build another community platform for end customers.

Customers Get Involved

The next morning, the product development team had organized another workshop, this time with (end) customers of the Bourges Crédit Agricole branches. These customers were there at the invita-tion of the retail branch advisors who'd participated in the advisor workshop on the previous day. Many of the advisors also returned for the customer workshop because the co-creation process relies on learning from actual people interacting with one another in real life (another key difference from traditional market research where focus group populations are randomly chosen). As the workshop participants systematically examined the range of interactions involving the customer, it became clear that many customers lacked a basic understanding of financial products. There was massive confusion among this group of young professionals in Bourges on how they should go about beginning to save money, what products they should use to do so, and whom they should talk to about it. The more Predica or Crédit Agricole people at the workshop tried to explain, the more confused the customer group became, lost in a maze of risk-return, tax considerations, and life expectancy scenarios. "How can we help people learn about life insurance on their own terms?" Steinmann wondered.

In the group was a young woman who worked at the local welfare office. Aicha, a single mother, proceeded to explain that a few years back, she had bought a life insurance product to protect her daughter, and with great discipline had been putting a bit more money into it every month. Her words were simple, her story touching, and all listened to her intently. Although she was far from having a deep understanding of the product she'd bought, she knew enough to convey the essentials.

In those two minutes, Aicha had done more to explain the value of life insurance to a crowd of young prospects than any pitch by Crédit Agricole or Predica experts. That night, during the team debrief at the hotel room, the product management team started prototyping a web-based platform for customers, where people like Aicha could tell "my first savings" stories in their own terms (reflecting customer-think rather than company-think). In brainstorming the site, the team agreed that it should function partly like YouTube and partly like *American Idol,* with a customer voting system and prizes for the best story. They all agreed that Aicha's video should be the first loaded onto the site. The customer site has moved through various incarnations since then, with its co-creation content sometimes challenged by the more traditional desire to promote Predica offering in "push" fashion, but its co-created content is steadily increasing, particularly in some of the regional banks more advanced in their understanding of social networks.

This new method of informing customers about products is both more user-friendly and costs less. As Steinmann explains, "It is always hard to make money with these low unit-price life insurance products, because the minute you involve experienced advisors, we start losing money. But here, we are effectively getting 'lower-cost advisors' to sell the product, and on top of that, they teach each other how to do it! Our selling cost is lower to start with because we leverage the younger advisors, but as we get more and more customers to sell the product to each other through a community effect, we further reduce our selling cost."

Predica wins in this new system, but so do the retail branch advisors as individuals. The new web-based platform for customers also reduces their risk and the cost. Young advisors are particularly concerned about the risk of inadvertently misrepresenting the product and producing dissatisfaction, or worse yet a lawsuit, from a disgruntled customer. This is a source of great anxiety for them. The web-based platform allows them to check for best practices, receive tips on how other advisors sell products, and secure general guidance from experts at Predica on what to do and not do. Another risk for the retail branch advisors is failing to meet quota. The new web platform addresses that issue as well, as advisors share their recipes for sales success on it.

The new platform also allows some co-creation of training, producing a cost reduction for Predica and a higher-quality experience for the advisor. Traditionally, Crédit Agricole and Predica would publish written manuals, send trainers into the field, and run sessions with advisors all over the country, at a high total cost. But some young advisors have taken over some of that role. They're writing their own life insurance manual by accumulating best practice experiences—Predica sometimes refers to their compilation as "Wikidica," a Wikipedia-like accumulation of practical knowledge for Predica products, co-created by advisors. The risk of nonacceptance of training materials is also very low since the advisors are developing this material in the first place.

Co-Creating the Design with All Actors in the System

After the Bourges co-creation workshop, it was clear to the product management team that the young advisors much preferred to be more engaged in the design of products, and they were eager for Predica to open up the design of the Cap Découverte product to them. These advisors had many ideas and a good deal of passion about how to develop the offerings. One of the most telling moments was when advisors recommended *against* lowering the product-loading fee to match the ING offering. "The customers I'm dealing with won't be looking at us versus ING," a young advisor explained. "Most of the time, I will be educating my customers on life insurance. They won't come into the branch and demand a particular loading fee versus ING or whoever. They'll be learning to save with me. They will not care one bit about loads." For these customers, the quality of the interaction would outweigh any concern about fees. The Predica team was astounded by this perspective, having believed that advisors always wanted as cheap and competitive a product as possible.

This engagement platform for sharing advisor insights was decidedly low-tech. As of early 2010, the insights platform consisted of a simple process of periodic live meetings between all interested parties, including a library of edited videos from all the co-creation workshops and a rolling sample of retail branch advisors acting as "power users" on behalf of their colleagues. There are a few rules of engagement—e.g., how missing executives may or may not be represented at the meetings—and a few simple posted documents that anyone can consult and make inputs into. "Unlike the web-based community of advisors, this product co-creation platform involves no real technology, at least for now," Steinmann says.

A Better Experience for All and Success in the Market

Co-creation has been on a steady roll at Predica. "What a difference co-creation makes to the experience of all players along the activity chain, starting with our own product managers!" Steinmann says. "Not to mention the money we save by avoiding the constant reworking of designs we used to have."

For the junior advisors, these combined co-creation projects under way have increased their access to customers and reduced their cost in getting leads in the door and qualifying them, since the advisors can build on the market buzz around the Cap Découverte product to find more sales leads. And because customers are partly educating themselves through the community web platform, the new prospects are better qualified than cold leads. The risk of having an inconclusive discovery interview has been reduced, as has the risk of customers letting their policy lapse over time.

Predica measures how many advisors have participated in either live co-creation workshops or web platform interactions, and it tracks through a variety of formal and less formal measures the general excitement of retail branch advisors about Cap Découverte (and, more broadly, Predica). While much remains to be done to formalize this feedback process, Predica clearly has moved from the back of the pack among Crédit Agricole product divisions to one of the leaders in terms of appeal to advisors. The Cap Découverte product, in particular, has risen to the top of the list for entry-level advisors, who give it high marks on multiple dimensions, including personal interest about the product and the product's strategic role in advancing their knowledge.

The ultimate yardstick of success, however, is sales in the market. By that measure, Cap Découverte is considered a tremendous success. About 80 percent of the banks decided to sell the product in the first year, with all banks adopting it in the following year. This rate of adoption is much higher than for similar products. It has generated a lot of sales enthusiasm at the retail level. Predica sold 330,000 contracts in 2008, against a high-end estimate of 300,000 for the first year. This result is particularly remarkable given the extremely negative financial situation in 2008. By the end of 2009, more than 500,000 products had been sold. Co-creation is now embedded in Predica's ongoing product development process, and the different engagement platforms developed for Cap Découverte are being repurposed for the launch of several new products in 2010, including employer-sponsored savings plans, long-term disability insurance, and annuities.

The greatest value of the co-creation effort is in the continuous buildup of new strategic capital created through the increased engagement of all players. A key source of revenue growth is faster learning, and Predica has put in place a learning engine where new insights are continuously generated so that good new product ideas can be crafted. The new sales tools and communications packages can be updated and renewed continuously, and the Cap Découverte product (and future products) can be quickly redesigned as new ideas are generated. Customers continuously add to the collective body of knowledge of the firm, and the rate of learning of retail branch advisors is dramatically increased through the co-creation process that links them with Predica.

The New Frontier of Co-Creative Operations

As the example of Predica shows, the view of operations as co-created is a far cry from the way most operations are designed and run in organizations today. Most companies view their operations as a set of one-way processes that deliver value to customers based on some assessment collected from customers of what that value is. The traditional representation of a process is a left-to-right arrow where successive process owners optimize their processes to deliver the best possible value to the next operators in the value chain— the process customers—until the chain reaches the actual customer. Each process is arrayed to reduce cycle time, reduce cost, and minimize variations in output while delivering value as stated by the customer. In that sense, processes are "designed to customer specs."

In most organizations this is done through a continuous improvement approach that involves a rapid succession of execution phases—where process owners measure the effectiveness and stability of process outcomes—and design phases, where they try to improve the processes. We have a rich tradition of continuous improvement methods, from Kaizen to Lean and Six Sigma quality methods. These approaches all start with a definition of the needs of the process customer—internal or external—and involve groups of operators (and occasionally customers) in the design of processes that attempt to deliver against that identified need efficiently and predictably. This approach to process redesign has served us well and has brought about a dramatic improvement in efficiency in many organizations over the last forty years.

The limit to these approaches, though, is that they fail to recognize the fact that customers also have processes. In effect, the lines between process owners and process customers are increasingly blurred, making the concept of process owners and process customers largely irrelevant. Processes are no longer solely left-to-right—driven by the process owner—but increasingly also right-to-left—driven by the process customer. Customers—whether external or internal—no longer want to be passive recipients of process outcomes, but want to be engaged. Animated by a new sense of empowerment and enabled by technology, they want to engage on their terms and require that the organization adapt to their new context every time they interact.

In this view, processes should no longer be "designed to the customer's specs," but instead "designed to the customer's process," realizing that the customer does not want to "freeze" the definition of his own desired experience, but wants the producer's process to adapt to his own (customer) process in real time. In such a view, there is intelligence on both sides of the interaction at all times. The design focus is no longer solely on delivering a process outcome from which all variation has been rooted out, but on designing the platform of interaction that will allow both processes to come together in optimized fashion in each new context. In other words, managers tend to ask, What does this organization need to do to deliver fixed and predictable outcomes? But instead, they should also continuously ask, How do individuals view their engagement experiences in light of their interaction contexts, and how can those views be leveraged by the organization?

The new frontier in operations lies in engaging two (or more) parties at both ends of an interaction. The idea is to not only get them to devise the process jointly—continuous improvement methods have involved customers in process design for some time—but to also design the interaction in such a way that both parties can jointly devise desired *outcomes* every time they interact. In co-creation, both parties not only actively participate in the design of each new interaction, but also co-create a unique outcome every time they encounter each other. Co-creation puts human experiences (and expectations) at the center of process design and improvements—a radical and needed innovation. Managers have to distinguish between the quality of a process and human experiences. The latter must guide the former. Moreover, managers should seek to encourage variation in different types of valuable experiences (i.e., accommodate a wide variety of outcomes) while minimizing variation in the quality of underlying processes (e.g., classic Six Sigma) so as to ensure the consistency of engagement experiences.

Beyond co-creative operations lies the next frontier of management co-creation: opening up a firm's entire corporate strategy process, as discussed in the next chapter.

Chapter 10

Opening Up Strategy

A key component of an organization's transformation to a co-creative enterprise is the extent to which its own strategy is co-created. Effective strategy requires integrating multiple needs and perspectives. Success requires becoming more democratized and decentralized, making strategy as much bottom-up and "middle management–out," as being guided top-down. Leaders can no longer view themselves as the sole experts in developing, evaluating, and implementing strategy. The complex networked world in which corporate strategy is formed increases the urgency to introduce co-creation into this process. Co-created strategy brings together multiple constituencies—employees, customers, regulators, and other stakeholders—inside the process.

A number of firms are building live and web-based engagement platforms for this new form of strategy co-creation. While this development is a bit further on the horizon for some industries, we believe few companies will ultimately escape the call to co-create their strategy. Considering the economic and global pressures senior managers face in maintaining cohesion and morale among their ranks, the tools and methods of co-creative strategy increasingly will be in vogue.

In this chapter, we discuss the disguised example of how Kaiser Chemicals used co-creation to fashion a new set of primary strategies.[1] Kaiser shows that a co-creative process, rather than a unilateral expert-driven, company-centric effort, can be highly effective. Kaiser's experience yielded insights they might not have come to otherwise, or not as quickly. It also fomented new types of strategic partnerships. There are obvious limits to sharing strategic information with others and constraints in determining the boundaries of each co-creator's intellectual property. But these problems can be solved through the proper identification of the rules of governance at the outset. The more important step is heeding the core principle of co-creation in opening up the strategy management process: paying attention to people's experiences in engaging them to co-create strategy.

Co-Creating Strategy at Kaiser

Kaiser Chemicals is a global agricultural chemical firm, now turned "life sciences" company with the advent of genetically engineered seeds. The company has traditionally manufactured agrichemicals in large, capital-intensive plants, and technology and process efficiency have driven its competitiveness. For years, Kaiser's cash cow product was an herbicide called Flumisense, which recently lost its patent protection in many parts of the world, opening the way to generic versions of it manufactured in China and other low-cost countries. The number-one strategic question for Kaiser's CEO, Wolfgang Schumpeter, therefore, had become how to respond to the challenge of the generics.

But Schumpeter had other challenges, too. Led by Monsanto, the agricultural chemical industry had evolved from a sleepy process industry into a high-tech life sciences business, where seeds are no longer developed by seed growers, but are genetically manipulated to possess certain traits. These "input traits" make the farmer's job easier by, for example, naturally killing certain pests that damage plants. Monsanto had been the first company to invest in seed bio-technology, and it had captured the most valuable input traits early on. The company had then gone on a shopping spree, buying the leading seed companies in each major crop. Several competitors, including Kaiser, had engaged in a bidding war for the remaining seed companies. Kaiser had snapped up a few seed companies, but Schumpeter wondered whether he should continue to acquire more.

Yet another issue was the development of "output traits." For example, the oil content of corn could be genetically increased, a valuable feature given corn's use as animal feed (the richer the corn, the fatter the hog, and the higher the revenue for the hog farmer). Also, some fruit and vegetables could be made to stay fresh longer once picked. This proliferation of design traits led to the so-called stacking question. Agricultural life sciences competitors were developing multiple input and output traits, but in the end, the farmer would buy only *one* soybean or corn seed—presumably the one that would "stack" the most valuable traits. The personal computer industry served as an analog. Many applications had been developed for the PC, but there was one dominant operating system, Microsoft Windows. Since Microsoft was able to set the economics of the other players in the PC industry, Schumpeter had to decide whether to be Windows or whether the relatively late start of the company in the biotechnology field condemned it to being a "single trait" player.

Schumpeter also had to worry about the downstream food in-dustry. Cargill, Archer Daniels Midland (ADM), and the other big commodity companies that bought and processed crops were reluc-tant to set up segregated processing supply "pipes" to separate out crops with specific outputs, such as high-oil corn. But if Cargill was going to throw all corn into the same processing pipe, why would farmers bother buying the GMO seeds in the first place? Schum-peter wondered how Kaiser could talk the major commodity pro-cessors into trait preservation, but was not sure how to get there.

The thorniest issue Kaiser faced was consumer acceptance of genetically modified organisms (GMOs). Monsanto had proven to be a masterful strategist on all fronts except one. It had taken the aggressive position that the merits of biotechnology and the dramatic productivity gains it allowed would blow away any negative consumer sensitivity about genetically modified food. The firm's management had been able to persuade the U.S. Food and Drug Administration (FDA) that there was little difference between a seed grower crossing various seeds in a seed farm and a laboratory geneticist manipulating the genome of the seed. Monsanto had assumed the rest of the world would follow the FDA's early endorsement, ignoring the early mobilization of European activists against GMOs. Monsanto's bet proved ill advised. Activists launched a large-scale campaign against "Frankenfoods," leading several European legislators and retailers to limit the use of GMOs and in some cases prohibit them outright. Many countries in Latin America and Asia were on the fence, not sure whether to adopt the full-speed-ahead attitude of the United States or the highly guarded European position.

Making Strategy Inclusive

Confronting this maze of strategic issues, Schumpeter trusted Kaiser's head of Strategy, Andreas Becker. Schumpeter had a PhD in chemistry and believed in the merit of an expert approach. He liked people who could present facts and articulate recommendations based on them, and he was tempted to do the usual thing: assign Becker the strategic planning task, encourage him to hire a global consultant, challenge the leaders of each major division in fact-based reviews of their business, and make decisions based on the outcome of the review process.

Schumpeter was troubled by one thing, however: "Monsanto, the industry leader, has some of the best brains in the industry," he said. "They've had more foresight than anybody else in seeing the power of biotechnology, in figuring out how to link chemicals and seeds, in convincing the regulators in the United States to adopt their vision. They have shaped the market and transformed farming as we knew it. They have done just about everything right, yet in the end, they botched the consumer acceptance issue. Why did the strategy process of such brilliant people miss something as retrospectively evident as that?"

His question was not rhetorical. He genuinely wanted to know. With the benefit of hindsight, it was pretty clear that Monsanto should have found a way to make the overseas public comfortable with genetically modified foods. "They were not customer-focused enough. They're engineers and biotechnologists who do not pay enough attention to customers," ventured an executive. But would Kaiser fare any better? After all, their culture was also dominated by engineers and biotechnologists. Schumpeter kept pushing the group on the issue, asking, "How should they have engaged with consumers?" More and more discomfort developed in the room.

As the management team talked, their view of strategy began to evolve, as they discussed the value of engaging multiple constituencies all along the agriculture and food chain. There was something scary about this new view of strategy as a process engaging multiple stakeholders. Becker was particularly skeptical, pointing to the danger of having nonexpert people, each with an agenda and a narrow fact base, influencing something that, to him, should have been decided by the top management of the firm. "Aren't we abdicating some of our responsibilities?" was the undertone of his comments to Schumpeter. Yet Schumpeter had become convinced that enlightened democratic leadership was needed. He wanted a big, open strategy process involving many people inside and outside the organization. He painted a picture of a "collective sense and respond" system where the relevant protagonists in the value chain would bring their own insights to the strategy formulation process.

"Our customers know more about trends or competitive moves than our internal experts," he argued. "They also know more about their needs than our marketing guys. So why not engage them into the process? This will be the 'collective sensing' part. And when it comes to understanding our own capabilities, let's work directly with the people who embody these capabilities at Kaiser and get them involved. This will be the 'collective respond' part. Yes, at the end of the day, we will make big decisions. But we will make them in a more participative manner than we currently do."

But now Schumpeter wanted to invite stakeholders into the firm's inner sanctum of strategy, believing their participation would reduce the implementation cost as well as the risks of the strategy. If Kaiser's stakeholders had ownership over the firm's strategy, he reasoned, they'd also be active in ensuring that it worked.

Mobilizing Teams Around Strategic Themes

The burden of formulating this new process fell on Becker. To generate a high-quality strategic *dialogue* with other stakeholders, he reasoned, Kaiser's management had to provide an interactive framework for discussion. He began by laying out Kaiser's definition of strategy: the identification of a limited number of themes that show where external trends are driving an emerging set of customer needs, which the firm can respond to better than competitors through the development of processes and capabilities, resulting in extraordinary financial returns.

Schumpeter coached Becker on how they might approach redesigning their process to involve co-creation. He suggested identifying the key strategic themes to begin a discussion among stakeholders. How they structured those themes required careful attention. Landing on a strategy would require hypothesizing how the three external factors (trends, emerging customer needs, and competitive moves) could provide a powerful driver of strategy (the "outside-in" part of the process) and how the company could harness its internal competences (processes, capabilities, and financial outcomes) to execute on that strategy (the "inside-out" part of the process).

Becker thought it would be helpful to devote two separate teams to the process. One would examine the outside-in component of the strategy. The other team would search for inside-out ideas. Then both teams would align their conclusions in the end. The outside-in team would identify all the trends relevant to the firm, all the emerging customer needs, and all the competitive moves being made by others. At the same time, the inside-out team would start with an

internal inventory of the company's core processes, core capabilities, and stated financial outcomes and would build an internal
theme-based logic between them. Identifying emerging customer
needs would be the point at which the outside-in and inside-out
teams would come together, with both the internal and external
stakeholders contributing their knowledge.

An Explosion of Market Trends

To identify key trends, Becker and his team ran a two-day trends
workshop in all regions where Kaiser had operations, inviting research, manufacturing, marketing, and salespeople from the firm,
as well as several agricultural dealers they felt close to. In three of
the four regions, they also hired local experts in new farming methods, seeds technology, biotechnology research, global food issues,
and emerging countries development.

They started close to home, focusing on trends pertaining to Flumisense, the company's cash cow. Of course, the expiring patent
was a major consideration since it threatened the economic model
of the firm. But a research scientist in Latin America pointed out
that someone in Brazil was already in the process of patenting a new
chemical route to the same molecule, which might also disrupt the
production economics of the product if the new approach proved
viable. It was the first time Becker and his management team had
heard of this. "Collective sensing" was already paying off.

The team discussed issues in farming trends. Some farmers
pointed out that weeds were beginning to develop resistance to
Monsanto's premier product, Roundup, generating concern over
the ability to control them in the future (as with germs and an-
tibiotics, weeds adapt to survive). The discussions also revealed
that farmers had a new awareness of economics and were building
sophisticated models of their farms. Many of them in the United
States had college degrees and ran their farms using sophisticated
software, regulating their tractors in order to optimize the dispens-
ing of seeds and herbicides in the field. Farmers also had new access
to information: data-rich websites providing deep product and ap-

plication information, detailed weather data, and crop yield bench-marks for their farm. Each of these trends was a potential starting point for a new strategy.

The team tracked biotechnology trends. They investigated how new gene-stacking technologies were producing an arms race between competitors trying to establish the Windows-like "operating system" for seeds. They also identified a rush toward new partnerships with universities, with biologists attached to universities suddenly finding themselves courted by major corporations offering to finance their research in exchange for the rights to use the commercial applications of their work.

The strategy team addressed seed trends. In general, farmers were rapidly adopting hybrid seeds globally. The economics of GMO seeds were simply proving too good for farmers to pass up wherever consumers or legislators had not limited their use. There were some complaining about the software-like licensing agreement that had been pioneered by Monsanto—seeds were technically licensed rather than owned by the farmer. All in all, though, hybrid seeds had led to tremendous improvement in productivity, leading to more hybrid seeds being available in the market.

Turning to the assessment of customer needs, Kaiser was particularly interested in the trend toward biotechnology-enabled farming in emerging markets. Areas of extreme poverty, such as Brazil's Cerrado or sub-Saharan Africa, could now potentially become farmland through the new productivity allowed by GMO seeds. The Kaiser team was interested in experimenting with new economic models in those areas. In addition, new actors in India, such as ITC e-Choupal, were beginning to equip Indian farmers with new knowledge about how to run their farms. Several experts also pointed out the key role of farming in the industrial policy of emerging countries, since farmers were the dominant segment of the population, which made lifting farmers out of poverty a prime consideration for economic development within those countries.

Returning to developed economies, Becker and his process also uncovered trends about the structure of the farming market. Farmers were often squeezed between large companies like Monsanto and John Deere selling them seeds, chemicals, and equipment, and huge commodity traders such as Cargill or ADM buying their crops. They were left with little room for negotiating prices for either the "input" or "output" of their goods. Farmers particularly feared the "chicken model," wherein chicken farmers had lost all freedom to negotiate, being essentially told by the big chicken processing companies what price they would get, what grain to buy and at what price, and how to run their chicken farms. This "contract farming" had a mixed record, with farmers frustrated by having so little say about their operations.

The last family of trends identified by Becker and the team involved consumers and regulation. This was the big one, the one Monsanto had missed. The first topic mentioned was always the lingering legacy of mad cow disease in Europe. This heightened the politically charged issue of public acceptance of GMOs, which took on different facets in various parts of the world, with, as already mentioned, the United States generally pro-technology, Europe highly suspicious, and Latin America and Asia somewhere in the middle. Across the world, consumers were choosing healthier and more nutritious foods. Finally, several countries in North America and Europe were developing a new regulatory framework for "nutraceuticals," i.e., food products thought to provide beneficial health effects. It was not yet clear what claims these products could make legally nor whether regulators would treat them as foods or as pharmaceuticals.

Competitors on the Move

Kaiser had long used a standard method for keeping up with what its competitors were up to, maintaining a competitor database, mostly a library of consulting reports about global players in the industry. These reports were jealously kept in the Strategy Department—after all, they cost a lot of money and contained significant proprietary information. Few people ever read them beyond the top executives who had commissioned them. In the spirit of democratizing strategy, Becker decided to take a different approach and tap the minds of all local people who, day-in and day-out, were in contact with competitors (e.g., salespeople who competed against them, dealers and customers who bought from them, and experts who interacted with them). In each of the trends workshops Becker ran across the globe, he included a half day dedicated to competitive intelligence, asking people to share their views of what competitors were doing. This produced a treasure trove of facts.

First, they learned competitors were increasing capacity in Flumisense's core market. This was bad news right there. They also discovered Monsanto was moving massively into farming data mining, hoping to unlock "productivity reservoirs" through predictive yield models of farm practices. Mergers and acquisitions (M&A) activity among competitors had also increased, producing an explosion in the price for seed companies. Competitors were also fighting for talent. The competition was particularly keen to recruit biotechnology PhD scientists.

A lot was also happening on the downstream part of the value chain. The beef and pork processing industries were consolidating rapidly, which meant the buyer of commodity grains could potentially gain the upper hand over Kaiser and other upstream companies. Food processors were becoming involved in branded foods, with traditional commodity-trading companies trying to become fast-moving consumer goods companies. In Brazil, Becker's team heard about a "blow-your-mind" move, attributed to Monsanto. Monsanto was rumored to be considering building an entire railway system all the way to the Brazilian port of Paranaguá (in partnership with the state of Paraná) to foster the export of the soybeans its farmers would produce with its new transgenic seeds. This was a far cry from Kaiser's original business of manufacturing a chemical in an efficient set of pots and pans!

By now, Becker knew the data he'd gathered was valuable. Even more important, though, was the fact that he'd mobilized a large number of people inside and outside Kaiser who wanted to engage with the strategy process. This is where the real energy was. There seemed to be no end to the desire of people to contribute new facts and new insights. While he did not yet have a formal system to capture all these items, he realized he'd stumbled onto something powerful: *a strategy co-creation platform.* He felt both exhilarated and intimidated after the first round of workshops. On one hand, all participants felt extraordinarily engaged in the process, proud to share what was happening in their geographies and curious to know what was happening in other parts of the world. This was the exhilaration part. On the other hand, the workshops had created expectations that there was going to be a continuous process of strategy co-creation, and Becker wondered, "How are we going to do that?" He knew the challenge was to provide a structure for the strategic dialogue. What he came up with involved a second round of workshops and the launch of a web-based platform.

Strategy Co-Creation Comes Together

Before embarking on the second round of global workshops, Becker and his team spent the next two months talking with others in the company—not just his strategy team and senior management, but also some trusted people in the regions, including retailers and farmers—in order to make sense of the data. They did a great deal of analysis themselves but also relied on the interpretive power of these internal and external stakeholders.

Most people were surprised to see Becker and his team return to their territory for the second workshops. They had assumed it would be like many other sessions, i.e., they would not get any feedback on their contribution, let alone be invited to think about the corporate strategy itself. They were even more surprised to see Becker come back with a small IT team in tow, whose role was to devise an IT-enabled "strategy co-creation platform" aimed at making the process continuous and evergreen.

This was a new role for Becker. He was no longer expected to spout wise strategic recommendations to his boss Schumpeter, but was now a facilitator linking stakeholders and their insights. It required leaving one's ego at the door, but he was beginning to like it. Most important, he felt he was contributing a lot more to the organization than before. Upon completion of his second world tour, Becker synthesized the new set of insights and identified eight strategy co-creation themes.

The first was "improve Flumisense competitiveness," which would be their highest priority, since Flumisense was the economic foundation of the company. At the workshops, attendees had pretty consistently made the point that the process through which Flumisense was losing its patent in each country would need to be closely monitored and also that the new chemical routes to making Flumisense that were being patented in Brazil and elsewhere must be understood. They needed to keep especially close tabs on the new Chinese capacity. They grasped their mandate to continuously reduce the cost of Flumisense to the farmer and improve the dealer's margin in these sales, since farmers would shortly have generic options.

Becker brought the people at the plant into the process. The plant staff in America was made aware of how dealers and farmers in Brazil were seeing a new opportunity due to the patent erosion and the new Chinese capacity in generics. The plant staff had long lived in the protected cocoon of their U.S. factory, but now they sat at the same workshops with these customers and dealers in far-flung parts of the world, could watch them on film, or blog with them on the new co-creation platform. This had a powerful effect. The teams at the plant proposed to redesign their manufacturing process and accelerate the bringing online of their new Argentinean plant, in order to lower the overall cost of the product.

"Improve Flumisense competitiveness" was the most operational of the eight themes. Theme 2 reached slightly higher strategic ground: fostering new farming practices. The essential idea was to engage multiple stakeholders, including farmers, dealers, farming data houses, and the agronomic departments of universities, in developing the next farming practices in tandem with Kaiser's agronomic specialists. This included widespread adoption of the "no-till" approach, where farmers do not till soils in the off-season.

218

No-till preserves valuable roots in the ground and has the advantage of encouraging the use of Flumisense, which obviously would help Kaiser. The Kaiser group saw the importance of no-till practices in light of global concerns regarding the sustainability of agriculture. This theme also brought together the farmers' new awareness of scientific information, their better understanding of their economic models, and Kaiser's need to challenge Monsanto on the farming data-mining terrain.

For this theme, the Kaiser sales force and the dealers they sold to became the primary actors. Salespeople and dealers took it upon themselves to promote no-till practices, to advocate the use of Flumisense in no-till fields, and to deliver field-specific recipes to farmers. Kaiser's management committed to building a database of best farming practices, promising to co-create it with farmers and dealers, rather than make it proprietary as Monsanto had done.

Theme 3 was about developing new biotechnology traits involving a partnership with universities, genomic data houses, and the scientific community within Kaiser. Theme 4 addressed building the seeds network and involved engaging seed companies still available on the market in a co-creative "dance" with Kaiser, in effect building a common future together. Theme 5 was built to preserve product identity downstream by engaging food-processing and branded-food companies in a discussion of how dedicated "pipes" might preserve new output traits, in spite of the heavy infrastructure investment already made in a commodity supply chain. Theme 6 was to engage beef-, pork-, and chicken-processing companies in a discussion of the future food chain, including commodity traders and contract farmers in the discussion, in the hope of co-creating a new market where meat-processing companies would benefit from the emergence of new crop traits developed in conjunction with Kaiser. Theme 7 involved creating foods with therapeutic value and greater nutritional value. It engaged the public at large with branded-food companies in the identification and possible development of nutraceuticals that would improve individual health.

Theme 8 was the most ambitious of all, "influencing the global food supply." For many people inside and outside Kaiser, this represented "the vision." It was not a vision in the classic strategic sense, in that it did not offer a deterministic, prescriptive view of what the company intended to do. Instead, it involved a broad engagement process linking governments of several emerging countries, farmer communities in those countries, local agronomists, and experts with the scientific and marketing community of Kaiser. The blueprint involved harnessing the emergence of global agricultural markets like India's, using biotechnology to allow farming in new areas such as Brazil's Cerrado, and recognizing the key role played by farming in the industrial policy of emerging countries. Kaiser's ambition was to increase farmer income in developing countries. This involved developing global projects, partnering with selected government and nongovernment entities, and identifying regions which biotechnology might make cultivable. The ultimate intent, of course, was for Kaiser to increase sales and profit in those emerging countries.

The strategy team thought of these themes as a "stairway to heaven," a layering of eight strategic themes of increasing ambition, with the capabilities built at each step allowing them to jump onto the next one. There was excitement both about the vision implied in the higher steps, and the orderly process through which they were going to try to get there. Each theme was a structured co-creative experiment, in that the strategic outcome of each theme was far from known in advance. They now had a structure linking the formal experiment with a group of internal and external people passionate about that experiment. Their new strategy process not only identified the exciting new ideas, it also mobilized the human energy to power them.

Strategy as a Co-Creative Discovery Process

In this chapter, we saw that strategy is itself a process that can be opened to co-creation. Frequent objections to this idea come from the confidentiality requirements of strategy. If strategy is openly discussed with a large group of internal and external stakeholders, will competitors learn what the company is up to, and will it therefore destroy the value of the moves being contemplated? While not all aspects of strategy can be co-created, we have generally found that many more aspects of strategy can be fruitfully opened up than is generally believed. Traditional strategic thinking is largely focused on competitors and largely built around M&A activity, which does indeed require some secrecy to avoid being preempted or triggering bidding wars. In co-creation, though, strategic moves involve a redefinition of key interactions among stakeholders, which requires a more continuous process of engagement between those stakeholders. This process of engagement is often itself the source of competitive advantage, because companies viewing strategy in the more traditional way find it hard to imitate.

More broadly, the traditional view of strategy is that companies can shape the evolution of their industry and the expectations of customers and stakeholders more or less autonomously, subject only to the actions of competitors. In strategy co-creation, external customers and stakeholders can have a significant influence on strategy options. While a firm's broad strategic direction may be obvious, strategy is a continuous process of ongoing experimentation, risk reduction, and minimizing investment while maximizing market impact.[2] It is a process of discovering value co-creation opportunities and connecting them with the firm's resource networks through an inclusive, collective, collaborative process, as we saw in the Kaiser example.

On the practical level, leaders can encourage the continuous co-creation of strategy by constructing themes bringing together external facts (trends, competitor moves, emerging and customer needs) and internal capabilities of the firm (competencies, processes, and financial models). Each theme can be structured as an experiment launched between the management of the company and the people who have the most at stake—namely, the employees and customers of the firm, with participation from business partners and other stakeholders. These themes can be in increasing order of ambition, leading to a possible co-created vision of the company.

In the next and concluding chapter, we discuss how co-creation can enable institutional change, and enhance the trust between individuals and institutions in society.

Chapter 11

Co-Creating Institutional Change

In this concluding chapter, we will share several ways that co-creation can be a powerful catalyst in bringing about institutional change that is transformational. Co-creation has the power to transform relationships and our social realities, changing the identity of the system we live in and the quality of our human experiences.[1] Co-creation is a means by which enterprises have transformed themselves into positive forces for social good, thereby enhancing their social legitimacy. Co-creation is also a means by which the institutions of public governance and civic engagement can be transformed, making governments more attuned and responsive to social needs and demands. It is the key to rebuilding the trust that institutions have lost in the new millennium.

We begin this chapter with the example of **Caja Navarra,** which illustrates how co-creative transformation of a bank can create continuous and resilient growth in an entire civic system. **OASIS,** an initiative in Seoul, South Korea, shows how public enterprises can allow the mass of citizens to have a more accessible and accountable government and take a more involved role in influencing and co-shaping policy making. **Rio Grande do Sul** illustrates how stakeholders can be made part of a continuous governance process to develop a joint national agenda, coordinate activities, and build political consensus. Finally, **SEBI** suggests how the public sector and the private sector can co-shape and co-evolve regulatory processes.

Co-Creating Philanthropic and Civic Change at Caja Navarra

Caja Navarra (CAN) is a savings bank based in Pamplona, in the Navarre region of northern Spain.[2] Like other Spanish savings banks, or *cajas* (pronounced "ca-has"), CAN is a regional, not-for-profit bank designed to support its local communities through social contributions, based on a dual financial and social mission, with part of its profits allocated for society's development and well-being. Incorporated under the legal form of "private foundations with a social purpose," cajas are actually full-credit institutions with freedom to act and compete operationally on par with the rest of the financial institutions in the well-developed Spanish banking system, which serves more than 45 million people. In this era when Western democracies are grappling with deep, persistent anger over the misguided operations and aftermath of mega-global banks, CAN's profitability and customer engagement is worthy of in-depth study and replication.

In 2002, CEO Enrique Goñi arrived at Caja Navarra and immediately sought to differentiate the bank in a crowded market of more than sixty savings banks, all of which made social investments (ranging from about 17 to 30 percent of profits for the major banks). CAN's social investment at that time was in the model of all cajas: the bank's board decided where the money went, in a highly political decision. Goñi approached the board with a proposal to put CAN's social investments in the hands of customers, in effect saying, "Those who decided had to stop deciding." In January 2004, the new initiative, dubbed You Choose: You Decide, allowed customers to specify their preferences among the seven initiatives of social action traditionally supported by CAN. CAN personalized customers' credit cards to show their choices, reinforcing their identification with the initiative and generating a strong emotional connection.

The results of this initiative were startling. Customers chose to direct the profits they generated for CAN to needs- and people-based projects such as disability and care (e.g., 34 percent chose this category in the first year) rather than to activities and things that CAN's board had chosen (e.g., they had allocated 35 percent of the budget for sport, leisure, and welfare). The top five investment categories were completely reordered: whereas the bank had chosen welfare, sport, and leisure; culture; disability and care; research; and heritage conservation, in that order, customers allocated funds to disability and care; cooperation; welfare, sports, and leisure; research, and environment, respectively. This was a startling contrast between conventional "institutional-think" and "customer-think." Like all people, managers at CAN had been shaped by their socialization—by the dominant logic of banking and managerial attitudes, behaviors, and assumptions they learned from their business environments. Managerial thinking, naturally, is conditioned by the routines, systems, processes, and incentives that institutions pursue within the traditional framework of value creation. However, engaging customers and other stakeholders in a process of co-creation enables institutions to overcome these limitations. Doing so requires that enterprises give customers and stakeholders the tools to "help them help organizations" understand them better.

Through a customer-facing engagement platform, implemented both online and at its branches, CAN let customers choose categories of investment *and* specific organizations and projects. Called You Choose: You Decide, bank customers revealed that their most popular project in 2006 was emergency aid in natural disasters and crises, with 12,099 supporting this. CAN invested €42 million (about $60 million), or 30 percent of its after-tax profits in 2006, in such social programs (the other 70 percent was reinvested in the business). By 2007, more than 530,000 customers (almost 88 percent of the customer base) had chosen which social initiatives to fund (with a total of €50.25 million, or about $71 million). More than 460,000 customers had selected specific projects from a portfolio of 2,707 projects proposed by 2,133 organizations. CAN's goal in 2010 was to have more than 700,000 customers deciding from over 4,000 projects.

From Conventional to Civic Banking

The You Choose: You Decide initiative was the original driving force behind the concept of CAN's civic banking—empowering people with new rights, as Goñi puts it. As CAN's pioneering initiative evolved, the bank positioned it as a customer right for Responsible Banking, giving customers a degree of insight into and control over CAN's social investment. Since then, CAN has launched five more customer rights, continuing its relentless pursuit of customer rights and co-creation opportunities that extend beyond customers to its ecosystem at large.

It was the second customer right, Civic Accountability, that truly began CAN's journey toward becoming a co-creative enterprise. The first customer right, remarkable as it was, did not provide full transparency to customers on the amount they individually contributed, which resulted in them not being fully aware of the consequences of their decisions. So in 2007, more than 650,000 customers received letters explaining how much profit CAN had made from their money and how much each customer had contributed to the projects they had chosen—in cash figures.

As Pablo Armendariz, CAN's head of Innovation, who works closely with Goñi in co-shaping the initiatives, puts it, "Everything is in on view, just like it is at CAN's branches. We undertake to work . . . without hiding anything, protecting our customers' interests at all times." Information on profitability—whether by region, product, segment, or individual customer—is usually one of the best-kept secrets at any bank. But CAN made its banking transparent, consistent with its strategic intent of social responsibility and its new perspective on the rights of customers. It provided prospective customers with an online tool to estimate how much money it will make with them, and therefore how much money the customer could direct to social projects. Besides creating a strong emotional connection with the bank (yes, a bank), CAN provided its customers with a platform to get more engaged in their community. The platform enables responsible, transparent, and innovative banking for multiple co-creators, ranging from the bank's consumers and business customers to volunteers (including company employees) and nonprofit organizations that contribute to the pool of social projects. CAN's business customers can and do use the philanthropic platform to conduct their own corporate social responsibility (CSR) activities. In effect, CAN is co-creating CSR activities with its consumers, business customers, and social project partners.

At the same time, CAN's employees have become more engaged in their daily work. James Gardner, head of innovation and research at Lloyds TSB in London, put it this way in a blog post: "This is a testament to the power of the new world of work and inclusionism. An example of what can happen when everyone is engaged in a worthwhile journey, rather than being limited to their traditional role-defined corporate box. It is also an example of the way that customers working as partners can drive a change in the nature of the relationship."[3] Both CAN's customer satisfaction and employee satisfaction measures have increased continuously, to the benefit of CAN's reputation with customers and employees. In 2007, CAN enjoyed 8.5 percent customer growth, with more than 75 percent of employees satisfied with their professional, personal, and social situation. Generating employee happiness by making banking more human is a laudable accomplishment indeed.

About 40 percent of CAN's business comes from organizations, making the bank as much B2B as B2C. Through its Viálogos platform, CAN engages in active dialogue with businesses—an open, live engagement platform where issues that affect business professionals can be dealt with, reflecting their needs, wishes, criticisms, and suggestions. Each Viálogos forum is focused around an important business sector. About five or six forums are held each year, with attendance averaging 200 to 250 people. CAN interacts with participating professionals in advance and then chooses a handful of issues to focus on. The key is that CAN makes public its commitments to the responses at the forum, the implementation of which it is publicly accountable for. It also encourages business professionals to share ideas with one another between forums, thereby seeding the formation of a community.

Not content with simply being transparent, CAN introduced its third right, Project Accountability, in 2007. The bank requires organizations running the social projects it supports to be accountable to its customers. It asks organizations to explain how they have invested their money, who has benefited from it, and to present the results "in person." CAN enables the engagement platform for these partners through its branches, where it organizes the live meetings, in addition to other meeting points where the project organizations can inform the public about their work. In 2007, more than two hundred social organizations went to CAN branches to inform customers what they had done with the money they had been given.

CAN has also transformed about half of its existing 351 branches into *canchas*—branches for social commitment (in Spanish *dar cancha* means to give an opportunity and to give exposure), thereby reinforcing yet another expression of CAN's civic banking philosophy. CAN views its 175 canchas (with about forty to fifty more opening each year) as places where people share, the branch belonging as much to the customers as to the bank. Besides making financial transactions at canchas, customers and noncustomers alike can have a coffee, read books or newspapers, connect to the internet with free Wi-Fi, and enjoy shows, talks, and concerts. There are magic shows, clowns, and puppets for children, and book groups are encouraged. For example, more than 65,000 people have visited CAN's Pamplona cancha, surfed the internet for more than 18,000 hours, enjoyed some 12,000 hours of reading, played 47,000 hours of children's games, and engaged in more than 1,500 activities, and more than 20,000 have chosen their charitable and benevolent projects in this cancha alone.

CAN also leverages its cancha-based platforms online to loop in recipients of social projects, who can then share their actual experiences as recipients of funding from project partners. This transparency, access, and dialogue foster collective accountability in the entire system, and they mitigate business risks of misappropriation and inefficiencies in the system. Moreover, given full transparency, individuals can make their own judgments about the relationship between the risks they might undertake in supporting certain projects and its rewards. The operating costs for each cancha are about 12.5 percent higher than for a traditional branch; however, the costs are more than balanced by efficiency gains and effectiveness in CAN's engagement with project partners. What's more, CAN sees increased sales through word-of-mouth referrals by the partners themselves and through their viral impact in the local communities. It is an investment with nonlinear market and partner impact. CAN's strategic capital is enhanced as well, through understanding and insights gained by employees from their social interactions with customers and noncustomers.

Thus, CAN's customer engagement platforms epitomize how customers can choose, decide, know, become involved, and take an active part in core company operations. CAN customers know how many euros they contribute for social projects, and how this money becomes drinking water for a village in Africa, a grant for research into cancer, or the smile on the face of a child with a disability. By exercising their customer rights, CAN's customers can strengthen their commitment to the projects they have chosen. Through direct conversations with social organizations at the canchas, they can know what has actually been done with their money.

Customers, as well as employees, can even visit the project and help out as volunteers via the VolCan engagement platform, through which CAN puts individuals in touch with nonprofits. VolCan is a manifestation of the bank's fourth customer right, Involved Banking. In 2007, 7,000 volunteer positions were offered through VolCan, with 2,750 people working as volunteers for 22,000 hours. A further 405 people were trained in five voluntary-work courses organized through VolCan. Armendariz says, "We are heading toward a new society, and at CAN we are building the future together."

Caja Navarra has also created Eurecan, a community engagement platform of mentors, social networks, and training for business entrepreneurs. Eurecan Copiloto is a community of prominent businesspeople on this platform who offer advice to entrepreneurs, who can learn from their collective experiences about failures and successes. Eurecan facilitates networking of entrepreneurs, making it easy for them to find appropriate partners, suppliers, and support. It also holds training days exclusively for entrepreneurs, known as Eurecanforma, and facilitates an annual get-together. CAN also engages other companies (e.g., automotive firms) to offer tailored products and services for its customers and stakeholders (e.g., loans for secondhand vehicles).

Caja Navarra continues to innovate relentlessly. Its fifth customer right is Know and Decide. CAN tells each customer what it does with his or her savings and lets each customer choose where these specific funds should be invested. Customers are given categories for investment, including clean energy, youth, training and employment, family help, and entrepreneurs and innovation. Customers who invest larger sums with CAN are allowed to choose specific social projects that their funds go to, from more than a thousand projects located both inside and far outside Spain.

The lucidity and responsibility engendered by Know and Decide has inspired nonprofit organizations to start sending their patrons to Caja Navarra. Churches, music bands, museums, artists, retirement homes, sporting associations, and many other organizations have become advocates of the bank. For example, the head of a youth association described CAN as "making it quicker, easier, and more effective for youth to engage parents in influencing CFOs and persuading them to work with CAN (and choosing their own youth projects) than to fill out forms asking for government financing." As organizations around the globe face rising pressures for responsible investing, CAN has taken a direct step with the construction of its civic banking strategy. This is downright extraordinary by any governance standards. The implications of this initiative are quite significant for corporate and nonprofit governance—not to mention forms of direct democracy such as public initiative and referendum.

In 2009, Caja Navarra rolled out its sixth right, Connecting Customers with Each Other—those who want to help with those who need it. CAN now puts people who want a loan in contact with people who can finance them, in peer-to-peer fashion. People can post their loan request on CAN's web platform. Anyone who wants to finance them can link their deposits to the loan. CAN handles the risk through an "advanced election loan" product it has designed for this purpose, with the loan rates depending on many variables such as CD rates, loan guarantees, and payment track records. CAN's customers, the customer's borrower, and CAN are once again involved in creating mutual value. In January 2010, nearly 5,000 people received loans totaling €344 million. In keeping with its commitment to transparency, CAN lists each loan on its website.

The financial results for Caja Navarra have been nothing short of remarkable. Over the six years from 2001 to 2007, profits grew 2.8 times (from €64 million to €182 million), credit investment grew 2.8 times (from €4.5 billion to €12.5 billion), resources managed grew 1.8 times (from €6.5 billion to €11.86 billion), and ROE (return on equity) grew from 8 to 17 percent. (Credit investment refers to the total amount of loans invested by CAN, while the resources managed are the bank's total deposits excluding funds from the central bank.) CAN's efforts have led to an increase of 6 percent per year of the bank's customer base. By 2006, CAN had exceeded its objectives set in the 2003–2007 strategic plan. In 2007, CAN moved from the sixteenth rank to fifth in margin per employee, and from forty-first to fourth in ROE, among savings banks in Spain.

The financial crisis and economic downturn of 2008–2009, which was particularly pronounced among Spanish banks, showed that this success was no mirage. Caja Navarra's financial results and bond rating remained relatively strong, in part because of its unusually tight connection with customers, who continued to flock to the bank: funds under investment in CAN's Basque home region grew 30 percent in the first half of 2009, and the volume of funds invested in the bank's mutual funds grew 8 percent. CAN invested €120 million (about $171 million) in 2008 to support its growth. It has kept the flow of money running with more than €3.3 billion in loans in 2008, up 18.6 percent in the business sector alone. Miguel Sesma, president of CAN, notes, "We might say that 2008 was the year of change; the financial sector is never going to be the same again. At CAN, in this key year, we have attained a historic record by topping the 200 million mark (about $285 million] in net profit. This has allowed us to make voluntary provisions totaling 40 million euros for an increasingly uncertain future."[4]

Building a Strategic Architecture for the Co-creative Enterprise

CAN illustrates the building of a *strategic architecture* for its co-creative enterprise through a portfolio of engagement platforms and initiatives that are linked together—from civic accountability, canchas, project accountability, and Viálogos, to VolCan, Eurecan, Know and Decide, and peer loans. This strategic architecture generates "win more–win more" opportunities that expand mutual value, bringing together all its co-creators—from customers, employees, business entrepreneurs, and professionals, to social project partners, recipients of project funding, noncustomers, prospective employees, and all other stakeholders in a self-reinforcing, co-creative ecosystem. It also fosters collective action, as communities of individuals can rally around a common cause. CAN is attuned to the collective engagement experiences of individuals, so that it can continuously monitor and learn from them.

While most banks struggle to find ways to roll out even simple innovations, Caja Navarra launched fifty-two new products in 2007 and sixty-six new products the previous year. In 2004, seeking to create an innovative culture, Goñi decreed that the bank must be able to launch one new product per week. The time-to-market for new products and services has dropped to two to three weeks, versus three to six months before the CEO's directive. Although the bank's innovation group started small in 2005 with only three people, CAN's organizational identity rests on social innovation. It is expressed in people, products, technology, processes, and social innovation initiatives that permeate all areas and aspects of the bank. Employees must devote the equivalent of twenty minutes each day to innovative ideas. As Armendariz notes, CAN's co-creative organizational model embeds innovation at every step, making its employees at all levels in the organization key stakeholders of the innovation process.

CAN intends to build new relationships among its multiple stakeholders across the business and social ecosystem, co-creating the CAN brand experience even as it continues expanding its social and economic impact in Spain and across the globe. In March 2009, Goñi announced plans to bring CAN's civic banking model to the United States, signaling a radical change in the way the financial services world might work in the future. As Goñi has said, "In the future, financial institutions will have to be civic. . . . Society no longer wants outdated economic models. We have learnt that, all of a sudden, we can no longer just look to shareholders. From now on, companies will look after the profits generated by all of the role players with whom they deal, because this is the only way of guaranteeing their sustainability. . . . In civic banking everyone provides and everyone wins, and that is why it works. This business model attains economic and social results, which is what drives us. . . . Now we want to get out there and 'pollinate' the world with our way of understanding financial relations."[5]

The "Seoul" of Citizen Engagement in Policy Making

Seoul, South Korea, is one of the most technologically advanced cities in the world. In October 2006, Mayor Oh Se-hoon launched an online suggestion platform called OASIS to "enhance creativity and imagination in administration"—together with citizens as active participants in government policy and decision making. Its genesis was an intranet initiative dubbed Creative Seoul Project Headquarters, where the mayor encouraged civil servants to suggest ideas on three topics: improvement of working practice, encouragement of citizen's participation, and transparent city administration.[6] More than 3,000 ideas per month were suggested in the first year and evaluated by the Seoul Development Institute. The institute forwarded the best ideas to the relevant civil servants. The performance evaluation system for city employees, which previously had been based on seniority, was revamped to include a merit rating system that included enactment of ideas from the intranet. This move paved the way for opening up the idea process to citizen engagement at large.

The new portal was named Ten Million Imaginations OASIS to invite creative policy-making ideas from the 10.3 million citizens of Seoul. Between October 2006 and May 2009, more than 4.25 million citizens visited OASIS, submitting 33,737 ideas (about 1,050 ideas per month on average). OASIS (oasis.seoul.go.kr) is more than a static suggestion system. It is a dynamic engagement platform involving three key constituencies: citizens, civic servants, and the public enterprise. Citizens are encouraged to participate in policy- and decision-making processes by engaging in open discussion with local government officials. First, in the Ideas & Suggestions phase, any citizen can suggest any idea to improve policies. Citizens can also show their interest by replying to ideas proposed to others. The Seoul city government uses these inputs to understand civic needs and gauge citizens' interest in each idea. Furthermore, when an idea is posted, the relevant city department is notified and it is its duty to comment on the idea's feasibility.

Next comes the Online Discussion phase. A select group of prequalified participants, including policy experts, civil servants, and a volunteer Citizen Committee assess and develop ideas. Citizens are qualified for the committee based on their participation in the OASIS process, from idea submission to review and discussion, through a point system. The Citizen Committee has six subgroups: economics, culture, transportation, environment, well-being, and citizens. As of 2009, there were more than 450 members, with membership being renewed every six months. Of the 1,050 ideas proposed per month in OASIS, about 120 ideas on average, make it to the discussion phase. OASIS consolidates similar ideas at this point. For instance, in one of these rounds citizens suggested 741 ideas related to a better bicycle environment, including 145 for bicycle-only lane construction, 237 on improving bicycle lanes, and 139 on better maintenance of bicycle lanes. These ideas were submitted in the context of a Bicycle Friendly Plan announced by the Seoul Metropolitan Government in October 2008.

The third phase of OASIS is an Offline Preliminary Examination, where selected ideas are evaluated based on feasibility and responses from citizens. About forty ideas per month get to this phase. The top levels of city government take part in a brainstorming process to develop the ideas into policies. The director general, directors, and external experts participate, and the deputy director in charge of implementing the idea and policy joins at the appropriate time. After the discussion, the city government holds a working level meeting to decide on feasible ideas to be brought to the final policy adoption meeting. About seven ideas make it through this stage, on average.

The fourth and final phase of the engagement process is the Seoul Policy Adoption meeting, a live public meeting that brings together around 200 people, including the idea provider, Citizen Committee members, nongovernmental organizations (NGOs), external experts, citizens, and the city's top officials. The meeting is chaired by the mayor and broadcast in real time over the internet. The citizen who originated the idea kicks off the discussion. For instance, in a recent policy adoption meeting, a Mr. Kang, who suggested adding English subtitles to Korean films, related how the idea came to him from his experience as a visitor in other countries. In India and Japan, he looked for a cinema with English subtitles without success, and he felt isolated as a foreigner and disappointed. Kang thought that subtitling Korean films in English would not only be attractive to Korea's 5 million tourists and help them appreciate Korean culture, but would also help in expanding the export of Korea's entertainment and pop culture around the world. After Kang's introduction, the floor was opened to comments of "netizens" at large. One person commented that English subtitles of films would help Koreans learn English. The floor was then opened up to Citizen Committee members, who in this case voted almost unanimously to enact the idea. One of them suggested extending the policy to TV shows. Then the civil servants weighed in, explaining the setup of the film infrastructure for the subtitling process, proposing a pilot program in select theaters, and discussing special theaters for preserving traditional content from the perspective of promoting Korean culture. In early 2009, the subtitles idea was implemented on a trial basis.

As of May 2009, more than seventy-five ideas had been adopted through the OASIS program, with more than fifty-five of them completed and implemented. OASIS led to the implementation of ideas such as free baby carriages and wheelchairs in parks, narrowing of gratings of drain covers, and a footbridge across the Han River. The adopted ideas are posted on the OASIS website with a due date and progression bar showing percentage of completion. Once ideas are adopted, the citizens who generated them are awarded about $100 per idea, with each idea eligible for a further award for creativity ranging from $500 to $3,000. Ideas not adopted are also posted on the website, with an explanation and details on any alternate policies in process. The website allows further discussion on alternate solutions to realize the basic idea or for related problems.

While other "e-government" systems around the world tend to focus on citizens' complaints, usually on a one-off basis, OASIS enables continuous administrative reform, enhancing the image of civil servants and improving citizens' trust in government at large.

Agenda 2020 in Rio Grande do Sul

Rio Grande do Sul, one of Brazil's richest states, nearly went bankrupt in 2005, as public investment reached its lowest level in thirty-five years. Since 1970, one government after another had failed to implement necessary state reforms to reduce public debt. By 2004, 32 percent of tax revenues were tied to the pension burden and 13 percent to the increasing public debt. In the early 1990s, Brazilian commodity export–oriented states like Rio Grande do Sul suffered not only from the negative impact of the overvalued national currency but also from a severe decline in agricultural production due to recurring droughts. It became increasingly clear that no single entity by itself could solve the state's major structural problems. The remedy lay in a co-creative governance model to develop a shared national agenda.

In late 2005, the Brazilian National Confederation of Industry (NCI), a powerful pan-business group, proposed a draft agenda to begin dialogue on setting goals for Brazil's sustainable development. Several state governments and administrative departments adopted the concept, including the state of Rio Grande do Sul. In 2006, leading entrepreneurs in the state rallied civic leaders to propose a comprehensive program for economic and social recovery. The industrial state federation (FIERGS), three trade associations (FDCL, Fecomercio, and Federasul), and an entrepreneurs association (FARSUL) got together to begin deliberations on reversing the state economic situation. Far from taking a passive role with public policy, these agents decided to propose a deep process for social and economic recovery.

The groups dubbed the initiative Agenda 2020, aiming to engage not only members of the sponsoring organizations, but also trade unions, NGOs, government, political leaders, and educators, among others. (Fully 30 to 40 percent of the identified programs in the NCI agenda draft were being undertaken by private entities and NGOs.) Yet addressing constituents' disparate interests is a major challenge facing government officials and legislators—and often the greatest source of political paralysis. It can take many years to reach consensus on complex issues and formulate solutions through law, public policy, or programs.

To begin the Agenda 2020 process, leaders set up a "live" engagement platform for engaging different stakeholders, building political consensus, and coordinating lobbying activities. The goal of this preliminary platform was to discuss government programs, which naturally called for a process of consensus building and democratic goal setting by diverse stakeholders who collectively represented the interests of the public. It was coordinated and facilitated over multiple phases by volunteers, economists, politicians, and external consultants.[7]

When developed within government, a public agenda involves only leaders and civil servants who address economic and social issues from the top down. When initiated outside of government, the agenda requires engagement of diverse stakeholders—business leaders and entrepreneurs, politicians, workers, educators, social activists, and others—to articulate a common vision and strategic objectives. All these parties must co-shape a system to manage and measure progress and hold elected officials accountable. When co-created, the agenda becomes in effect a societal referendum, representing a consensus view of challenges, goals, and recommended actions. When the government sector and the private sector work cooperatively on a common strategic agenda, better outcomes of mutual value can emerge.

In the first phase of Agenda 2020, 950 people met in person, representing all social segments ranging from community, union, and association representatives, to business and academic leaders, to NGO personnel and government officials. Dubbed The Future Vision of Rio Grande do Sul 2020 (the Rio Grande That We Want), the meeting mobilized the leaders and citizens to explore their past, present, and desired future as a backdrop to formulating a vision for the state.

In the next phase, participants sought to shape a shared vision and strategic agenda entailing goals, objectives, targets, and actions for current and future generations, while still keeping the government focused on strategic priorities. People generally agreed it was important to bring a long-term perspective on economic and social programs, since a return on education and infrastructure programs can take ten or more years. At the same time, a governance agenda can maintain the commitment to initiatives and reduce the likelihood of discontinuity from one administration to the next, thereby ensuring that a fifteen-year plan of action is actually accomplished. The agenda had to identify a societal vision and a corresponding set of long-term objectives, targets, and actions in a framework that could be created either within government or outside of it by a coalition of stakeholders.

From co-creative leadership forums around eleven themes—market development, regional development, innovation and technology, public administration, infrastructure, institutional and regulatory environment, financial resources availability, citizenship and social responsibility, environment preservation, education, and health—a draft of the strategic agenda emerged. More than 5,000 people and 200 municipalities provided input, with 400 people focusing on each theme. This shared agenda was meant to serve as a legitimate tool for monitoring performance—either by the government, which could use the agenda to monitor itself, or by the public, which could use it to pressure government leaders to stay on track. Metrics for the agenda included the UN Human Development Index (a quality-of-life measure), the Gini indicator (a measure of income inequality), and GDP growth. The forum participants used the metrics to transparently monitor the results and track the various initiatives. In October 2006, the strategic agenda was presented to the two state government candidates, who each committed themselves in front of more than 1,000 people and the media to implement its targets.

Strategic Agenda 2020 then began its third phrase: system-wide implementation and performance management. The agenda was discussed in "road shows" and communication efforts and campaigns all over the state, including public discussions with newly elected government officials and a review of initiatives and their collective progress. The coordinating group undertook a strategic prioritization of projects, creating a website (www.agenda2020 .org.br) that included an online public forum and open access to every presentation or discussion topic from the agenda, to democratize the governance process in action. In this way, the agenda has become a "public observatory" for governance and performance management that encourages every public and economic entity to align its own agenda with the larger strategy, while also fostering collective public debate and dialogue. There is periodic "feedback on the feedback" via newsletters and blogs as part of an ongoing conversation and continuous recalibration of the state agenda. Strategic Agenda 2020 is a refreshing example of a concerted effort by the public and private sectors to engage jointly in co-shaping a national strategic governance agenda.

Balancing the Invisible Hand with the Visible at SEBI

Leaders, media, analysts, and business experts worldwide paid considerable attention to the relative resilience of India's economy and its financial sector following the 2008–2009 financial crisis. India's banking and financial systems benefited from a strong regulatory framework, which took shape in the early 1990s, through the Securities and Exchange Board of India (SEBI)—the equivalent of the Securities and Exchange Commission (SEC) in the United States. Former SEBI director Pratip Kar described to one of us how SEBI developed its framework for governance and regulation. Its work offers an important lesson in public-private engagement and how to govern stakeholders in co-shaping and co-evolving regulatory processes.[8] As Kar noted, when SEBI engaged its stakeholders, it was not only prior to the advent of web-based technologies, but they did not even realize that they were actually working on governance in a co-creative manner. The engagement process seemed natural and the only logical way forward. Stretch goals, constraints, pressure for accountability, and urgency formed a potent mix for co-creating regulatory governance.

The securities market in India is more than 130 years old, the oldest in Asia. Yet it was a backwater within India's financial system until the mid-1980s, when the securities market began to expand.

In 1988, the government of India set up SEBI as an autonomous regulatory body for the securities market, and in 1992 SEBI became a statutory body under the SEBI Act of the Parliament of India, with the twin objectives of investor protection and market development through regulation.

SEBI sought to install a new governance framework that would anticipate and be responsive to the needs of the Indian economy, which at that time experienced a sweeping and historic reformation. In some places, regulations existed but needed redesigning; in other places, a new regulatory design had to be crafted. Change threatens the status quo, of course, and the Indian stock market in 1992 was no exception. SEBI's first step was to identify the stakeholders of the regulatory architecture, who included:

- Investors, because they invest their savings in stocks to make money
- Firms, because they need capital for growth
- Intermediaries, because as agents or service providers they arrange or facilitate securities transactions between buyers and sellers
- Institutions like the stock exchanges to provide the marketplace
- Regulators of all parts of the financial market (because money is fungible and flows seamlessly between markets in a liberalized economy, meaning that policies in one sector have an impact on other financial markets)
- Government, because it has to manage the economy and the stock market is central to it

Next, SEBI identified potential supporters among the stakeholders and recognized possible pockets of resistance. It quickly recognized the investor community as its primary constituency; investors are the bedrock of financial markets, and investor protection was the raison d'être of SEBI's existence. The regulatory architecture had to protect investors' rights, understand their problems, address their grievances, and sustain their confidence in the market. SEBI knew that its regulatory changes would not automatically enlist the support of the other stakeholders; for example, an elaborate disclosure requirement would be resisted by firms, and a strict compliance and risk-management regimen would be opposed by intermediaries, but both would serve the interests of investors.

SEBI's third step was to make the principal stakeholders a part of the change process and co-create the new regulatory architecture with them. Excessive regulation would lead to regulatory anarchy, as the market would look for opportunities for regulatory arbitrage. However, if the regulator and the regulated were part of the same reference framework, there would be a possibility of creating a mutually satisfying regulatory architecture that would maximize economic value.

SEBI then established engagement platforms the regulator and the stakeholders to exchange ideas. The Indian securities market had very few trappings of a modern securities market, such as electronic markets, trading systems, settlement cycles, risk management systems, regulations for takeovers, or insider trading regulations. The stakes were high for SEBI. It had to get things right the first time; failures would be expensive and could turn away domestic and international investors, disillusion firms that issue securities, and dishearten intermediaries.

Even before SEBI gained statutory powers in 1992, it used the media to reach out to investors and learn about their grievances against security market transactions against any listed companies, brokers, or other intermediaries. They heard only a few complaints in the first few weeks of the media campaign, but the number of investors writing to SEBI picked up in later months. SEBI began to publish names of companies and intermediaries against whom there were complaints and highlighted the top ten offenders. This initiative helped SEBI understand the nature of investor problems and what needed to be mended, and that, in turn, helped SEBI prioritize its agenda, while investors were able to express their concerns and problems.

Before SEBI was formed, a few investor NGOs had looked after investor grievances, sometimes using moral persuasion and sometimes legal action on behalf of investors. Once SEBI became a statutory body, it began to recognize formally these investor associations across the country (using strict eligibility criteria). SEBI held periodic meetings with these groups, sometimes at their request, sometimes at the request of SEBI. These live meetings provided another engagement platform for interaction with investors.

Of course, the stock exchanges were themselves a live engagement platform. SEBI used the exchanges to organize meetings not only with brokers but also with issuers, investors, and other intermediaries. India's Chambers of Commerce and Industries were another engagement platform, which helped SEBI and industry to understand each others' viewpoints.

Finally, advisory committees set up by SEBI for consultation on regulatory policy interventions became the most interactive and powerful engagement platforms. These committees comprised representatives of all stakeholders in the regulatory process, including the stock exchanges, investor associations, intermediaries, mutual funds, listed firms, academics and other experts, professional bodies, fellow regulators, and government representatives. The advisory committees discussed problems in the market, new areas of development, market needs, and areas in which regulatory policy intervention was required or an existing policy needed change. SEBI officials attended the advisory committee meetings only to give clarifications if requested by committee members or to help prepare minutes and reports of the committee, but not to give SEBI's views on issues. Any committee member was free to place any agenda item for discussion, as is SEBI.

Today, SEBI places advisory committee reports on its public website and circulates them to all the stakeholders across the country, requesting their comments back within three weeks. SEBI sometimes meets with the stakeholder groups to discuss draft reports. Often some of the stakeholder groups will hold their own meetings and invite SEBI. On occasion SEBI facilitates meetings between the

243

stakeholder groups and the advisory committee concerned. SEBI collates the views from these meetings and sends notes back to the advisory committee to prepare a final report. This process enables the SEBI board to make decisions based on inputs from all stakeholders, which ensures that the final policy announced by SEBI minimizes surprises to the market. Many of SEBI's major public policy decisions have been adopted through this engagement process, including policies on takeover regulations, framing the integrated risk management system for the securities market, corporate governance norms, a change in governance structure of the stock exchanges, a policy of dematerialization of securities and electronic share transfer, a change in settlement cycles from account period to rolling settlement, and the introduction of derivatives trading.

SEBI continues to evolve all its engagement platforms to frame the governance for securities market development. The strength of co-creative governance is that ideas and initiatives emanating from the intersection of all stakeholder interests, recognizing different perspectives, mixing diverse interests, and blending and synthesizing them, are able to gain broad consensus. Corporate scandals, like India's Satyam accounting debacle in 2008–2009, have only reinforced the need for more intense and broader co-creation beyond the regulatory architecture. Shareholder activism coupled with media and public scrutiny brought this debacle into the open.

Toward a Co-Creative Economy

Our society is witnessing a structural change in the relationship between institutions and individuals. Properly harnessed, we believe the co-creation paradigm can usher in a new era of wealth creation through new economics of interactions and human experiences that goes beyond the conventional paradigm of goods and services exchange. Our primary goal in this book has been to help you see and think differently about value creation opportunities through the co-creation paradigm, and equip you with concepts and ideas to act as a co-creative enterprise. We believe that for organizations to sustain themselves in the future, they must institutionalize co-creative thinking and a co-creation culture in their organizations. As evidence mounts of superior and more sustainable success from co-creation, it will spread in organizations, as occurred with the quality movement. Over time, the movement toward co-creation can help create a new basis for the social legitimacy of all large institutions in our society—and, we hope, the emergence of a truly democratic global society in which human rights, needs, and values are predominant. All enterprises, whether private, social, or public, must learn to engage people, individually and collectively. To borrow Abraham Lincoln's words, enterprises must be designed by the people, for the people, of the people, and we might add, co-creating value with the people.

In January 2008 at the World Economic Forum in Davos, Switzerland, Microsoft chairman Bill Gates called for a new approach to capitalism—"creative capitalism"—where businesses, governments, and nonprofits will work together so that more people can make a profit or gain recognition in doing work that eases the world's inequities.[9] According to Gates, "The genius of capitalism lies in its ability to make self-interest serve the wider interest." Gates went on to quote Adam Smith, the father of modern capitalism, from *The Theory of Moral Sentiments*: "How selfish soever man may be supposed, there are evidently some principles in his nature, which interest him in the fortunes of others, and render their happiness necessary to him, though he derives nothing from it, except the pleasure of seeing it."[10]

Gates continued: "Creative capitalism takes this interest in the fortunes of others and ties it to our interest in our own fortunes in ways that help advance both. This hybrid engine of self-interest and concern for others serves a much wider circle of people than can be reached by self-interest or caring alone." However, philosophers such as Plato have long recognized the plight of the human condition in reconciling self-interest with morality. We believe that people may not necessarily go beyond their self-interest if left to themselves, unless the *joint interest* is itself shown to be in the *self-interest* of the individual and the *collective* self-interest.

Call it the makings of a *co-creative economy*—the convergence of private, social, and public sector enterprises around meaningful human experiences and the realization of human potential. The advent of the web and ubiquitous connectivity in the hands of millions of citizens has ushered in new social interactions and unleashed a democratic and decentralized force of participation in society, beyond institutional boundaries. These forces continue to spawn new ways of collective engagement, collaboration, and value co-creation. The single most important shift that leaders must make is to recognize the centrality of individuals, whether in their role as customers, employees, or any other stakeholder, and their human experiences as the new basis of value creation. Business and society are moving toward an individual- and experience-based view of co-creative engagement among individuals and institutions—outside and inside enterprises. It's a change with profound implications for the human experience, with a future that nobody can yet fully anticipate.

As Peter Drucker reputedly said, "The best way to anticipate the future is to create it." Even better, co-create it.

Epilogue: A Co-Creation Manifesto

Here's a summary of the key takeaways, which cuts across all the examples in this book.

1. Co-creative enterprises follow a simple principle: they focus their entire organization on the experiences of all their customers and stakeholders that stem from *interactions* with products, processes, and people. They design these interactions with participants through engagement platforms. The new experiences and the improved economics constitute the fruit of this process, while the engagement platforms are like the trees that bear the fruit.

2. There are three equally important aspects to co-creation: engagement platforms, human experiences, and the collaborative process of creating with individuals.

3. *Engagement platforms* come in all forms, from the product itself, to live meetings, websites, retail stores, and mobile phones, to call centers, private community spaces, and open community spaces. The technology does not matter as much as the philosophy that drives the engagement. Some

247

sophisticated websites are highly company-centered, while live meetings can be highly co-creative. However, large-scale transformation to co-creation typically requires some form of technology intermediation, as the cost of human interactions tends to become prohibitive in large numbers.

4. *Human experiences* come from interactions. If managers accept experiences as the basis of value, then they must design their organization's products, processes, and management functions to change the nature of interactions, and enable compelling and meaningful experiences of value. Managers need to adopt an experience mind-set rather than focus on goods and services.

5. Since the value of experiences vary from context to context and from individual to individual, by definition, enterprises must create value *together with* individuals—including customers and all other external stakeholders, and employees and all other internal stakeholders. The immense power of co-creation arises from combining engagement platforms, experiences, and a collaborative process that harnesses the insights, knowledge, skills, and ingenuity of all participants, in a mutually valuable manner.

6. The totality of human experiences (current and possible) transcends any enterprise's view of human experiences. In any organization, no matter how focused it is on the experiences of co-creators, there are *insights* to be gained through real-time visualization and dialogue about experiences. These insights help enterprises learn smarter and faster and minimize the likelihood of not connecting with human experiences.

7. The commonly used term *users* limits people's potentially creative roles, as well as the significance of their personal human experiences. The language that managers use often reinforces a mind-set, in this case of design being enterprise- and product-centric, rather than *human- and experience-centric*. The latter is what constitutes co-creative design.

8. The design of engagement platforms must constantly evolve as a function of the co-creative process it fosters. Co-creative design thinking is critical to *keeping engagement platforms alive.* As enterprises open up their innovation process to tap into talent from all over the world, this process can be made better and more effective by applying co-creative design thinking. The key is to view the innovation process as a co-creative process of interactions, with customers and participants, and using the power of experience visualization to generate new insights about what aspects of offerings and experiences are of value.

9. *Co-creative design thinking* continuously expands the experience mind-set of platform designers inside the enterprise, enabling them to gain insights through the lens of participants and thereby make more meaningful changes to their offerings and processes that augment mutual value. Co-creative design increases value creation efficiency and effectiveness in the long run, in the process mitigating business and societal risks.

10. Going beyond crowdsourcing and mass collaboration, *innovation co-creation* builds the innovation process *with* participants. Moreover, innovation co-creation incorporates the experiences of people and talent *inside* the enterprise as much as those of outsiders. Co-creation of innovation works regardless of whether a company's resulting offerings are standard, customized, or personalized. Enhance engagement experiences all around, and co-creative innovation will flow in the business network.

11. Propelled by rapid advances in tools for collaboration, information networking, and communication, enterprises are developing new styles of engagement in business networks. Different players in the value chain come together to create, improve, and deliver new product and service offerings—often through a *nodal enterprise* that provides the leadership and facilitates execution. Each of the parties in a company's business network engage in multiple types of interactions.

Making these interactions co-creative provides new pathways to expanding mutual value in business networks.

12. Successful nodal enterprises facilitate shared engagement platforms in the business network, engaging vendors and partners on the one hand, and end customers and users on the other. They take co-creation to new levels, *by linking upstream co-creation with downstream co-creation,* transforming value creation on both the supply side and the demand side.

13. Reaping the full benefits of co-creation across the business ecosystem requires the building of engagement platforms that multiple types of stakeholders can easily plug into. Nodal enterprises bring unique capabilities and enlightened leadership to the design of these platforms. By *seamlessly connecting experiences* across the different engagement platforms, new types of mutual value can be unleashed altogether.

14. By building social ecosystems through continuous engagement with multiple socially responsible stakeholders, co-creation enables a more efficient discovery and development of *sustainable* growth opportunities. Companies can use co-creation to better manage the triple bottom line that balances economic success, environmental stewardship, and social progress. Co-creation in the citizen sector can energize the motivation of participants, especially volunteers, by enhancing their interactions and making their human experiences more meaningful.

15. Building effective social ecosystems requires going beyond an enterprise-centric view of "doing well by doing good." All stakeholders must have a say in and benefit from outcomes. By creating more value with others, the "win more–win more" nature of co-creation simultaneously generates better economics for enterprises and reduces societal business and societal risk. Co-creation ultimately enhances the *social legitimacy* of all enterprises, whether private, social, or public.

16. Successful change management is best achieved *through engagement of those affected by change.* Leading the trans-

formation to a co-creative enterprise can, however, occur in middle-out, bottom-up, or top-down fashion. A key role of senior management leadership is to enable organizational linkages between employee/internal co-creation, customer/ community co-creation, and partner/network co-creation.

17. Leaders in most established organizations need not attempt to "boil the ocean," but instead identify "wellsprings" of co-creation opportunities that make strategic sense to them and build the requisite capabilities to evolve over time toward a co-creative enterprise. The key is the capacity to experiment, learn, and execute with supportive co-creative management processes.

18. Managing innovation by everybody is a big organizational and social challenge. The technologies enabling the innovation co-creation process, and for realizing the innovations, must be agile and capable of enabling co-creative interactions on a large scale.

19. Leaders must adopt a distributed view of strategy involving a process of engaging multiple constituencies in the interactive resolution of complex issues, and encourage the continuous co-creation of strategy across a wide spectrum of themes and supporting initiatives, launched between themselves and the people who have the most at stake with the company— namely the customers and employees of the firm, with creative inputs from partners and other stakeholders.

20. Companies increasingly have to redefine themselves away from single-company performance models toward ecosystem-based performance management systems. Joint performance models can be co-created through multi-stakeholder engagement platforms.

21. If individuals can be viewed at the center of performance management processes, co-created personal scorecards can be developed between key individuals and the firm. Individual goals can be defined and aggregated in "bottom-up" fashion into an enterprise's overall scorecard, which ulti-

mately results in a more "bought in" co-created performance management system.

22. An organizational capacity to learn, nurture, share, and deploy knowledge across traditional boundaries (both personal and institutional) will be a major co-creation capability in strategic risk management for companies that can develop it.

23. The strategic engagement architecture of the co-creative enterprise rests on interaction capabilities and linkages—among its multiple engagement platforms involving customers, employees, and all other external and internal stakeholders. It must emphasize the importance of social linkages of human capital inside the organization. For organizations to co-create a unique customer experience, it must co-create a unique employee experience inside the organization. Management co-creation inside the enterprise must support customer engagement. Linkages between external value co-creation and management co-creation inside the enterprise generate the capacity for continuous and resilient growth.

24. Governance must evolve toward working together in transparent fashion to maximize mutual involvement and consensus building of joint solutions. Governments can become co-creative by moving from one-way systems, in which they hand down laws and provide services to citizens, to a co-creative system in which citizens, corporations, and civil organizations create mutual value together. Public-private co-creation has the potential to balance the role of the visible hand of government with the invisible hand of free markets, and of citizens' expectations of more responsive government.

25. The co-creative enterprise has the power to transform relationships among individuals and institutions. The evolution toward a co-creative economy rests on the convergence of private, social, and public sector enterprises around productive and meaningful human experiences, and the realization of human potential.

Acknowledgments

A book about co-creation has many co-creators. Many people have given their time and energy to document and share their examples in this book. Our heartfelt thanks go to all of you who are mentioned in the book and on the book's website.

We first want to thank the many people who have inspired us. They include: Pablo Armendariz (Head of Innovation, Caja Navarra), Frances Bell (SAP) for organizing the special session on Co-Creation at the 2008 SAP CEO Forum, Pankaj Bhargava (Principal, People Builders, and former Head of HR, Marico), Tim Brown (CEO, IDEO), Henri de Castries (CEO, Axa), Bernard Charlès (CEO of Dassault Systèmes), John Chambers (Chairman and CEO, Cisco), Yasayuki Cho (GM, Wacoal Japan), Adi Godrej (Chairman, Godrej Group), Kris Gopalakrishnan (CEO, Infosys), Subu Goparaju (Head, SETLabs Infosys), Anders Gronstedt (The Gronstedt Group), Diane Hessan (CEO, Communispace), Henning Kagermann (former CEO of SAP), S. Karun (Head, Sustainability, ABB India), Larry Keeley (President, Doblin), Jørgen Knudstorp (CEO, LEGO), Shelly Lazarus (Chairman and CEO, Ogilvy and Mather), Anand Mahindra (Vice Chairman and Managing Director,

Mahindra), Harsh Mariwala (Chairman and Managing Director, Marico), N. R. Narayana Murthy (Founder-Chairman and Chief Mentor, Infosys), Rakesh Pandey (CEO, Kaya Skin Clinic), Dr. João Polanczyk (CEO, Hospital Moinhos de Vento), K. K. Rajesh (Hindustan Unilever), Zilea Santos (Head, Operations Support and Technology, Real Tokio Marine Vida e Previdência), S. Sivakumar (Head, ITC-IBD), V. Sriram (CEO, Infosys Japan) for organizing the CIO Forum session in Japan, and Jean-Pascal Tricoire (CEO, Schneider Electric).

We are indebted to our consulting clients who believed in our ideas early on and were willing to share our common work in this book: at Credit Agricole, Jean-Yves Hocher, Isabelle Steinmann, and Nicole Derrien; at ERM, Pete Regan and John Alexander; and at La Poste Retail, Jacques Rapoport, Marc Zemmour, Fabien Monsallier, Julien Tétu, Michel Garnier, and Béatrice Tourette. Two of our colleagues at Experience Co-Creation Partnership deserve special mention: Frédérique Bouty for leading the relationship with Predica (Credit Agricole) and being such a wonderful friend, and Moira O'Leary for spearheading the work at La Poste.

We want to thank PRTM for supporting and disseminating the ideas with its global client base. We are particularly indebted to Mark Deck for his personal commitment to our work and engaging his partner colleagues in this adventure, and to Roger Wery for getting us involved in the firm's high-tech practice, to Doug Billings for his vision of co-creation in health care, and to Mark Strom for his invaluable support.

We also want to thank André Coutinho, Mathias Mangels, and Patricio Guitart at Symnetics/Tantum Group for being such strong partners in the implementation of co-creation in Latin America. We are also indebted to Sofia Medem for pioneering the use of co-creation in Spain.

We would also like to send our heartfelt thanks to several people who took time to read various portions and versions of the manuscript, giving us often detailed comments and being actively involved in the shaping of it. They include Melanie Barnett, Ron

Bendersky, Mark Frigo, Ganesh Jayaram, M. S. Krishnan, Manjunatha Kukkuru, Kerimcan Ozcan, Venkatesh Rajah, S. Sivakumar, and Richard Wolfe.

Getting from concept to a book draft is a long, arduous process. As many people shared their examples with us, we needed a co-creator who was not only intimately familiar with the content domain but also brought strong research and editorial skills. Edward Prewitt was that person. We are indebted to him for both his "behind-the-scenes" project management and his "onstage," intense co-shaping of the book. Ed worked long hours and went far beyond his content and research responsibilities at the ECC Partnership, with a passion we are deeply grateful for. We also thank Katie Sasser for her support with graphics, events, and managing partner relations.

Getting from a book draft to a compelling manuscript is a unique process. Herb Schaffner is the person who made this book real. With his great editorial skills and experience of the publishing business, Herb is more than an agent and media partner. He brought his passion for the subject matter of the book and was deeply involved in the transformation of the book draft into a manuscript. We also thank M. S. Krishnan for connecting us with Herb.

Emily Loose, our Free Press Editor, went far beyond the role of the traditional editor, and truly co-created the book with us. Emily dug into the manuscript incisively with a keen sense of where the message had to be. In many instances, Emily challenged us to see the forest for the trees while keeping alive the spirit of the book. Her insistence on using simple language was challenging, yet her deep personal belief about the distinctiveness of this book, and her willingness to endure rewrites, helped tremendously.

We hope this book inspires you to become a co-creator in your own life, and to help your organization become a co-creative enterprise.

Notes

Chapter 1: Becoming a Co-Creative Enterprise

1. See C. K. Prahalad and Venkatram Ramaswamy, "Co-opting Customer Competence," *Harvard Business Review,* January–February, 2000; C. K. Prahalad and Venkatram Ramaswamy, "The Co-Creation Connection," *Strategy and Business,* summer 2002; C. K. Prahalad and Venkatram Ramaswamy, "The New Frontier of Experience Innovation," *Sloan Management Review,* summer 2003, winner of the MIT PriceWaterhouseCoopers Award for Best Article in 2003 that most contributed to the enhancement and advancement of management practice; C. K. Prahalad and Venkatram Ramaswamy, (2004), "Co-creation Experiences: Convergence of Markets and Value Creation," *Journal of Interactive Marketing;* C. K. Prahalad and Venkat Ramaswamy, "Co-creating Unique Value with Customers," *Strategy and Leadership,* 32, 3, 2004.

2. C. K. Prahalad and Venkat Ramaswamy, *The Future of Competition: Co-Creating Unique Value with Customers,* Harvard Business School Press, 2004. C. K. Prahalad, one of the world's most dynamic strategists, was a close friend and mentor to the authors of *The*

Power of Co-Creation, and we are grateful to him for his contributions in this area.

3. Mark McClusky, "The Nike Experiment: How the Shoe Giant Unleashed the Power of Personal Metrics," *Wired,* June 22, 2009.

4. See also Venkat Ramaswamy, "Co-creating Value Through Customers' Experiences: The Nike Case," *Strategy & Leadership,* 36, 5, 2008.

5. An engagement platform is a set of virtual and/or physical environments entailing technology and human-enabled processes/activities, stakeholders/communities, products/artifacts, and spaces/interfaces designed to engage individuals in creating valuable experiences.

6. Mark McClusky, "The Nike Experiment: How the Shoe Giant Unleashed the Power of Personal Metrics," *Wired,* June 22, 2009.

7. Nike worked in close collaboration with its agency partner R/GA to bring the Nike+ concept to life. Together, they continue to evolve the Nike+ platform, innovating and improving experiences with new social media extending the Nike+ experience beyond Nikeplus.com into a runner's overall digital life that creates deeper customer connections to the brand and expanding mutual value.

8. "The Consumer Decides," Nike, Inc. *Investor Days,* Feb. 6, 2007.

9. Louise Story, "The New Advertising Outlet: Your Life," *New York Times,* Oct. 14, 2007.

10. Mark McClusky, "The Nike Experiment: How the Shoe Giant Unleashed the Power of Personal Metrics," *Wired,* June 22, 2009.

11. Sean Gregory, "Cool Runnings," *Time,* Oct. 4, 2007.

12. Jay Greene, "This Social Network Is Up and Running," *BusinessWeek,* Nov. 17, 2008.

13. Mark McClusky, "The Nike Experiment: How the Shoe Giant Unleashed the Power of Personal Metrics," *Wired,* June 22, 2009.

14. Bonnie Goldstein, "The Starbucks Stops Here," Slate.com, Mar. 9, 2007.

15. Jeff Jarvis, "'Hey, Starbucks, How About Coffee Cubes?'" *BusinessWeek,* Apr. 15, 2008.

16. Ibid.

17. Lindsay Gorton, "Starbucks Revamps Menu with Healthier Fare," *Brandweek*, June 30, 2009.

18. Phil Mathew, "Starbucks Sets Eco-Friendly Goals for New Store," *Brandweek*, June 26, 2009; "Starbucks New Store Designs Highlight Coffee, Community, and the Environment," Starbucks press release (undated).

19. "Connecting customers and partners through V2V," Starbucks press release (undated).

20. "Starbucks to Open Regional Farmer Support Center in Rwanda," Starbucks press release, Dec. 5, 2007.

21. Claire Cain Miller, "Now at Starbucks: A Rebound," *New York Times*, Jan. 20, 2010.

22. Julie Jargon, "Latest Starbucks Buzzword: 'Lean' Japanese Techniques," *Wall Street Journal*, Aug. 4, 2009.

23. Jay Miller, "Starbucks Lifts Forecast as Net Rises," *Wall Street Journal*, Jan. 20, 2010.

24. "A Letter from Jeff Immelt," www.ge.com/citizenship/priorities_engagement/resetting_resp_immelt.jsp.

25. IBM Innnovation Discovery website.

26. In this book, we present an expansive view of the co-creation paradigm and what we believe is the next-generation co-creative enterprise. Needless to say, there are several intersecting strands of thoughts and ideas from the collective wisdom on this planet, and we humbly stand on the shoulders of all those before us. Rather than an extensive bibliography and comparative comments that would still be incomplete, we have chosen to keep the endnotes brief, citing contextual references and recognizing the contributions of our co-creators. In an internet-worked age of hyperlinked abundance, we recognize that active readers can explore on their own terms and invite you to contribute and participate at **powerofcocreation.com** once you are done reading this book.

Chapter 2: The Co-Creation Principle

1. The authors are grateful to our co-creator Katsutoshi Murakami for his contribution to this example.

2. Despite this growth, Club Tourism has had to manage a slowdown in demand, like many other travel companies, following the global economic downturn of 2008–2009.

3. Jon Fortt, "Michael Dell 'Friends' His Customers," *Fortune,* Sep. 4, 2008.

4. You can read about Jeff Jarvis's experience and how he was just the "tip of the iceberg" on his archived BuzzMachine blog.

5. See archived discussions on Jeff Jarvis's BuzzMachine blog.

6. Jeff Jarvis, "Dell Learns to Listen," *BusinessWeek,* Oct. 17, 2007.

7. Don Tapscott and Anthony Williams, "Hack This Product, Please!" *BusinessWeek,* Feb. 23, 2007.

8. Jeff Jarvis, "Dell Learns to Listen," *BusinessWeek,* Oct. 17, 2007.

9. Jon Fortt, "Michael Dell 'Friends' His Customers," *Fortune,* Sep. 4, 2008.

10. Jeff Jarvis, "Dell Learns to Listen," *BusinessWeek,* Oct. 17, 2007. See also "Dell, Starbucks, and the Marketplace of Ideas," BuzzMachine blog, Apr. 21, 2008.

11. Matthew Yeomans, "How Dell Got Out of Hell," *The Big Money,* Dec. 14, 2009.

12. Katie Hafner, "Inside Apple Stores, a Certain Aura Enchants the Faithful," *New York Times,* Dec. 27, 2007.

13. Randall Stross, "Apple's Lesson for Sony's Stores: Just Connect," *New York Times,* May 27, 2007.

14. Brooks Barnes, "Disney's Retail Plan Is a Theme Park in Its Stores," *New York Times,* Oct. 13, 2009. Sony does not release data on the sales or profits of its Sony Style stores. See also Jerry Useem, "Apple: America's Best Retailer," *Fortune,* Mar. 8, 2007.

15. ZDNet Between the Lines blog, July 25, 2007.

16. Gartner Inc. "Personal Computer Quarterly Statistics," June 26, 2009.

17. Jerry Useem, "Apple: America's Best Retailer," *Fortune,* Mar. 8, 2007.

18. The authors thank Jørgen Knudstorp, CEO of LEGO Group, for his insights into LEGO's success in co-creation.

19. Jørgen Knudstorp and Andrew O'Connell, "LEGO CEO Jørgen Vig Knudstorp on Leading Through Survival and Growth," *Harvard Business Review,* Jan. 1, 2009.

20. Indirect Collaboration blog, "Q&A with Cecilia Weckstrom of The LEGO Group," Mar. 4, 2010.

21. "Virtual world is LEGO's latest brick trick," Reuters Newswire, May 1, 2008.

22. Jennifer LeClaire, "Analysts Expect Apple to Exceed iPhone Sales Goals," Newsfactor.com, June 18, 2008.

23. Apple Inc. press release, "Apple's App Store Downloads Top Two Billion," Sept. 28, 2009.

24. Chin Wong, "The Mac Clone Myth," Digital Life blog, Apr. 22, 2008.

25. The authors are grateful to our co-creator Katsutoshi Murakami for his contributions to the Nestlé example.

26. The authors appreciate the efforts of Bimal Rath, then head of Human Resources, and Sanjeev Sharma in working with us to experiment with co-creation.

27. Communispace case study, "GlaxoSmithKline Consumer Healthcare: Making Customers the Center of Gravity to Develop a Blockbuster Drug Launch."

28. "Communispace Connections" newsletter, June 2007.

29. "Study Results Reveal Alli Patient Satisfaction Linked to Weight Loss Achieved; Not Treatment Effects," Medical News Today, Oct. 23, 2007.

30. "Communispace Connections" Newsletter, June 2007.

31. GlaxoSmithKline press release, "2 Million People Partner with Alli," Oct. 24, 2007.

32. Personal communication with Julie Schlack at Communispace. We also thank Debi Kleiman for her contributions to the GSK Alli example.

33. Bruce Horovitz, "'Two Nobodies from Nowhere' Craft Winning Super Bowl Ad," USA Today, Dec. 31, 2009.

34. "Power to the People! Doritos User-Generated Ads Score Big Again, Crowned #1 Spot According to TiVo," TiVo Inc. press release, Feb. 8, 2010.

35. The authors are grateful to our co-creators K. K. Rajesh, who was involved with this initiative within HUL, and Manish Srivastava, for his assistance with this example.

36. Al Bawaba, "SAP Launches New Social Media Tools for SAP Community Network," Aug. 29, 2009.
37. Scott Cook commenting on Intuit company wiki "The Contribution Revolution."
38. For more on the concept of experiences, see the discussion of experience innovation, experience personalization, and experience networks in C. K. Prahalad and Venkat Ramaswamy, *The Future of Competition* (Harvard Business School Press, 2004); staging and authenticity of experiences in B. Joseph Pine II and James H. Gilmore, *The Experience Economy; Work Is Theater and Every Business a Stage* (Harvard Business School Press, 1999), and James H. Gilmore and B. Joseph Pine II, *Authenticity: What Consumers Really Want* (Harvard Business School Press, 2007); and the transformative nature of experiences in Albert Boswijk, Thomas Thijssen, and Ed Peelen, *The Experience Economy: A New Perspective* (Pearson Education, 2007).

Chapter 3: Innovation Co-Creation

1. The authors are grateful to our co-creators Fabio Lazarini and André Coutinho of Symnetics for their insights into the Camiseteria example.
2. Personal communication by Fabio Seixas with Symnetics.
3. The authors are grateful to our co-creator Yasuyuki Cho for sharing Wacoal's experimentation with opening up the product development process, and his passion for and personal experience of co-creation.
4. The authors are grateful to Alban Martin for sharing the Orange story and his passionate co-creative spirit. See also Alban Martin, *L'Âge de Peer* (Village Mondial, 2006).
5. Jacky Abitbol, SanDisk, cited on "Orange Partner Camp, Cape Canaveral, U.S.," Orange Partner website, www.orangepartner.com/site/enuk/news/events/orange_partner_camp/orlando/p_orlando.jsp.
6. Bruce Renny, Rok Entertainment Group, cited on "Orange Partner Camp, Faro, Portugal, 14–16 April 2008," Orange Partner website, www.orangepartner.com/site/enuk/news/events/orange_partner_ca mp/faro/p_develop_and_test.jsp.
7. Tom McNichol, "The Wales Rules for Web 2.0," *Business 2.0*, Feb. 2007.

8. Lenny T. Mendonca and Robert Sutton, "Succeeding at Open-Source Innovation: An Interview with Mozilla's Mitchell Baker," *McKinsey on Business Technology,* fall 2008, p. 30.

9. Forrester Research, "The Total Economic Impact of InnoCentive Challenges," May 2009.

10. Jeff Howe, "The Rise of Crowdsourcing," *Wired,* June 2006.

11. Warren Berger, "InnoCentive: When Being Part of the Crowd Pays Off," GlimmerSite blog, Nov. 19, 2009.

12. Brent Schlender, "How Big Can Apple Get," *Fortune,* Feb. 21, 2005.

13. The authors are grateful to our co-creators Manjunatha Kukkuru of SETLabs and Dr. Sougata Ray of the Indian Institute of Management, Kolkata, for their contributions to the Infosys example. We also thank Krishnan Narayanan and Jacob Varghese.

14. The authors are grateful to Jade Nguyen Strattner for her contribution to the IBM example.

15. Bob Andelman, "Big Blue's World Jam," *Corporate Meetings and Incentives,* Oct. 1, 2001.

16. Samuel J. Palmisano, "Fix the Bridges but Don't Forget Broadband," *Wall Street Journal,* Feb. 18, 2010.

Chapter 4: Engaging People among Business Networks

1. See Chapter 6, "Experience Networks" in C. K. Prahalad and Venkat Ramaswamy, *The Future of Competition* (Harvard Business School Press, 2004), and chapter 1, "Transformation of Business," in C. K. Prahalad and M. S. Krishnan, *The New Age of Innovation* (McGraw-Hill, 2008).

2. The authors are grateful to our co-creator Katsutoshi Murakami for his contribution to the Brother Industries example.

3. Fara Warner, "Learning How to Speak to Gen Y," *Fast Company,* June 2003.

4. Keith Naughton, "Hot Wheels," *Newsweek,* Aug. 21, 2006.

5. "The Art of Creating a Social Media Campaign for Toyota," Viva la Revolución blog, Strawberry Frog, July 6, 2008.

6. Ibid.

7. Elin McCoy, "Do-It-Yourself Wine," Bloomberg.com, May 2008.

Chapter 5: Building Social Ecosystems

1. "A Special Report on Corporate Social Responsibility," *The Economist,* Jan. 2008.

2. The authors are grateful to our co-creator Shiv SivaKumar of ITC Agri Business for his contributions to the ITC e-Choupal example. See also C. K. Prahalad, *The Fortune at the Bottom of the Pyramid: Eradicating Poverty Through Profits* (Wharton School Publishing, 2004).

3. Rohit Saran, "To Boldly Go Where . . . ," *India Today,* Dec. 13, 2004.

4. Ibid.

5. The authors are grateful to our co-creator Hugo Villena of Symnetics and Gabriela Rojas of BEME for their contributions to the BEME example.

6. The authors are grateful to S. Karun for sharing ABB's environmental co-creation efforts as part of its sustainability initiatives.

7. Communication with the authors.

8. Communication with the authors.

9. The authors are grateful to our co-creators Blair Miller and Lei Duran for their contributions to the Ashoka example. See also David Bornstein, *How to Change the World: Social Entrepreneurs and the Power of New Ideas* (Oxford University Press, 2004).

10. Ashoka website.

Chapter 6: Designing Engagement Platforms

1. The authors are grateful to our co-creators David Ward and Jonathan Banas for their contributions to the AmazonFresh example.

2. "Children of the Web," *BusinessWeek,* July 7, 2007.

3. The authors are grateful to our co-creator Ganga Venkatasubramanian for his contribution to the Google enterprise search example.

4. The authors are grateful to Ted Zhou and Chuanfeng Lang, co-creators of the Jabil Circuit example.

5. We thank Bernard Charlès for his open discussion with the authors. See also Thomas K. Grose, "3D comes to Web 2.0," *Time,* May 13, 2008.

6. See also Tim Brown, *Change by Design: How Design Thinking Transforms Organizations and Inspires Innovation* (HarperBusiness, 2009) and Roger Martin, *The Opposable Mind: How Successful Leaders Win Through Integrative Thinking* (Harvard Business School Press, 2007).

Chapter 7: Transforming the Enterprise Through Co-Creation

1. The authors are very grateful to Jacques Rapoport, Marc Zemmour, Fabien Monsallier, Julien Tétu, and Béatrice Tourette for their contributions to the La Poste example.

Chapter 8: Leading the Co-Creative Enterprise

1. Bronwyn Fryer and Thomas Stewart, "The HBR Interview: Cisco Sees the Future," *Harvard Business Review,* Nov. 1, 2008. Emphasis is added.
2. Jena McGregor, "Smart Management for Tough Times," *BusinessWeek,* Mar. 12, 2009.
3. Bronwyn Fryer and Thomas Stewart, "The HBR Interview: Cisco Sees the Future," *Harvard Business Review,* Nov. 1, 2008.
4. Jena McGregor, "Smart Management for Tough Times," *BusinessWeek,* Mar. 12, 2009.
5. Bronwyn Fryer and Thomas Stewart, "The HBR Interview: Cisco Sees the Future," *Harvard Business Review,* Nov. 1, 2008.
6. Ellen McGirt, "How Cisco's CEO John Chambers Is Turning the Tech Giant Socialist," *Fast Company,* Nov. 25, 2008.
7. Joe McKendrick, "Cisco Practices What It Preaches, Crosses Boundaries with SOA," ZDNet Service Oriented blog, Sep. 23, 2009.
8. Moryt Milo, "Not the Cisco You Think You Know," Portfolio.com, Dec. 31, 2009.
9. The authors thank Nick Watson, vice president of Strategic Accounts at Cisco, for his comments.
10. Ellen McGirt, "How Cisco's CEO John Chambers Is Turning the Tech Giant Socialist," *Fast Company,* Nov. 25, 2008.
11. This example is based on personal discussions, interviews, and interactions with CEO Vineet Nayar and other senior management of

HCL Technologies. The authors are grateful to our co-creators Priya Ranjan Dass, Vineet Kumar, Debashish Sinha, and Meena Vaidyanathan. See also Venkat Ramaswamy, "Leading the Transformation of Value," *Strategy & Leadership,* 37, 2, 2009.

12. David Kirkpatrick, "The World's Most Modern Management—in India," *Fortune,* Apr. 14, 2006.

13. Vineet Nayar, "The Reincarnate CEO," Fortune Brainstorm Tech blog, Sep. 9, 2009.

14. The authors are grateful to Pete Regan and John Alexander for sharing the story of ERM's co-created performance management system.

Chapter 9: Going Beyond Processes to Co-Creative Engagement

1. The authors are very grateful to Jean-Yves Hocher, Isabelle Steinmann, and the co-creation teams across Predica for their contributions to this example.

Chapter 10: Opening Up Strategy

1. In the Kaiser example, the name of the company and its cast of characters are all disguised. The authors do want to thank all those with whom we have worked in this business, however. You know who you are.

2. See chapter 11, "Strategy as Discovery" in C. K. Prahalad and Venkat Ramaswamy, *The Future of Competition: Co-Creating Unique Value with Customers* (Harvard Business School Press, 2004).

Chapter 11: Co-Creating Institutional Change

1. The authors thank our co-creator Manish Srivastava for his valuable insights into transformational change.

2. The authors are grateful to Pablo Armendariz, head of Innovation at Caja Navarra, for sharing the story of the bank's co-creation journey and his contributions. We also thank Sofia Medem of the Palladium Group for facilitating this process. See also C. Aranda, J. Arellano, and A. Davila, "Caja Navarra: Reporting Customer Profitability . . . to Customers" (IESE Business School, Sep. 2008), which provides more details into CAN's individual-level analytics capabilities.

3. James Gardner, comment on "Caja Navarra: A Bank at the Centre of Its Community," Bankervision: opinions on retail banking and technology blog, comment posted Aug. 14, 2007.

4. President's letter, Caja Navarra annual report, 2008.

5. Managing Director's letter, Caja Navarra annual report, 2008.

6. The authors thank our co-creator Sookyung Cho for her contributions to the Seoul OASIS example.

7. The authors are grateful to our co-creator André Coutinho of Symnetics (a member of Tantum Group) for his contributions and insights into the Rio Grande do Sul example.

8. The authors are very grateful and indebted to our co-creator Pratip Kar, who was a co-author of the SEBI example.

9. David Kirkpatrick, "In Davos, Gates Calls for 'Creative Capitalism,'" *Fortune*, Jan. 24, 2008.

10. Bill Gates, "A New Approach to Capitalism in the 21st Century," World Economic Forum 2008.

Index

About the Authors

Venkat Ramaswamy is Hallman Fellow of Electronic Business and Professor of Marketing at the Ross School of Business, University of Michigan, Ann Arbor. He is a globally recognized thought leader, idea practitioner, and eclectic scholar with wide-ranging interests in innovation, strategy, marketing, branding, IT, operations, and the human side of the organization. He is a prolific author of numerous articles—including the popular *Harvard Business Review* article "Co-opting Customer Competence" and the MIT-PricewaterhouseCoopers award-winning *Sloan Management Review* article "The New Frontier of Experience Innovation" (both coauthored with C. K. Prahalad) as well as the Emerald Literati award-winning *Strategy & Leadership* article "Leading the Transformation to Co-Creation of Value"—and is also a sought-after speaker and mentor to global firms. His award-winning book, *The Future of Competition* (with C. K. Prahalad), introduced co-creation as a revolutionary business concept. He has helped several organizations across the United States, Europe, Asia, and Latin America conceive and execute new business ideas through co-creation, and build management capabilities for co-creation inside their organizations. Venkat lives in Ann Arbor, Michigan. He can be reached at venkatr@umich.edu and blogs at venkatramaswamy.com.

Francis Gouillart is President and Founder of the Experience Co-Creation Partnership, a firm dedicated to the practice of co-creation (www.eccpartnership.com). He is considered one of the leading authorities on the building of strategy, innovation, and transformation capabilities, using co-creation as the core framework. He has been a sought-after consultant and teacher around the globe to many firms in diverse industries. He coauthored (with James Kelly) the bestselling book *Transforming the Organization* and the popular *Harvard Business Review* article "Spend a Day in the Life of Your Customers" (with Frederick D. Sturdivant). Francis lives in Concord, Massachusetts. He can be reached at fgouillart@eccpartnership.com and blogs at francisgouillart.com.